Samsung® Galaxy Tabs

FOR DUMMIES®

A Wiley Brand

by Dan Gookin

FOR DUMMIES®
A Wiley Brand

Samsung® Galaxy Tabs For Dummies®

Published by: **John Wiley & Sons, Inc.,** 111 River Street, Hoboken, NJ 07030-5774, www.wiley.com

Copyright © 2014 by John Wiley & Sons, Inc., Hoboken, New Jersey

Published simultaneously in Canada

No part of this publication may be reproduced, stored in a retrieval system or transmitted in any form or by any means, electronic, mechanical, photocopying, recording, scanning or otherwise, except as permitted under Sections 107 or 108 of the 1976 United States Copyright Act, without the prior written permission of the Publisher. Requests to the Publisher for permission should be addressed to the Permissions Department, John Wiley & Sons, Inc., 111 River Street, Hoboken, NJ 07030, (201) 748-6011, fax (201) 748-6008, or online at http://www.wiley.com/go/permissions.

Trademarks: Wiley, For Dummies, the Dummies Man logo, Dummies.com, Making Everything Easier, and related trade dress are trademarks or registered trademarks of John Wiley & Sons, Inc. and may not be used without written permission. Samsung Galaxy is a registered trademark of Samsung Electronics Co. Ltd. All other trademarks are the property of their respective owners. John Wiley & Sons, Inc. is not associated with any product or vendor mentioned in this book.

LIMIT OF LIABILITY/DISCLAIMER OF WARRANTY: THE PUBLISHER AND THE AUTHOR MAKE NO REPRESENTATIONS OR WARRANTIES WITH RESPECT TO THE ACCURACY OR COMPLETENESS OF THE CONTENTS OF THIS WORK AND SPECIFICALLY DISCLAIM ALL WARRANTIES, INCLUDING WITHOUT LIMITATION WARRANTIES OF FITNESS FOR A PARTICULAR PURPOSE. NO WARRANTY MAY BE CREATED OR EXTENDED BY SALES OR PROMOTIONAL MATERIALS. THE ADVICE AND STRATEGIES CONTAINED HEREIN MAY NOT BE SUITABLE FOR EVERY SITUATION. THIS WORK IS SOLD WITH THE UNDERSTANDING THAT THE PUBLISHER IS NOT ENGAGED IN RENDERING LEGAL, ACCOUNTING, OR OTHER PROFESSIONAL SERVICES. IF PROFESSIONAL ASSISTANCE IS REQUIRED, THE SERVICES OF A COMPETENT PROFESSIONAL PERSON SHOULD BE SOUGHT. NEITHER THE PUBLISHER NOR THE AUTHOR SHALL BE LIABLE FOR DAMAGES ARISING HEREFROM. THE FACT THAT AN ORGANIZATION OR WEBSITE IS REFERRED TO IN THIS WORK AS A CITATION AND/OR A POTENTIAL SOURCE OF FURTHER INFORMATION DOES NOT MEAN THAT THE AUTHOR OR THE PUBLISHER ENDORSES THE INFORMATION THE ORGANIZATION OR WEBSITE MAY PROVIDE OR RECOMMENDATIONS IT MAY MAKE. FURTHER, READERS SHOULD BE AWARE THAT INTERNET WEBSITES LISTED IN THIS WORK MAY HAVE CHANGED OR DISAPPEARED BETWEEN WHEN THIS WORK WAS WRITTEN AND WHEN IT IS READ.

For general information on our other products and services, please contact our Customer Care Department within the U.S. at 877-762-2974, outside the U.S. at 317-572-3993, or fax 317-572-4002. For technical support, please visit www.wiley.com/techsupport.

Wiley publishes in a variety of print and electronic formats and by print-on-demand. Some material included with standard print versions of this book may not be included in e-books or in print-on-demand. If this book refers to media such as a CD or DVD that is not included in the version you purchased, you may download this material at http://booksupport.wiley.com. For more information about Wiley products, visit www.wiley.com.

Library of Congress Control Number: 2013949559

ISBN 978-1-118-77294-2 (pbk); ISBN 978-1-118-77295-9 (ebk); ISBN 978-1-118-77371-0 (ebk)

Manufactured in the United States of America

10 9 8 7 6 5 4 3 2 1

Table of Contents

Introduction

*I*t's not a smartphone. It's not a computer. It's the latest craze: the tablet. It exists somewhere between the traditional computer and the newfangled smartphone. That makes the tablet kind of an oddball, but quite a popular oddball.

Samsung's solution to your mobile, wireless, communications, information, and entertainment needs comes in the form of two tablets: the Samsung Galaxy Note and the Samsung Galaxy Tab. These gizmos do so much, yet they come with such scant documentation that you would lose the thing should there be a strong wind.

Anyone wanting more information about how to get the most from his or her Samsung Galaxy tablet needs another source. This book is that source.

About This Book

This book was written to help you get the most from your Galactic tablet's massive potential. It's a reference. Each chapter covers a specific topic, and the sections in each chapter address an issue related to the topic. The overall idea is to show how things are done on the tablet and to help you get the most from it without overwhelming you with information or intimidating you into despair.

Sample sections in this book include

- Making a home for the tablet
- Obtaining a Google account
- Importing contacts from your computer
- Reading e-mail
- Running Facebook on your tablet
- Talking and video chatting
- Placing a Skype phone call
- Shooting a panorama
- Traveling, Galactic style

You have nothing to memorize, no sacred utterances or animal sacrifices, and definitely no PowerPoint presentations. Instead, every section explains a topic as though it's the first thing you read in this book. Nothing is assumed, and everything is cross-referenced. Technical terms and topics, when they come up, are neatly shoved to the side, where they're easily avoided. The idea here isn't to learn anything. This book's philosophy is to help you look it up, figure it out, and get on with your life.

This book follows a few conventions for using a Galaxy tablet. First of all, I refer to your device as the *Galaxy Note* or the *Galaxy Tab* throughout the book. I might also write *Galaxy tablet* or even, occasionally, *Galactic tablet*. Generally speaking, all the information here applies to both tablets. Information specific to one or the other is pointed out in the text.

The way you interact with the tablet is by using its *touchscreen,* the glassy part of the device as it's facing you. The device also has some physical buttons, called *keys.* It also features some holes and connectors. All those items are described in Chapter 1. You can touch the screen in various ways, which are explained and named in Chapter 3.

Chapter 4 discusses tablet text input, which involves using an onscreen keyboard. You can also input text by speaking to the tablet, which is also covered in Chapter 4.

This book directs you to do things by following numbered steps. Each step involves a specific activity, such as touching something on the screen; for example:

    2. Choose Downloads.

This step directs you to touch the text or item labeled *Downloads* on the screen. You might also be told to do this:

    3. Touch Downloads.

 Some options can be turned off or on, as indicated by a gray box with a green check mark in it, as shown in the margin. By touching the box on the screen, you add or remove the green check mark. When the green check mark appears, the option is on; otherwise, it's off.

Other options are on-off buttons, as shown in the margin. Touch the button to turn it on, in which case it turns green. A button that's off is a dull blue color. You can either touch the button or slide it a wee bit by dragging your finger across the touchscreen.

Foolish Assumptions

Even though this book is written with the gentle hand-holding required by anyone who is just starting out, or who is easily intimidated, I've made a few assumptions. For example, I assume that you're a human being and not the emperor of Jupiter.

My biggest assumption: You have a Samsung Galaxy tablet of your own. Although you could use this book without owning such a tablet, I think the people in the Phone Store would grow tired of you reading it while standing in front of the demo model.

A variety of Galaxy Note and Galaxy Tab tablets are available. This book covers them all, no matter the tablet's dimensions or whether the device receives the cellular data connection or is a Wi-Fi–only version. Which cellular provider you're using also doesn't matter.

You don't need a computer to use this book, although having one does let you do certain things. The times that you could use a computer are noted in the text. The computer can be a desktop or laptop, and a PC or Macintosh. Oh, I suppose it could also be a Linux computer. In any event, I refer to the computer as "a computer" throughout this book. When directions are specific to a PC or Mac, the book says so.

Finally, this book doesn't assume that you have a Google account, but already having one helps. Information is provided in Chapter 2 about setting up a Google account — an extremely important part of using the Galaxy Note or Galaxy Tab. Having a Google account opens up a slew of useful features, information, and programs that make using your tablet more productive.

Icons Used in This Book

This icon flags useful, helpful tips or shortcuts.

This icon marks a friendly reminder to do something.

This icon marks a friendly reminder not to do something.

This icon alerts you to overly nerdy information and technical discussions of the topic at hand. Reading the information is optional, though it may win you the Daily Double on *Jeopardy!*

Beyond the Book

Bonus information for this title can be found online. You can visit the publisher's website to find an online cheat sheet at

    www.dummies.com/cheatsheet/samsunggalaxytabs

Supplemental online material has been created for this book. Because the book can only be so big, but also because the publisher is making me do it, seeing how people are growing more and more fearful of printed material, that supplemental stuff can be found at

    www.dummies.com/extras/samsunggalaxytabs

Updates to this book might someday be found at

    www.dummies.com/extras/samsunggalaxytabs

Beyond the stuff that the publisher requires me to write about, I do my own updates, blog posts, alerts, and helpful information. It's updated more frequently than the publisher's website because I'm an individual and the publisher is a big corporation. You can find my own information at

    www.wambooli.com

Specific support for the Galaxy Tab and Galaxy Note is found here:

    www.wambooli.com/help/tablets/galaxy

My e-mail address is dgookin@wambooli.com. Yes, that's my real address. I reply to all e-mail I get, and you'll get a quick reply if you keep your question short and specific to this book. Although I do enjoy saying "Hi," I cannot answer technical support questions, resolve billing issues, or help you troubleshoot your Galaxy Tab or Galaxy Note. Thanks for understanding.

Enjoy this book and your Galactic tablet!

Where to Go from Here

Start reading! Observe the table of contents and find something that interests you. Or look up your puzzle in the index. When these suggestions don't cut it, just start reading Chapter 1.

Part I
A Galaxy in Your Hands

getting started

with

the Galaxy Note

and Galaxy Tab

In this part...

- Get started with Samsung Galaxy tablets.
- Work through the setup of your Samsung Galaxy tablet.
- Learn how to use your Samsung Galaxy tablet.
- Discover the parts of the Samsung Galaxy tablets.

A Quick Orientation

I thoroughly enjoy getting a new gizmo and opening its box. Expectations build. Joy is released. Then frustration descends like a grand piano pushed out a third-story window. That's because any new electronic device, especially something as sophisticated as a Samsung Galaxy tablet, requires a bit of hand-holding. You have a lot of ground to cover, but it all starts with opening the box and reading this gentle introduction.

Set Up Your Galaxy Tablet

The folks who sold you the Galaxy tablet may have already done some configuration before you left the store. That's great if it happened, but not terrible if it didn't. A cellular (LTE) tablet has most likely been unboxed and manhandled by the Phone Store people — maybe even in front of your own eyes! That step is necessary before you can use an LTE tablet — even though it might have broken your heart (as it did mine).

✔ Chapter 2 details how the setup process works. It also covers the basic on-off operations for your tablet.

✔ The initial setup identifies the tablet with the cellular network, giving it a network ID and associating the ID with your cellular bill.

✔ The Wi-Fi tablet doesn't require setup with a cellular provider, but it does require a Wi-Fi signal to use many features. See Chapter 16 for information on configuring your tablet for use with a Wi-Fi network.

Opening the box

Both the Galaxy Note and Galaxy Tab fit tight and snug inside their boxes. You'll find yours lying right on top. Remove the device by locating and lifting the cardboard tab on one side of the box.

After liberating the tablet, remove the plastic sheet that's clinging to the device's front, back, rear camera lens, and maybe even sides. Toss out those pieces, unless you're enrolled in a college art class, in which case you can turn in the plastic sheeting for credit as an interpretive sculpture project.

In the box's bottom compartment, you may find

✔ **A USB cable:** You can use it to connect the tablet to a computer or a wall charger.

✔ **A wall charger:** It may be a single brick or come in two pieces. You'll find a USB connector on the charger, as well as a gizmo for plugging the thing into a wall socket.

✔ **Pamphlets with warnings and warranty information:** If your tablet is like mine, you'll find that the safety and warranty information is far more extensive than the setup guide. See the priority our culture places on lawyers versus technology writers?

✔ **The 4G SIM card holder:** For the cellular tablet, you'll need a 4G SIM card. The Phone Store people may have tossed its holder into the box as well. You can throw it out.

✔ **Jimmy Hoffa:** The former labor leader disappeared in 1975, and no one has ever been able to find him. Look in the bottom of the box to see whether Hoffa's body is there. You never know.

Go ahead and free the USB cable and power charger from their clear plastic cocoons. If necessary, assemble the power charger's two pieces, which fit so snugly together that you'll probably never be able to pry them apart.

Keep the box for as long as you own your tablet. If you ever need to return the thing or ship it somewhere, the original box is the ideal container. You can shove the pamphlets and papers back into the box as well.

Charging the battery

The first thing that I recommend you do with your Galaxy tablet is give it a full charge. Obey these steps:

1. **Assemble the wall adapter that came with the tablet.**

2. **Attach one end of the USB cable to the tablet.**

   The cable attaches to the tablet's bottom edge; the hole cannot be mistaken and the connector plugs in only one way.

3. **Attach the other end of the USB cable to the wall adapter.**

4. **Plug the wall adapter into the wall.**

Upon success, you may see a large Battery icon on the Galaxy tablet touchscreen. The icon gives you an idea of the current battery-power level and lets you know that the tablet is functioning properly. Don't be alarmed if the Battery icon fails to appear.

If the Welcome screen appears when you charge the tablet, you can proceed to the installation and setup, which are covered in Chapter 2. Or you can wait and finish reading this chapter first.

- ✔ Most tablets come partially charged from the factory. However, I still recommend giving your tablet an initial charge just in case, as well as to familiarize yourself with the process.

- ✔ The USB cable is used for charging the Galaxy tablet and for connecting it to a computer to share information or exchange files, as covered in Chapter 17.

- ✔ The tablet's battery charges also when connected to a computer's USB port, providing that the computer is on. However, charging the tablet by plugging it into a wall socket is more effective.

- ✔ Neither the Galaxy Note nor the Galaxy Tab tablets feature removable batteries.

Know Your Way around the Galaxy

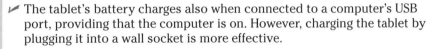

"Second star to the right and straight on till morning" may get Peter Pan to Neverland, but you need more specific directions for navigating your way around your Galaxy tablet.

Finding things on the tablet

Many interesting and useful items festoon the front, back, and perimeter of your Samsung Galaxy tablet. Figure 1-1 is my attempt at illustrating a few of the items you can find. Different tablets place some features in different locations, however, as shown by the horizontal and vertical orientation of the different tablets. Due to the differences, ensure that you properly locate everything on your tablet, even if it's not specifically called out in the figure.

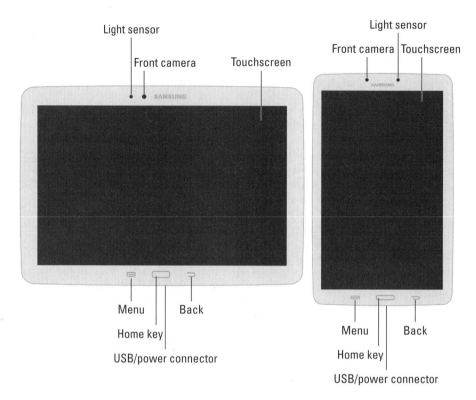

Figure 1-1: Things on the Galaxy tablet.

Touchscreen display: The biggest part of the tablet is its touchscreen display, which occupies almost all the territory on the front of the device. The touchscreen display is a see-touch thing: You look at it and also touch it with your fingers to control the tablet.

Front camera: The Galaxy tablet's front-facing camera is centered above the touchscreen. The camera is used for taking self-portraits as well as for video chats.

Light sensor: Just next to the front camera is a teensy light sensor. It's used to help adjust the brightness level of the touchscreen. It is not a second camera.

Home key: Found at the bottom center of the tablet, the Home key serves many important functions. Its use is covered in Chapters 2 and 3.

Menu and Back buttons: To the left and right of the Home key are the Menu and Back buttons, respectively. These are touch buttons, not physical buttons like the Home key. They also serve important functions, covered in Chapter 3.

Power/USB connector: The Power/USB jack is located on the tablet's edge, below the Home key. This is where you attach the USB cable to the tablet. It's also where the tablet connects to an optional docking stand, keyboard, or other fun doodad as discussed in the later section, "Getting optional accessories."

Beyond the features shown in Figure 1-1, you'll find a variety of buttons, holes, connectors, and other important thingamabobs on your tablet. The location of these items varies depending on the tablet's size and whether it's a cellular or Wi-Fi tablet. Take a moment to locate and identify the following items:

Power Lock key: The Power Lock key may or may not be labeled. If it is, it's labeled with the universal power icon, shown in the margin. If not, look for two buttons on the side of the tablet; the Power Lock key is the smaller one. (The other one is the Volume key.)

Press the Power Lock key to turn on the tablet, to lock it (put it to sleep), to wake it up, and to turn it off. Directions for performing these tasks are found in Chapter 2.

Volume key: The tablet's volume control is two buttons in one. Press one side of the key to set the volume higher, and the other side to set the volume lower. This key is found next to the Power Lock key.

Headphone jack: On the top of the tablet, or high up on one of the sides, you find a hole where you can connect standard headphones.

S Pen: The Galaxy Note features a digital stylus, which inserts into the side of the tablet. Locate the S Pen but keep it in its snug cubby for now.

SIM card cover: This spot is used to access the cellular tablet's SIM card, which is inserted into a slot beneath the cover.

Media card slot: Lift the cover on this slot to add or remove a microSD memory card. See the next section.

Speaker(s): Stereo speakers are located left and right on the tablet, either on the sides or on the bottom edge.

Microphone: A tiny hole on the tablet serves as the device's microphone. The hole's location may not be apparent — it's about the diameter of a pin — but it's there.

Rear camera: The rear camera is found on the back of the tablet. It's the only thing back there, and it's kind of lonely, which is why I don't feature an illustration of it.

- ✔ Be careful not to confuse the SIM card with the removable storage media (microSD card). They're not the same thing. You'll rarely, if ever, access the SIM card.

- ✔ SIM stands for Subscriber Identity Module. The SIM card is used by your cellular provider to identify your tablet and keep track of the amount of data accessed by the tablet. Yep, that's so you can be billed properly. The SIM also gives your cellular tablet a phone number, though that number is merely an account and not something you can dial into or send a text message to.

- ✔ Don't stick anything in the microphone hole. The only things you need to stick into the tablet are the USB cable (or the connector on the dock) or headphones.

Inserting and removing a microSD card

You can easily expand your tablet's storage capacity by installing a microSD card. The card stores photos, music, and other information, supplementing the tablet's internal storage. You can use the card also to exchange files between the tablet and other devices, including a computer.

You can insert the microSD card into the tablet whether the device is on or off. Heed these directions:

1. **Locate the microSD card hatch on the tablet's edge.**

   Figure 1-2 illustrates the hatch's appearance, although it may look subtly different on your tablet. The hatch is labeled *microSD;* don't confuse it with the SIM card cover.

Lift here

Figure 1-2: Opening the memory card hatch.

2. **Insert a fingernail into the slot on the teensy hatch that covers the microSD slot, and then flip up the hatch.**

   The slot cover has a fingernail-size indentation, similar to what's shown in Figure 1-2. When pressure is applied, the hatch that covers the slot pops up and kind of flops over to the side. The slot cover doesn't come off completely.

3. **Orient the microSD card so that the printed side is up and the teeny triangle on the card is pointing toward the open slot.**

4. **Use your fingernail or a bent paperclip to gently shove the card all the way into the slot.**

The card makes a faint clicking sound when it's fully inserted.

If the card keeps popping out, you're not shoving it in far enough.

5. **Close the hatch covering the microSD card slot.**

If the tablet is on (and has been configured), you may see a prompt regarding the MTP application needing to restart after you successfully insert the card. If so, touch the OK button on the tablet's touchscreen.

To remove the microSD card, follow these steps:

1. **If the tablet is on, unmount the microSD card. If the tablet is off, skip to Step 2.**

   Before you attempt this process, reading Chapter 2 and 3 and helps.

   a. At the Home screen, touch the Apps icon to visit the Apps screen.

   b. Open the Settings app.

   c. On the left side of the screen, choose the Storage category.

   If you can't find the Storage category, touch the General tab found at the top of the Settings app screen.

   d. Under the SD Card heading on the right side of the screen, choose Unmount SD Card.

   e. Ignore the warning, and then touch the OK button.

   A message appears briefly atop the touchscreen, telling you that it's okay to remove the microSD card; proceed with Step 2.

2. **Open the little hatch covering the microSD card slot.**

3. **Using your fingernail or a bent paperclip, press the microSD card inward a tad.**

   The microSD card is spring-loaded, so pressing it in pops it outward.

4. **Pinch the microSD card between your fingers and remove it completely.**

When the tablet is turned off, you can insert or remove the microSD card at will. Refer to Chapter 2 for information on turning off your Galaxy tablet.

✔ Odds are good that your tablet didn't come with a microSD card, so run out and buy one!

✔ The microSD cards are teensy. To use the card on a computer or another electronic device, get an SD card adapter.

✔ The Galaxy Note accepts microSD cards up to 64GB in capacity; the Galaxy Tab accepts cards up to 32GB. Lower-capacity cards are cheaper, although they store less information.

✔ GB is an abbreviation for *gigabyte,* which is one billion characters of storage. One gigabyte is enough storage for about an hour of video, or a week's worth of music, or a year's worth of photographs. It's a lot of storage.

✔ SD stands for *Secure Digital.* It is but one of about a zillion different media card standards.

✔ The tablet works with or without a microSD card installed.

✔ Refer to Chapter 17 for more information on storage.

Getting optional accessories

You can find a galaxy of accessories for your Galaxy tablet. Of the lot, I recommend the following:

Earphones: You can use earphones from any standard smartphone or portable media player with your tablet. Simply plug the earphones into the headphone jack and you're ready to go.

Cases: Various cases and case stands are available for the Galaxy tablet. Some are mere enclosures, like a portfolio. Other cases can also be used as stands to prop up the tablet for easy viewing.

Docking stands and keyboards: Several types of keyboards are available for your tablet, from the case keyboard to keyboard docking stands or keyboards. They can both prop up the tablet for easy viewing as well as allow for faster typing than can be done on a touchscreen.

USB adapter: This USB adapter isn't the same thing as the USB cable that came with your tablet. It's a dongle that plugs into the tablet's power/USB jack that allows the tablet to host a USB device, such as a keyboard, a mouse, a modem, or an external storage device (hard drive or optical drive).

HDMI adapter: The adapter plugs into the power/USB jack. Into the adapter, you can plug an HDMI cable (which you buy separately) so that you can view the tablet's output on an HDMI-compatible monitor or television.

Screen protectors: You affix these plastic clingy things to the front of the tablet, right over the touchscreen. They help protect the touchscreen glass from finger smudges and sneeze globs while still allowing you to use the touchscreen.

Vehicle charger: You can charge the Galaxy tablet in your car when you buy the vehicle charger. This adapter plugs into your car's 12-volt power supply, in the receptacle once known as the cigarette lighter. The vehicle charger is a must-have if you plan to use the Galaxy tablet navigation features in your auto or you need a charge on the road.

Additional accessories may be available. Check the location where your Galaxy tablet was sold to inquire about new items.

- ✔ None of this extra stuff is essential to using the tablet.

- ✔ If the earphones feature a microphone, you can use the microphone for dictation and audio recording on the tablet.

- ✔ If the earphones feature a button, you can use the button to pause and play music. Press the button once to pause and again to play.

- ✔ The set of screen protectors I purchased also came with a microfiber cloth to help clean the tablet's screen, plus a special cleaning-solution wipe. See Chapter 20 for more information about cleaning the tablet's screen.

- ✔ See Chapter 16 for more information on pairing your tablet with Bluetooth devices, such as a Bluetooth keyboard.

Where to Keep Your Tablet

Like your car keys, glasses, wallet, and light saber, you'll want to keep your Galaxy tablet in a place where it's safe, easy to find, and always handy whether you're at home, at work, on the road, or in a galaxy far, far away.

Making a home for the tablet

I recommend keeping your Galaxy tablet in the same spot when you've finished using it. My first suggestion is to make a spot next to your computer. Keep the charging cord handy or just plug the cord into the computer's USB port so that you can synchronize information with your computer regularly and keep the tablet charged.

Another handy place to keep the tablet is on your nightstand. See Chapter 14 for information on using the tablet to satisfy your nighttime reading or video watching. It can also serve as an alarm clock.

If you have a docking stand, plug your tablet into it when you're not toting it about.

Avoid keeping the tablet anyplace where it may get too hot. Keep the tablet visible. Don't put it where someone might sit on it, step on it, or otherwise damage it. For example, don't leave the tablet under a stack of newspapers on a table or counter, where it might get accidentally tossed out or recycled. Never leave your tablet unattended on the planet Venus.

As long as you remember to return the tablet to the same spot when you're done with it, you'll always know where it is.

Taking the tablet with you

If you're like me, you probably carry your Galactic tablet with you around the house, around the office, at the airport, in the air, or while you're in the car. I hope you're not using the tablet while you're driving! Regardless, have a portable place to store your tablet while you're on the road.

The ideal storage spot for the tablet is a specially designed Galaxy Note or Galaxy Tab carrying case or pouch, such as the type of pouches mama kangaroos have, but without the expense of owning a zoo. A case keeps the tablet from being dinged, scratched, or even unexpectedly turned on while it's in your backpack, purse, carry-on luggage, or wherever you put the tablet when you aren't using it.

Also see Chapter 18 for information on using your Galaxy tablet on the road.

The On and Off Chapter

In This Chapter

▶ Setting up and configuring the tablet
▶ Turning on the tablet
▶ Unlocking the screen
▶ Adding accounts
▶ Locking the screen
▶ Shutting down the tablet

I remember reading my very first computer book, back during the Steam-Powered Microcomputer Era. The book had clever and humorous directions for turning on the computer. When it came time to turn off the computer, there was nothing. No information on the proper method for shutting down the silly thing. No details. No humor. Apparently, you turned off the beastie by thunking the big red switch or yanking the plug from the wall socket.

Technology books are better today. As an example, I point to this chapter, which not only shows you how to turn on your Galaxy tablet but also offers directions on locking the thing *and* turning it off. As a bonus, I've tossed in some setup information as well. And, no, I didn't forget the humor.

Hello, Tablet

In all the effort made by engineers and wizards to make technology easier, one area where they fail is in the basic way you turn on a gizmo. Take the typical Galactic tablet: It can be turned on in two ways, plus special bonus goodies happen the *first* time it's turned on, plus it can be unlocked in several ways. This section discusses the details.

✔ Initial tablet setup works best when you already have a Google, or Gmail, account. If you lack a Google account, see the "Obtaining a Google account" section, later in the chapter, for details.

✔ If you have a Wi-Fi–only tablet, you'll skip the cellular network activation stage during setup.

✔ See Chapter 16 for information on connecting your tablet to a Wi-Fi network.

✔ The tablet doesn't start unless the battery is charged. See Chapter 1.

Turning on your Galaxy tablet (for the first time)

The very, very first time your Galaxy tablet is turned on is a special event because setup and configuration takes place. You need to do this procedure only once. If the tablet has already been set up and configured, skip to the next section, "Turning on your tablet."

The specifics for the setup and configuration process may change. As this book goes to press, the following are general steps for configuring the Galaxy Note or Galaxy Tab.

I recommend reading through these steps first, before turning on the tablet and working through them. The process goes kind of fast, and the screen may dim if you spend too much time waiting between steps.

1. **Turn on the tablet by pressing the Power Lock key.**

   You may have to press the key longer than you think; when the tablet's logo appears on the screen, the tablet has started.

   It's okay to turn on the tablet while it's plugged in and charging.

2. **Choose your language (if necessary), and then touch Next.**

   Yes, if you're reading this in English, you choose English as the language for your tablet. Если ты говоришь русский, выбрать Русский язык.

3. **Activate the cellular tablet.**

   This step was most likely done at the Phone Store. If it wasn't, follow the directions on the screen and wait for the connection to be made.

4. **Select a Wi-Fi network, entering the network password if prompted.**

   You see a list of available Wi-Fi networks. To connect with one, do the following:

   a. Choose the Wi-Fi network name as shown in the list.

   b. Type the network password by using the onscreen keyboard.

   c. Touch the Connect button.

   For help using the onscreen keyboard, see Chapter 4; Chapter 16 covers Wi-Fi networking.

   Upon success, you'll see the list of networks redisplayed. The word *Connected* appears below the Wi-Fi network that the tablet is using.

5. **Touch the Next button.**

6. **Confirm that the date and time are correct.**

   If not, touch the screen to set the date and time. I recommend setting the time zone before you set the time.

7. **Touch the Next button.**

   The next step is to agree to the terms and conditions, which seems like an option but isn't.

8. **Touch the box to agree to the terms and conditions.**

   A check mark appears. You can't touch the Next button (Step 9) until you select the box.

9. **Touch the Next button.**

   You'll be asked whether you want to sign in to a Samsung account or create a new one.

10. **If you already have a Samsung account and enjoy using it, sign in.**

    Otherwise, if you want to create one (later), touch the Skip button to skip this step.

     You can add the Samsung account — or any online account — at any time after the initial setup is complete. See the later section "Adding accounts to the tablet."

    The next step is required to connect your tablet to your Google account. Again, you can skip this step, but I recommend signing in with a Google account to fully exploit your tablet's capabilities. It is, after all, a Google device.

11. **If you have a Google account, sign in.**

    If you don't yet have a Google account, you can sign up for one later. Don't worry about skipping this step! See the later section "Account Creation and Configuration."

    a. *Touch the Yes button if you already have a Google account.*

    b. *Type your Gmail account name and password.*

       Type using the onscreen keyboard. Press the Next button on the keyboard to hop from the Email field to the Password field.

    c. *Touch the right-facing triangle (shown in the margin), and then touch the OK button to submit to Google's tyrannical terms.*

12. **Ensure that all items are selected on the next screen.**

    The items, specifically Backup and Location, relate to Google services. You may see all the items on one screen, or you may have to wade through several screens. Regardless, ensure that all items are selected.

13. **Touch the right-facing triangle.**

    If you have another Android mobile device, or use any of Google's online services, your account information is updated and synchronized with your new Galaxy Note or Galaxy Tab. For example, existing contacts are updated on the tablet, and settings made on other Android devices are copied to your new tablet. This process may take a few minutes.

14. **Continue working through the installation process.**

    At this point, a number of things could happen, depending on which tablet or cellular provider you have. Continue answering questions, touching the Next or right-facing triangle, until the process is over.

    Eventually, you will . . .

15. **Touch the Finish button.**

The good news is that you're done. The better news is that you need to complete this setup only once on your Galaxy tablet. From this point on, starting the tablet works as described in the next few sections.

- Most of the settings, choices, and options you've made during the initial setup process can be changed later.

- You may be asked various questions or prompted to try various tricks when you first start to use the tablet. Some of those prompts are helpful, but it's okay to skip things or select the Do Not Show Again box.

- App is short for *application*, which is like a computer program but one that runs on a tablet. Part of the setup process (Step 13 in the preceding list) involves synchronizing your new Galaxy tablet with apps you've previously obtained for an Android mobile device.

- See Chapter 15 for information on obtaining apps from the Google Play Store.

- See the later sidebar "Who is this Android person?" for more information about the Android operating system.

Turning on your tablet

To turn on your Galaxy tablet, press and hold down the Power Lock key. After a few seconds, you see the tablet's start-up logo and then some hypnotic animation. The tablet is coming to life.

Eventually, you see the main unlock screen, similar to what's shown in Figure 2-1. The screen may appear in a vertical orientation, depending on how you've oriented the tablet.

Slide your finger across the screen, just above the text *Swipe Screen to Unlock.* The tablet unlocks and you can start using it.

You probably won't turn on your Galaxy tablet much in the future. Mostly, you'll unlock the gizmo. See the later section "Unlocking the tablet."

Swipe your finger across here

Start-up apps

Figure 2-1: The basic unlocking screen.

Working the various lock screens

The standard swipe unlock screen isn't a difficult lock to pick. In fact, it's labeled the *No Security* screen lock. If you've added more security, you might see any one of several different lock screens on your tablet, each illustrated in Figure 2-2.

PIN   Pattern   Password   Face

Figure 2-2: Various unlocking screens.

The PIN lock requires that you type a secret number to unlock the tablet. Touch the OK button to unlock the tablet, or use the Del (X) icon to back up and erase.

To work the Pattern lock, you trace your finger over the nine dots that appear on the screen (refer to Figure 2-2) according to a preset pattern. Upon matching the pattern, the tablet is unlocked.

The Password lock requires that you type a multicharacter password to unlock the tablet. Touch the Done button on the keyboard to accept the password and unlock the tablet.

Finally, the Face lock screen works when you hold up the tablet and gaze at the touchscreen. If the voice option has been added, you'll be prompted to utter a vocal password, such as "open sesame." This option may not be available on all tablets.

Whether or not you see these various lock screens depends on how you've configured your tablet's security. Directions for setting the locks as well as for removing them and returning to the standard screen lock are found in Chapter 19.

> ✔ The Pattern lock can start at any dot, not necessarily the upper-left dot, as shown in Figure 2-2.

> ✔ For additional information on working the onscreen keyboard, see Chapter 4.

Unlocking the tablet

You'll probably leave your Galaxy Note or Galaxy Tab on all the time. The tablets are designed that way and the battery supports keeping it on for lengthy periods of time. When your tablet is bored or you've ignored it for a while, it locks itself in a manner similar to a computer entering sleep mode. When locked, the touchscreen turns off to save power.

> ✔ To unlock the tablet, press the Power Lock key. Unlike when turning on the tablet, a quick press is all that's needed.

> ✔ You can unlock the tablet also by pressing the Home key.

> ✔ On the Galaxy Note, you can unlock the tablet by removing the S Pen.

After unlocking the tablet, you see the unlock screen (refer to Figure 2-1). Or if you've configured the tablet for more security, you see one of the unlocking screens (refer to Figure 2-2). Simply unlock the screen, and you can start using the device.

See the section "Locking the tablet," later in this chapter, for information on how to lock the tablet.

Who is this Android person?

Just like your computer, your Samsung tablet has an operating system. It's the main program in charge of all the software, or apps, inside your tablet. Unlike on your computer, however, Android is a mobile device operating system, designed primarily for use in tablets and smartphones.

Android is based on the Linux operating system, which is also a computer operating system. Linux is much more stable and bug-free than Windows, so it's not as popular. Google owns, maintains, and develops Android, which is why your online Google information is synced with the Galaxy

tablet. The Android mascot, shown here, often appears on Android apps or hardware. He has no official name, though most folks call him Andy.

Unlocking and running an app

Your lock screen might be adorned with certain start-up apps, such as the five app icons shown in Figure 2-1. You can immediately start one of those apps when the Swipe lock is set by touching the app icon and swiping the screen.

Only the Swipe lock lets you unlock the tablet and immediately start an app.

Account Creation and Configuration

Your Samsung Galaxy Note or Galaxy Tab can be home to your various online incarnations, including your e-mail accounts, online services, subscriptions, plus other digital personas. I recommended adding those accounts to your tablet to continue the setup and configuration process.

Obtaining a Google account

Although it's possible to use your Galaxy tablet without a Google account, you'd be missing out on a buncha features. So if you don't already have one, drop everything (but not this book) and follow these steps to obtain a Google account:

1. **Open your computer's web browser program.**

   Yes, these steps work best if you use your computer, not the tablet.

2. **Visit the main Google page at www.google.com.**

   Type www.google.com in the web browser's address bar.

3. **Click the Sign In link or button.**

   Another page opens, and on it you can log in to your Google account, but you don't have a Google account, so . . .

4. **Click the link to create a new account.**

   The link is typically found below the text boxes where you would log in to your Google account. As I write this chapter, the link is titled Sign Up.

5. **Continue heeding the directions until you've created your own Google account.**

Eventually, your account is set up and configured.

To try things out, log off from Google and then log back in. That way, you ensure that you've done everything properly — and remembered your password. Your web browser may even prompt you to let it remember the password for you.

I also recommend creating a bookmark for your account's Google page. The Ctrl+D or ⌘+D keyboard shortcut is used to create a bookmark in just about any web browser.

Your next step is to make your new Google account known to the tablet. Keep reading.

Adding accounts to the tablet

You don't have to add all your online accounts during the tablet setup and configuration process. If you skipped those steps, or when you have more accounts to add, you can easily do so. With your tablet turned on and unlocked, follow these steps:

1. **Touch the Apps icon.**

   The Apps icon is located on the Home screen. Its icon is shown in the margin.

2. **Open the Settings app.**

   You may have to swipe the screen right or left to find the Settings app.

   After touching the Settings icon, the Settings screen appears. It contains commands for configuring and setting tablet options.

3. **Select the Accounts category.**

   You may have to touch the General tab to find that category, as shown in Figure 2-3. If you don't see any tabs across the top of the Settings app screen, scroll the list on the left side of the screen until you find the Accounts category. (Not every Galaxy tablet has the same Settings app.)

4. Touch Add Account (next to the green plus sign).

5. Select an account from the list that appears.

Don't worry if you don't see the exact type of account you want to add. You may have to add an app before a specific account appears. Chapter 15 covers adding apps.

6. Follow the directions on the screen to sign into your account.

The steps that follow depend on the account. Generally speaking, you sign in using an existing username and password.

When you're done, press the Home key to return to the Home screen, or you can continue adding accounts by repeating these steps.

- ✔ See Chapter 6 for specific information on adding e-mail accounts to your Galaxy Note or Galaxy Tab.

- ✔ Chapter 8 covers social networking on your tablet. Refer to that chapter for information on adding Facebook, Twitter, and other accounts.

- ✔ See Chapter 3 for information about the Home screen and using the Apps icon.

- ✔ Swiping the screen, as well as other touchscreen techniques, is also covered in Chapter 3.

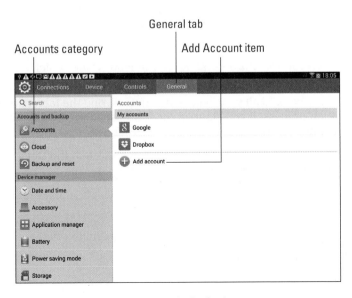

Figure 2-3: The Accounts category in the Settings app.

Farewell, Tablet

I know of three ways to say goodbye to your Galaxy tablet, and only one of them involves a trained elephant. The other two methods are documented in this section.

Locking the tablet

To lock the tablet, simply press the Power Lock key. The touchscreen goes dark; the tablet is locked.

> ✔ The tablet still works while it's locked; it still receives e-mail and can still play music. But it's not using as much power as it would with the display on.
>
> ✔ Your tablet will probably spend most of its time locked.
>
> ✔ Locking doesn't turn off the tablet.
>
> ✔ Any timers or alarms you set still activate when the tablet is locked. See Chapter 14 for information on setting timers and alarms.
>
> ✔ To unlock the tablet, press and release the Power Lock key. See the "Unlocking the tablet" section, earlier in this chapter.

Controlling the lock timeout

You can manually lock the Galaxy Note or Galaxy Tab at any time by pressing the Power Lock key. That's why it's called the Power *Lock* key. When you don't manually lock the tablet, it automatically locks itself after a given period of inactivity.

You have control over the automatic lock timeout value, which can be set from 15 seconds to 30 minutes. Obey these steps:

1. **At the Home screen, touch the Apps icon.**

2. **Touch the Settings icon to open the Settings app.**

3. **If you see tabs across the top of the screen, touch the Device tab.**

   Not every version of the Settings app displays tabs across the top of the screen (refer to Figure 2-3).

4. **On the left side of the screen, select Display.**

   You may have to swipe down the left side to find the Display item.

5. **Choose Screen Timeout.**

6. **Select a timeout value from the list.**

   I prefer 1 minute. The standard value is 30 seconds.

7. **Press the Home key to return to the Home screen.**

The lock timer measures inactivity; when you don't touch the screen or tap an icon or a button, the timer starts ticking. About 5 seconds before the time-out value you set (refer to Step 6), the touchscreen dims. Then it turns off, and the tablet locks. If you touch the screen before then, the timer is reset.

Turning off your Galaxy tablet

To turn off the tablet, heed these steps:

1. **Press and hold down the Power Lock key.**

   You see the Device Options menu, shown in Figure 2-4.
   The Galaxy Tab 3 doesn't feature the Vibrate option, shown in the figure.

Figure 2-4: The Device Options menu.

 If you chicken out and don't want to turn off the tablet, touch the Back button to dismiss the Device Options menu.

2. **Touch the Power Off item.**

3. **Touch OK.**

   The tablet turns itself off.

The tablet doesn't run when it's off, so it doesn't remind you of appointments, collect e-mail, or let you hear any alarms you've set. The tablet also isn't angry with you for turning it off, though you may sense some resentment when you turn it on again.

 Keep the tablet in a safe place while it's turned off. Refer to Chapter 1 for storage suggestions.

Find Your Way around the Galaxy

In This Chapter

▶ Working the touchscreen

▶ Changing the volume

▶ Getting around the Home screen

▶ Using buttons and icons

▶ Running apps

▶ Checking notifications

▶ Finding all the apps

▶ Accessing recently used apps

▶ Using the S Pen

I'm not certain, but I believe that your Galaxy tablet is more powerful than all the technology in the bat cave from the 1960s TV show, *Batman*. Those computers were impressive, with lots of buttons and flashing lights. In today's high-tech world, however, sophisticated devices don't have a lot of buttons and flashing lights. In fact, the more sophisticated the device, the fewer buttons and lights.

To accommodate for the lack of buttons, both the Galaxy Note and Galaxy Tab feature a touchscreen. You use the touchscreen to control the tablet, which might be a new experience for you. To get you up to speed, and to get Batman up to speed should he be reading this book, I present this chapter on understanding the touchscreen interface.

Basic Operations

The first steps toward learning how to manipulate your tablet are truly simple. The terminology is most definitely not simple. This section helps iron things out.

Touching the touchscreen

Minus an ample supply of buttons and knobs, your tablet is controlled for the most part by manipulating things on the touchscreen. That manipulation happens by using one or two of your fingers. It doesn't matter which fingers you use, and feel free to experiment with other body parts as well.

Here are some of the many ways you can touch the touchscreen:

Touch: The simplest way to manipulate the touchscreen is to touch it. You touch an object, an icon, a control, a menu item, a doodad, and so on. The touch operation is similar to a mouse click on a computer. It may also be referred to as a *tap* or *press*.

Double-tap: Touch the screen twice in the same location. Double-tapping can be used to zoom in on an image or a map, but it can also zoom out. Because of the double-tap's dual nature, I recommend using the *pinch* or *spread* operation instead when you want to zoom.

Long-press: A long-press occurs when you touch part of the screen and hold down your finger. Depending on what you're doing, a pop-up menu may appear, or the item you're long-pressing may get "picked up" so that you can move it around. A *long-press* might also be referred to as *touch and hold down* in some documentation.

Swipe: To swipe, you touch your finger on one spot and then drag it to another spot. Swipes can go up, down, left, or right; the touchscreen content moves in the direction you swipe your finger. A swipe can be fast or slow. It's also called a *flick* or *slide*.

Pinch: A pinch involves two fingers, which start out separated and then are brought together. The effect is used to *zoom out,* to reduce the size of an image or see more of a map.

Spread: The opposite of pinch is spread. You start out with your fingers together and then spread them. The spread is used to *zoom in,* to enlarge an image or see more detail on a map.

Rotate: A few apps let you rotate an image on the screen by touching with two fingers and twisting them around a center point. Think of turning a combination lock on a safe, and you get the rotate operation.

You can't manipulate the touchscreen while wearing gloves unless they're gloves designed for using electronic touchscreens, such as the gloves that Batman wears.

Changing the orientation

Your Galaxy tablet features a gizmo called an *accelerometer.* It determines in which direction the tablet is pointed or whether you've reoriented the device from an upright to a horizontal position, or even upside down. That way, the information on the touchscreen always appears upright, no matter how you hold it.

To demonstrate how the tablet orients itself, rotate the device to the left or right. Most apps change their orientation to match however you've turned the tablet (see Figure 3-1).

Vertical orientation   Horizontal orientation

Figure 3-1: Galaxy tablet orientation.

The rotation feature may not work for all apps, especially games, which may present themselves in one orientation only.

✔ On some large-screen Galaxy tablets, the Apps icon stays in the lower-right corner when you rotate the device.

✔ You can lock the orientation if the rotating screen bothers you. See the "Making Quick Settings" section, later in this chapter.

✔ A nifty application for demonstrating the accelerometer is the game Labyrinth. It can be purchased at the Google Play Store, or the free version, Labyrinth Lite, can be downloaded. See Chapter 15 for more information about the Google Play Store.

Controlling the volume

Sometimes the sound level is too loud. Sometimes it's too soft. And rarely, it's just right. Finding that just-right level is the job of the Volume key that clings to the side of your Galaxy tablet.

If the Volume key is on top of your tablet, press the left part of the key to increase the volume and the right part to decrease the volume. If the Volume key is on the side of your tablet, press the top part to make the volume louder and the bottom part to make the volume softer.

As you press the Volume key, a graphic appears on the touchscreen to illustrate the relative volume level, as shown in Figure 3-2.

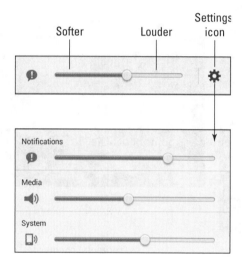

Figure 3-2: Setting the volume.

Touch the Settings icon, shown in Figure 3-2, to see more detailed volume controls. You can individually set the volume for notifications, media, and system sounds, as shown in the expanded onscreen volume control: Swipe the white dot left or right to set the volume.

✔ When the volume is set all the way down, the tablet is silenced. Some tablets may switch to vibration mode. (Not every Galaxy tablet features vibration mode.)

✔ The Volume key works even when the tablet is locked. That means you don't need to unlock the device to adjust the volume when you're listening to music.

Behold the Home Screen

The main base from which you begin exploration of your Galaxy Note or Galaxy Tab is the *Home* screen. It's the first thing you see after unlocking the tablet, and the place you go to whenever you quit an app.

To view the Home screen at any time, press the Home key, which is found on the front of the tablet, right below the touchscreen.

Touring the Home screen

The main Home screen is illustrated in Figure 3-3.

You'll find many fun and interesting things to notice on the Home screen:

Notification icons: These icons come and go, depending on what happens in your digital life. For example, icons appear whenever you receive a new e-mail message or have a pending appointment. The "Reviewing notifications" section, later in this chapter, describes how to deal with notifications.

Status icons: These icons represent the tablet's current condition, such as the type of network it's connected to, its signal strength, and its battery status, as well as whether the tablet is connected to a Wi-Fi network or using Bluetooth, for example.

App icons: The meat of the meal on the Home screen plate, app (application) icons are where the action takes place. Touching an app icon opens that app.

Widgets: A widget is a teensy program that can display information, let you control the tablet, access features, or do something purely amusing.

Folders: Multiple apps can be stored in a folder. Touch the folder to see a pop-up window that lists all the apps. Touch an app icon to start.

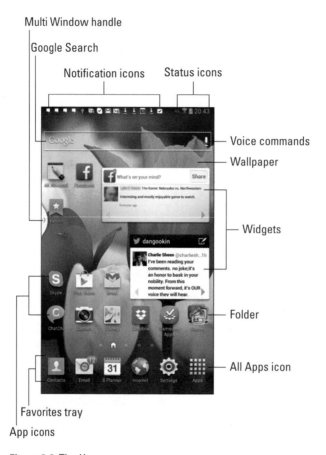

Figure 3-3: The Home screen.

Wallpaper: The background image you see on the Home screen is the wallpaper.

Favorites tray: The lineup of icons near the bottom of the screen consists of five slots for popular apps. This feature isn't found on every tablet's Home screen.

Apps icon: At the bottom right of the Home screen is the Apps icon. Touching this icon displays the Apps screen, which lists all apps installed on your tablet. See the later section "Visiting the Apps screen" for details.

Multi Window tab: This item appears only when the Multi Window feature is active. Touching the tab displays the Multi Window tray. See the later section "Playing with Multi Window" for information.

Ensure that you recognize the names of the various parts of the Home screen. These terms are used throughout this book and in whatever other scant Galaxy tablet documentation exists. Directions for using the Home screen gizmos are found throughout this chapter.

✔ The Home screen is customizable. You can add and remove icons, widgets, folders, and shortcuts, and even change wallpaper (background) images. See Chapter 19 for more information.

✔ When you rotate the tablet, the Home screen changes its orientation to match (refer to Figure 3-1).

✔ Touching a part of the Home screen that doesn't feature an icon or a control does nothing. That is, unless you're using the *live wallpaper* feature. In that case, touching the screen changes the wallpaper in some way, depending on the wallpaper that's selected. You can read more about live wallpaper in Chapter 19.

✔ You may see numbers affixed to some Home screen icons. Those numbers indicate pending actions, such as the unread e-mail messages indicated by the icon shown in the margin.

Accessing multiple Home screens

The Home screen is more than what you see. It's actually an entire street of Home screens, with only one Home screen *panel* displayed at a time.

To switch from one panel to another, swipe the Home screen left or right. The currently displayed Home screen can be determined by looking at the Home screen index, shown in Figure 3-4.

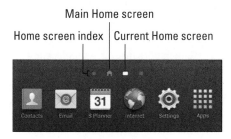

Figure 3-4: The Home screen index.

When you press the Home key, you're returned to the last Home screen panel you viewed. To return to the main Home screen panel, press the Home key a second time.

✔ Both the Galaxy Note and Galaxy Tab come with one panel to the left and right of the main Home screen panel.

✔ You can add more panels to the Home screen street; details are provided in Chapter 19.

Using common buttons and icons

Below the touchscreen, and to the left and right of the Home key, are two popular touch buttons, each adorned with its own icon. These buttons are used to control not only the Home screen but also apps.

 The Menu button displays a menu of commands. When no commands are available, touching the button does nothing.

 The Back button returns to the previous screen. It also closes or dismisses a menu, a pop-up window, or the onscreen keyboard. When there's nothing to go back to, the Back button does nothing.

If you touch and hold down the Back button and the Multi Window feature is active, the Multi Window tray pops out. (To find out about Multi Window, see the "Playing with Multi Window" section, later in this chapter.)

Beyond the Menu and Back buttons, various icons appear on the touchscreen while you use the tablet. Touch these icons to control and manipulate apps. Table 3-1 lists the most common icons and their functions.

Table 3-1		Common Icons
Icon	*Name*	*Function*
╋	Add	Adds or creates a new item. The plus symbol (+) may be used with other symbols, depending on the app.
🔖	Bookmark	Remembers the current item, such as a web page or app in the Play Store.
✕	Close	Closes a window or clears text from an input field.
🗑	Delete	Removes a selected item or is used in a drag operation to delete something.
🎤	Dictation	Lets you use your voice to dictate text. On the Home screen, dictation is used with the Google Search function.
✏	Edit	Lets you edit an item, add text, or fill in fields.
☆	Favorite	Flags a favorite item, such as a contact or web page.

Icon	Name	Function
▪▪▪	Menu	Displays an app's menu. Some apps use this icon in addition to the Menu button found below the touchscreen.
◢	More	Displays a pop-up menu. This teensy icon appears in the lower-right corner of a button.
⟳	Refresh	Fetches new or reloads existing information.
🔍	Search	Searches the tablet or the Internet for some tidbit of information.
⚙	Settings	Adjusts options for an app.
⤙	Share	Shares information stored on the tablet via e-mail, social networking, or other Internet services.
⟳	Sync	Synchronizes information, such as updating data shared on the Internet.

Various sections throughout this book give examples of using the icons. Their images appear in the book's margins where relevant.

Home Screen Chores

To become a cat, you must know how to perform several duties: Sleep, eat, catch critters, and cause mischief. A cat's life isn't difficult, and neither is your Galaxy tablet life, as long as you know how to do some basic duties on the Home screen. As with the cat, you need to know about only a few duties.

Starting an app

It's blissfully simple to run an app on the Home screen: Touch its icon. The app starts.

- ✐ Not all apps dwell on the Home screen, but they all appear when you display the Apps screen. See the "Visiting the Apps screen" section, later in this chapter.

- ✐ When an app closes, you're returned to the Home screen.

- ✐ App is short for *application*. It's another word for *program* or *software*.

Accessing a widget

Like apps, widgets can appear on the Home screen. To use a widget, touch it. What happens next depends on the widget and what it does.

For example, the YouTube widget lets you peruse videos. The Calendar widget shows a preview of your upcoming schedule.

Other widgets do interesting things, display useful information, or give you access to the tablet's settings or features.

> ✔ Just like apps, new widgets are obtained from the Google Play Store. See Chapter 15 for information.

> ✔ See Chapter 19 for details on adding widgets to the Home screen.

Reviewing notifications

Notifications appear as icons at the top left of the Home screen (refer to Figure 3-3). To review them, you pull down the notifications shade by dragging your finger downward from the top-left part of the screen. The notifications shade is illustrated in Figure 3-5.

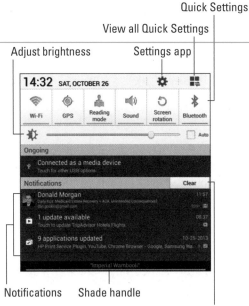

Figure 3-5: Reviewing notifications.

Touch a notification to deal with it. What happens next depends on the notification, but most often the app that generated the notification appears. You might also be given the opportunity to deal with whatever caused the notification, such as a calendar appointment.

Dismiss an individual notification by touching it and then swiping to the right or left. To dismiss all notifications, touch the Clear button. Some ongoing notifications, such as the USB notification in Figure 3-5, cannot be dismissed.

 When you're done looking, you can slide the notifications shade up again: Swipe the notifications shade handle by dragging your finger up the screen. If you find this process frustrating (and it is), touch the Back button.

✔ If you don't deal with notifications, they can stack up!

✔ Notification icons disappear after they've been chosen.

✔ Dismissing some notifications doesn't prevent them from appearing again in the future. For example, notifications to update your programs continue to appear, as do calendar reminders.

✔ The text above the notification shade handle refers to the currently connected Wi-Fi network. In Figure 3-5, it's "Imperial Wambooli," my office network.

✔ Some apps, such as Facebook and Twitter, don't display notifications unless you're logged in. See Chapter 8.

✔ The tablet plays a sound, or *ringtone,* when a new notification floats in. You can choose which sound plays; see Chapter 19 for more information.

Making Quick Settings

Many common settings and features for your Galaxy Note or Galaxy Tab can be found atop the notifications shade. These Quick Settings appear as large icons (refer to Figure 3-5).

To see all Quick Settings, swipe the row of icons left or right. Or you can reorient the tablet to a horizontal position. Touching the Quick Settings icon in the upper-right corner of the screen (refer to Figure 3-5) displays the whole lot of them.

To activate a setting, touch its icon. When the setting is on, it appears highlighted in green. Touch a highlighted setting to turn it off.

You find out how to use the various settings throughout the book. Generally speaking, any item that can be turned on or off — such as Wi-Fi, Bluetooth, Airplane Mode, Sound, and so on — can be accessed quickly from a Quick Settings icon.

Visiting the Apps screen

The icons you see on the Home screen don't represent all the apps in your tablet. Those icons aren't even apps themselves; they're shortcuts. To see all installed apps, you must visit the Apps screen. To do so, touch the Apps button on the Home screen. You see the first panel of the Apps screen, as shown in Figure 3-6.

View downloaded apps

Apps tab   Widgets tab

App screen index

Swipe to see more apps

Figure 3-6: The Apps screen.

You can find any additional apps by swiping the Apps screen to the left.

Even more apps might be found inside folders found on the Apps screen. An example of a folder icon is shown in the margin. To access apps in the folder, touch the icon.

To peruse installed widgets, touch the Widgets tab. Scroll to the left to view the various widgets.

As you install apps, they're added to the Apps screen. New apps are added to the end of the list or inserted alphabetically — that is, unless you change the way the Apps screen is viewed. Follow these steps:

1. **Touch the Menu button.**

2. **Choose the View Type command.**

3. **Select Alphabetical Grid to have the apps listed alphabetically.**

When Alphabetical Grid is selected, new apps are inserted in the Apps screen alphabetically.

If you choose the Customizable Grid option (Step 3), you can edit the order in which apps appear on the Apps screen. To edit, touch the Menu button and choose the Edit command. Then use your finger to rearrange the apps on the Apps screen.

See Chapter 15 for information on getting more apps for your Galaxy tablet.

Reviewing recent apps

If you're like me, you probably use the same apps over and over on your tablet. You can easily access that list of recent and currently running apps by pressing and holding down the Home key. When you do, you see a pop-up list of apps most recently accessed, similar to the list shown in Figure 3-7.

To reopen an app, choose it from the list. The app takes over the screen, in most cases picking up right where you left off.

✒ Apps on your Galaxy Note or Galaxy Tab tablet do not quit. They keep running, so using the recent apps list is a great way to switch between running apps.

✒ Don't fret that apps don't quit when you close them. Some apps do feature a Quit or Sign Off command. Even when they don't, the Android operating system shuts down apps you haven't used in a while or which are taking up too much memory. That process takes place automatically and no information is ever lost.

✒ You can quit a program by using Task Manager. Touch the Task Manager button (see Figure 3-7). You'll see a list of running apps. Touch the End button by an app to shut it down.

✒ For the programs you use all the time, consider creating shortcuts on the Home screen. Chapter 19 describes how to create shortcuts for apps.

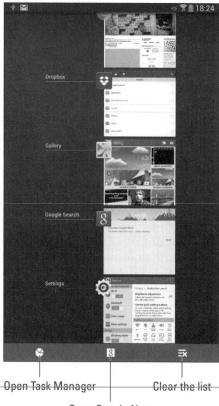

Open Task Manager   Clear the list

Open Google Now

Figure 3-7: Recently used apps.

Playing with Multi Window

Samsung Galaxy tablets feature a unique multitasking feature called Multi Window. It allows you to view two apps side-by-side on the touchscreen. This is opposed to how apps normally run, which is full screen.

Before you can use Multi Window, ensure that it's activated. The quick way to turn on this feature is to pull down the notifications shade and choose the Multi Window quick action. When it's activated, you'll see the Multi Window handle on the right side of the Home screen (refer to Figure 3-3).

To use Multi Window, tap the handle to view the various apps sitting in the tray. Drag an app icon from the tray out onto the screen to start that app. To start a second app, drag another icon from the tray onto the screen.

With Multi Window active, the Home screen is split horizontally or vertically, depending on the tablet's orientation. Each side of the split contains a running app, as shown in Figure 3-8, which illustrates the My Music and Gallery apps.

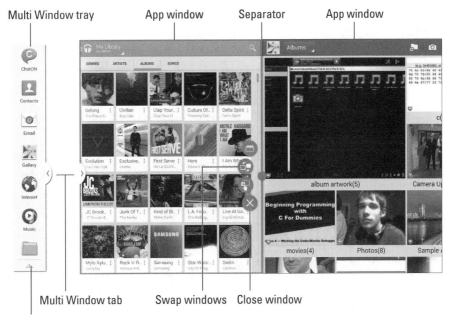

Multi Window tray   App window   Separator   App window

Multi Window tab   Swap windows   Close window

Show commands

Figure 3-8: Multi Window in action.

To adjust the window size, drag the separator left or right, or up or down when the tablet is oriented horizontally. The two windows need not be equal in size.

The control buttons let you manipulate the windows. For example, you can close a window or swap windows, as illustrated in Figure 3-8. To see those controls, touch the separator. Once a window is expanded full-screen or closed, you exit Multi Window and return to normal full-screen operation.

You can exit Multi Window mode at any time also by pressing the Home key.

✔ Only certain apps can run in Multi Window. The variety is seen by scrolling the Multi Window tray up and down.

✔ Touch the Edit button on the Multi Window tray to add or remove apps. You may have to touch the bottom of the tray to see the Edit button.

> ✔ You can keep Multi Window active yet hide the tab by long-pressing the Back button. To make the tab reappear, long-press the Back button again.

> ✔ Use your finger to drag the Multi Window tray from one side of the screen to the other.

> ✔ Android tablets always run multiple apps at once. The only benefit to Multi Window is that you can view two apps at the same time.

The Magical S Pen

The Galaxy Note comes with a handy stylus called the S Pen. It's probably the reason you chose the Galaxy Note over that silly, pen-less Galaxy Tab. Your tablet's S Pen opens a constellation of opportunities for tablet input and manipulation. Yes, it can do more than just draw mustaches on pictures.

> ✔ See Chapter 4 for information on writing text with the S Pen.

> ✔ Drawing mustaches on pictures isn't covered in this edition of the book.

Understanding the S Pen

To use the S Pen, slide it out of the tablet's case: Grab the cap and yank the thing out. If the tablet is locked, pulling out the S Pen unlocks the tablet. You'll still have to work the PIN, Pattern, or Password screen locks, but if your Note has only the Swipe lock, it's unlocked right away and ready for action.

Take a second to locate the S Pen button. It's found near the tip of the S Pen, illustrated in Figure 3-9. Use that button to help the S Pen perform some of its fancier tricks, but be aware that the button is found on only one side of the S Pen. That means that there's a right way and a wrong way to hold the thing.

It's here

Figure 3-9: Where to find the S Pen button.

You can use the S Pen at any time as a handy substitute for your finger. All touch-screen manipulations you can do with a single finger can be performed by using the S Pen; see the earlier section "Touching the touchscreen" for the list.

One S Pen feature you may notice right away is the Air Command control. Keep reading in the next section for more info.

> ✔ Always replace the S Pen when you're done. Stick it back in the slot. You do not want to lose the S Pen! Because . . .
>
> ✔ If you lose the S Pen, you can obtain a replacement from Samsung. It's not cheap. Well, not as cheap as it could be.

Using Air Command

Most of the fancy things you can do with the S Pen are easily accessed by using the Air Command dingus, shown in Figure 3-10.

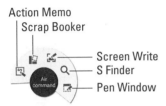

Figure 3-10: The Air Command dingus.

Air Command appears whenever you remove the S Pen from its launching tube. You can also make it appear by pointing the S Pen at the touchscreen (you don't need to touch the screen with it), and then clicking the S Pen button.

Here are brief descriptions of what the Air Command buttons do:

Action Memo: Choosing this item opens an Action Memo window into which you can jot notes. The notes are accessed from the Action Memo app, found in the Samsung folder on the Apps screen.

Scrap Booker: This feature allows you to copy chunks of the screen to the Scrapbook app. The chunks are graphic images, not the information you've circled by using the S Pen.

Screen Write: The Screen Write command takes a picture of the screen — a screen shot — and then lets you draw in it by using the S Pen. The saved images can be accessed from the Gallery app. See Chapter 12.

S Finder: Use this item to search your tablet — or the Internet — for specific tidbits of information.

Pen Window: After choosing this item, draw a rectangle on the screen, and then choose a mini-app to appear in that rectangle. Only a handful of apps are accessible through the Pen Window.

If you don't see the Air Command gizmus, ensure that it's activated on your Galaxy Note. Open the Settings app, found on the Apps screen. Touch the Controls tab and choose the S Pen category from the left side of the window. On the right side, ensure that the Air Command item has a green ON button to its right. If not, touch the button.

Doing some S Pen tricks

Those Galaxy Tab owners are going to laugh at you if you use the S Pen just as a substitute for your finger. Make those guys seethe with jealousy by showing them some of these fancy S Pen tricks:

Screen capture and scribble: To take a snapshot of the screen, press and hold down the S Pen button while long-pressing the S Pen to the touchscreen. After about two seconds, you'll hear a shutter click sound. The screen shot is saved. You're then given an opportunity to scribble on the screen shot and save it with your edits. This trick works just like the Screen Write command, covered in the preceding section.

Selective screen capture: Press and hold down the S Pen button and then draw around a chunk of information on the screen. That chunk — the exact size you drew around — is presented on the screen. Choose an app from the bottom of the screen and the chunk is sent to that app for further manipulation.

Quick launch the Action Memo app: When you're in dire need to access the Action Memo app and using the Air Command control is too bothersome, press the S Pen button and double-tap the screen. Voilà!

4

Typing and Text

In This Chapter

▶ Using the onscreen keyboard

▶ Accessing special characters

▶ Writing text with the S Pen

▶ Dictating text with voice input

▶ Editing text

▶ Selecting, cutting, copying, and pasting text

*D*on't bother looking for your tablet's keyboard. It's not there. The keyboard you'll use for your Galaxy Note or Galaxy Tab appears on the touchscreen, popping up whenever text input is demanded. Using such a keyboard may be strange for you. Editing text on a touchscreen may be odd. And voice input? That's unusual. All that weird stuff is gently presented in this chapter.

This Is a Keyboard?

To accommodate your typing needs, your Galaxy tablet displays an onscreen keyboard. Don't let it frighten you. If it does, read this section to discover a bit more about what the onscreen keyboard is and how it differs from the keyboards you use in the real world.

Using the onscreen keyboard

The onscreen keyboard reveals itself on the bottom half of the screen, similar to what's shown in Figure 4-1. If you find that keyboard comforting, you're getting ahead of yourself. That's because the keyboard may change its appearance and function as you use it. This feature can be useful but also disconcerting.

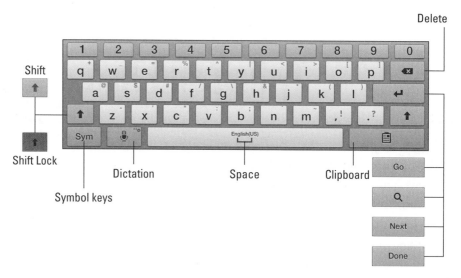

Figure 4-1: The onscreen keyboard.

In Figure 4-1, the onscreen keyboard is shown in alphabetic mode. You see keys from A through Z in lowercase. You also see a Shift key for producing capital letters, and a Delete key, which backspaces and erases.

The Enter key, which is below the Delete key, changes its look depending on what you're typing. Five variations are shown in Figure 4-1. Here's what each one does:

- **Enter/Return:** Just like the Enter or Return key on a computer keyboard, this key ends a paragraph of text. It's used mostly when filling in long stretches of text or when multiline input is needed.
- **Go:** This action key directs the app to proceed with a search, accept input, or perform another action.
- **Search:** You see the Search key when you're searching for something. Touching the key starts the search.
- **Next:** This key appears when you're typing information in multiple fields. Touching this key switches from one field to the next, such as when typing a username and a password.
- **Done:** This key appears whenever you've finished typing text in the final field of a screen that has several fields. Sometimes it dismisses the onscreen keyboard; sometimes not.

The large key at the bottom center of the onscreen keyboard is the Space key. The keys to the left and right may change depending on the context of what you're typing. For example, a www or .com key may appear to assist in typing a web page or an e-mail address. Other keys may change as well, although the basic alphabetic keys remain the same.

A real keyboard?

If typing is your thing and the onscreen keyboard doesn't do it for you, consider getting a real keyboard for your tablet. Official Samsung keyboard docks are available, including some Galaxy tablet combination keyboard covers. You can also use any Bluetooth keyboard with your Galaxy Note or Galaxy Tab. Those keyboards have the advantage of being wireless. Read more about Bluetooth in Chapter 16.

✔ To resummon the keyboard, touch any text field or spot on the screen where typing is permitted.

✔ To dismiss the onscreen keyboard, touch the Back button.

✔ If you pine for a real keyboard, one that exists in the fourth dimension, you're not out of luck. See the nearby sidebar, "A real keyboard?"

✔ The keyboard reorients itself when you rotate the tablet. The onscreen keyboard's horizontal orientation is the easiest to use.

Accessing special keyboard symbols

You're not limited to typing only the symbols you see on the alphabetic keyboard, shown in Figure 4-1. The onscreen keyboard has many more symbols available, which you can see by touching the Sym key. Touching this key gives you access to two additional keyboard layouts, as shown in Figure 4-2.

Figure 4-2: Number and symbol keyboards.

Touch the 1/2 or 2/2 key to switch between the symbol keyboards, as illustrated in Figure 4-2. Some of the symbols may not look the same on all tablets.

To return to the standard alpha keyboard (refer to Figure 4-1), touch the ABC key.

You can access special character keys from the main alphabetic keyboard, provided you know a secret: Long-press (touch and hold down) a key. When you do, you see a pop-up palette of additional characters, similar to the ones shown for the A key in Figure 4-3.

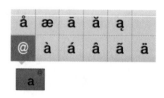

Figure 4-3: Special symbol pop-up palette thing.

Choose a character from the pop-up palette by keeping your finger down and sliding over the key you want. Or choose a highlighted key (the @ in Figure 4-3) by lifting your finger from the touchscreen. (If you accidentally type a special character, just touch the Delete key to erase it.)

Not every character sports a special pop-up palette.

The Old Hunt-and-Peck

The old mechanical typewriters required a lot of effort to press their keys: clackity-clack-clack. Electronic typewriters made typing easier. And, of course, the computer is the easiest thing to type on. A tablet? That device takes some getting used to because its keys are merely flat rectangles on a touchscreen. If this concept doesn't drive you nuts, typing on a tablet is something you should master with relative ease.

Typing one character at a time

The onscreen keyboard that appears on your Galaxy Note or Galaxy Tab touchscreen is pretty easy to figure out: Touch a letter to produce the character. In that respect, the onscreen keyboard works just like a computer keyboard.

As you type, the key you touch is highlighted. The tablet may give a wee bit of feedback in the form of a faint click.

- ✔ Above all, it helps to *type slowly* until you get used to the onscreen keyboard.
- ✔ When you make a mistake, press the Delete key to back up and erase.
- ✔ A blinking cursor on the touchscreen shows where new text appears, which is similar to how text input works on your computer.
- ✔ When you type a password, each character you type appears briefly, but for security reasons, it's then replaced by a black dot.
- ✔ See the later section, "Text Editing," for more details on editing your text.

Typing quickly by using predictive text

As you type, you may see a selection of word suggestions just above the keyboard. That's the tablet's Predictive Text feature. You can use this feature to greatly accelerate your typing.

In Figure 4-4, I typed the word *I.* The keyboard then suggested the word *thought,* which I chose from the Predictive Text list. Then I chose the word *I* again, and then the word *was.*

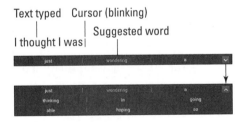

Figure 4-4: Predictive Text in action.

To see additional text, touch the arrow button, illustrated in Figure 4-4. You'll see more words that you can choose from. Touching a word inserts it in the text.

When your desired word doesn't appear, continue typing: The Predictive Text feature begins making suggestions based on what you've typed so far. Touch the right word when it appears.

To ensure that the Predictive Text has been activated on your tablet, follow these steps:

1. **Long-press the Microphone key on the onscreen keyboard.**

2. **From the pop-up menu, choose the Gear icon.**

The Gear icon represents settings. In this case, you see the Samsung Keyboard Settings screen.

3. Ensure that the button next to the Predictive Text option is green.

Green means on. If the button isn't green, touch it to turn it green and activate Predictive Text.

4. Touch the Back button to return to your typing.

Likewise, if you find Predictive Text boring and predictable, disable it by repeating these steps but turning off the option in Step 3.

Adding SwiftKey Flow

If you're really after typing speed, consider enabling the onscreen keyboard's SwiftKey Flow feature. It allows you to type words by swiping your finger over the keyboard, like mad scribbling but with a positive result. To enable this feature, follow these steps when the onscreen keyboard is visible:

1. Long-press the Microphone key.

2. Choose the Gear icon from the pop-up menu.

3. Ensure that the SwiftKey Flow item is selected.

Either place a check mark in the box or ensure that the SwiftKey Flow item is chosen from the list of options.

4. If you see a warning about disabling cursor control, touch the OK button.

See the later section, "Moving the cursor," for information on controlling the cursor.

When SwiftKey Flow is active, you type by dragging your fingers over letters on the keyboard. Figure 4-5 illustrates how the word *hello* would be typed in this manner.

Figure 4-5: Using SwiftKey Flow to type *hello*.

The SwiftKey Flow feature may not be active when you need to type a password or for specific apps on the tablet. If it doesn't work, use the onscreen keyboard one letter at a time.

Scribbling text with the S Pen

Another way to create text is to use the S Pen, although this trick isn't limited to the Galaxy Note. You can take a stab at scribbling input on a Galaxy Tab as well, although it's better to write with something more refined than a stubby finger.

 To draw text using the S Pen (or your finger), long-press the Microphone key on the keyboard. Choose the Pen Input icon (shown in the margin). The keyboard is replaced with a scribble pad. Use that area to write text.

You can print text or you can write in cursive. The better your penmanship, the more accurate the text reproduction. When Predictive Text is active, you can tap the word that appears above the scribble area.

To exit scribble input mode, touch the Keyboard icon. It's found just above the text input area.

 Cursive is a handwriting style popular in the twentieth century. If you're too young to understand this type of writing, well, that's really sad.

Google Voice Typing

Your Galaxy tablet has the amazing capability to interpret your utterances as text. It works almost as well as computer dictation in science fiction movies, though I can't seem to find the command to launch photon torpedoes.

Activating voice input

To ensure that the tablet's dictation feature is active, obey these steps:

1. **Display the onscreen keyboard.**

    Touch a text box or somehow get the onscreen keyboard to appear.

2. **Choose the keyboard notification icon.**

     Look up yonder in the notification area for an icon that looks similar to the one shown in the margin. Pull down the notification shade and touch that item, titled Select Input Method.

3. **Choose Google Voice Typing.**

    You're good.

Voice typing appears the instant you activate it. If you don't want to utter anything at the moment, tap the screen or touch the Back button.

Dictating input

Talking to your tablet really works, and works quite well, provided that you touch the Microphone key on the keyboard and properly dictate your text.

After touching the Microphone key, you see a special window at the bottom of the screen, similar to what's shown in Figure 4-6. When the Speak Now text appears, dictate your text; speak directly at the tablet.

As you speak, the Microphone icon on the screen flashes. The flashing doesn't mean that the tablet is embarrassed by what you're saying. No, the flashing merely indicates that your words are being digested.

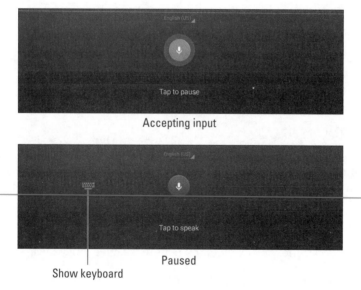

Accepting input

Show keyboard   Paused

Figure 4-6: Google Voice typing.

The text you utter appears as you speak. To pause, touch the Tap to Pause text on the screen. To use the keyboard, touch the Keyboard icon just to the left of the Microphone icon, shown in Figure 4-6. Or to continue dictation, touch the Tap to Speak text.

  ✔ The first time you try voice input, you might see a description displayed. Touch the OK button to continue.

  ✔ The better your diction, the better your results.

  ✔ You can't use dictation to edit text. Text editing still takes place on the touchscreen, as described in the later section, "Text Editing."

✔ Speak the punctuation in your text. For example, you would say, "I'm sorry comma and it won't happen again" to produce the text *I'm sorry, and it won't happen again.*

✔ Common punctuation you can dictate includes the comma, period, exclamation point, question mark, and colon.

✔ You can't dictate capital letters. If you're a stickler for such things, you'll have to go back and edit the text.

✔ Dictation may not work without an Internet connection.

*Uttering s**** words*

Both the Galaxy Note and Galaxy Tab feature a voice censor. It replaces those naughty words you might utter, placing the word's first letter on the screen, followed by the appropriate number of asterisks.

For example, if *spatula* were a blue word and you uttered *spatula* when dictating text, the dictation feature would place *s******* on the screen rather than the word *spatula.*

Yeah, I know: silly. Or s****.

The tablet knows a lot of blue terms, including the infamous "Seven Words You Can Never Say on Television," but apparently the terms *crap* and *damn* are fine. Don't ask me how much time I spent researching this topic.

See Chapter 21 if you really want the tablet to take naughty dictation.

Text Editing

You'll probably do more text editing on your Galaxy tablet than you realize. That editing includes the basic stuff, such as spiffing up typos and adding a period here or there as well as complex editing involving cut, copy, and paste. The concepts are the same as you find on a computer, but the process can be daunting without a keyboard and mouse. This section irons out the text-editing wrinkles.

Moving the cursor

The first part of editing text is to move the cursor to the right spot. The *cursor* is that blinking vertical line where text appears. On most computing devices, you move the cursor by using a pointing device. Your tablet has no pointing device, but you do: your finger.

To move the cursor, simply touch the spot on the text where you want to move the cursor. To help your precision, a cursor tab appears below the text, as shown in the margin. Move that tab with your finger to move the cursor around in the text.

After you move the cursor, you can continue to type, use the Delete key to back up and erase, or paste text copied from elsewhere.

By the cursor tab, you may see a pop-up containing a Paste command button. That button is used to paste text, as described in the later section, "Cutting, copying, and pasting."

You can move the cursor around also by dragging your finger over the onscreen keyboard. This trick doesn't work when the SwiftKey Flow feature is activated. See the "Adding SwiftKey Flow" section, earlier in this chapter.

Selecting text

Selecting text on your Galaxy tablet works just like selecting text in a word processor: You mark the start and end of a block. That chunk of text appears highlighted on the screen. How you get there, however, can be a mystery — until now!

Start selecting by long-pressing the text or double-tapping a word. Upon success, you see a chunk of text selected, as shown in Figure 4-7.

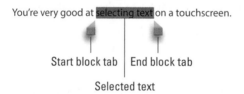

Figure 4-7: Text is selected.

Drag the start and end markers around the touchscreen to define the selected text.

To select all the text, touch the Select All command. It appears on the text selection toolbar that appears whenever text is selected on your tablet. One of two different text selection toolbars may appear; one is native to Android and the other from Samsung. Both are shown in Figure 4-8.

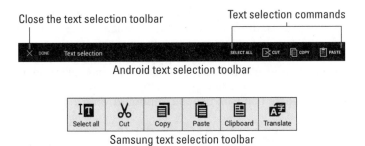

Close the text selection toolbar

Text selection commands

Android text selection toolbar

Samsung text selection toolbar

Figure 4-8: Text selection toolbar varieties.

The Galaxy Note's S Pen can also be used to select text, but there's no trick: It's used just like your finger: Long-press text with the S Pen to select a word. Using the S Pen is more civilized than using a finger, of course.

After you select the text, you can delete it by touching the Delete key on the keyboard. You can replace the text by typing something new. Or you can cut or copy the text. See the next section "Cutting, copying, and pasting."

To cancel text selection, touch the Cancel button, or just touch anywhere on the touchscreen outside the selected block.

Cutting, copying, and pasting

Selected text is primed for cutting or copying, which works just like it does in your favorite word processor. After you select the text, choose the proper command from the text selection toolbar: To copy the text, choose the Copy command. To cut the text, choose Cut.

Just like on your computer, cut or copied text on your is stored in a Clipboard. To paste any previously cut or copied text, move the cursor to the spot where you want the text pasted.

Figure 4-9: The Paste command button.

If you're lucky, you'll see a Paste command button appear above the blinking cursor, as shown in Figure 4-9. Touch that command to paste in the text.

If the Paste command button doesn't appear, touch the blue tab. If the command button still doesn't show up, text cannot be pasted for some reason.

Another way to paste text is to use the Clipboard, shown in Figure 4-10.

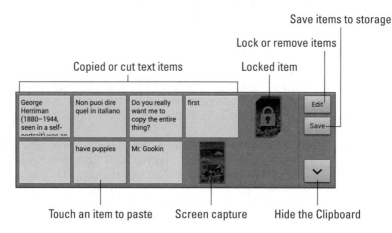

Figure 4-10: The Clipboard.

To summon the Clipboard, touch the Clipboard button on the onscreen keyboard, or touch the Clipboard icon on the Samsung text selection toolbar (refer to Figure 4-8). You see both text and graphics items that have been recently cut or copied, as shown in Figure 4-10.

To paste an item, position the cursor in the text and then choose something to paste from the Clipboard window. You can continue to choose items and they'll be pasted as long as you like. When you're done, touch the down-pointing arrow to hide the Clipboard.

You can paste text only in locations where text is allowed. Odds are good that whenever you see the onscreen keyboard, you can paste text.

Part II
Tablet Communications

Learn how to organize your apps into folders on the Apps screen at www.dummies.
com/extras/samsunggalaxytabs.

Apps   Widgets

Alarm   Calculator   Camera   ChatON   Chrom

Contacts   Down   ail   Flipboa

In this part...

- Understand how to deal with your friends.
- Work with messages of the electronic kind.
- Explore on the web.
- Discover your digital social life.
- Drool over text chat, video chat, and phone calls.

Gallery   Game Hub   Gmail   Google   Googl
                                                                 Setting

Google+   Group Play   Help   Internet   Loca

All Your Friends in the Galaxy

In This Chapter

▶ Exploring the Contacts app
▶ Searching and sorting your contacts
▶ Adding new contacts
▶ Editing and changing contacts
▶ Updating a contact's picture
▶ Deleting contacts

*W*hen I was a kid, I kept a dozen or so phone numbers in my head. That was enough to call someone in a pinch. Beyond that, there was the address book or numbers written down on the kitchen cabinet. Today, things are different. People typically have not only more than one phone number but also e-mail addresses, websites, and a host of other information. Why cram all that stuff inside your head when you have something handy like your Galaxy Note or Galaxy Tab to store it for you?

As a communications device, your tablet has a need to harbor information about all the people you know — specifically, those with whom you want to communicate electronically. From sending e-mail to social networking, you want to have access to your list of friends, pals, and cohorts. This chapter explains how to do that.

Meet the Tablet's Address Book

You may already have some friends in your Galaxy tablet. That's because your Google account was synchronized with the tablet when you first set up the device. Because all your Gmail and other types of contacts on the Internet were duplicated on the tablet, you already have a host of friends available. The place where you can access those folks is the Contacts app.

✔ If you haven't yet set up a Google account, refer to Chapter 2.

✔ Adding more contacts is covered later in this chapter, in the "More Friends in Your Galaxy" section.

✔ Many apps use contact information from the Contacts app, including Email, Gmail, Hangouts, as well as any app that lets you share information such as photographs or videos.

✔ Information from your social networking apps is also coordinated with the Contacts app. See Chapter 8 for more information on using the tablet as your social networking hub.

Using the Contacts app

To peruse your tablet's address book, start the Contacts app: Touch the Apps icon on the Home screen and then touch the Contacts app icon.

The Contacts app displays a list of all contacts in your Galaxy tablet, organized alphabetically by first name. Scroll the list by swiping the screen. Or you can swipe your finger on the left side of the screen to quickly scan through the list, as shown in Figure 5-1.

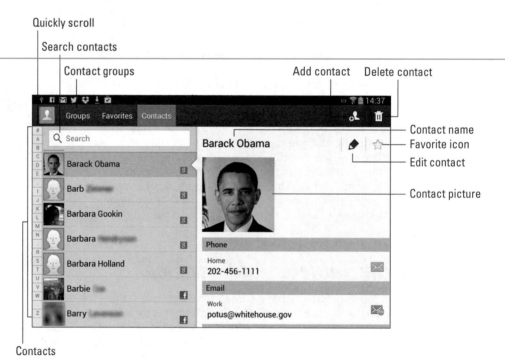

Quickly scroll

Search contacts

Contact groups   Add contact   Delete contact

Contact name

Favorite icon

Edit contact

Contact picture

Contacts

Figure 5-1: Your tablet's electronic address book.

To do anything with a contact, you first have to choose it: Touch a contact name, and you see detailed information on the right side of the screen, as shown in Figure 5-1. The list of activities you can do with the contact depends on the information shown and the apps installed on the tab. Here are some options:

- **Place a phone call:** Neither the Galaxy Note nor the Galaxy Tab is a phone, but if you install Skype, touching a contact's phone number activates that app. You can then use the tablet to make a call. See Chapter 9 for details.

- **Send e-mail:** Touch the contact's e-mail address to compose an e-mail message using either the Gmail or Email app. When the contact has more than one e-mail address, you can choose to which one you want to send the message. Chapter 6 covers e-mail.

- **View address:** When the contact lists a home or business address, you can choose that item and use the Maps app to view the address. You can then get directions, look at the place using the Street View tool, or do any of a number of interesting things, covered in Chapter 10.

- **View social networking status:** The current status of contacts who are also your social networking buddies is displayed on the right side of the screen when you view their information. See Chapter 8 for more information on social networking.

Some tidbits of information that show up for a contact don't have an associated action. For example, the tablet won't sing "Happy Birthday" when you touch a contact's birthday information.

- Not every contact has a picture, and the picture can come from a number of sources (Gmail or Facebook, for example). See the "Taking a picture of a contact" section for more information.

- When a contact is referred to as a *joined contact,* the information you see comes from multiple sources, such as Gmail and Facebook. See the "Joining identical contacts" section for information on joining contacts, as well as the "Separating contacts" section for information on splitting improperly joined contacts.

Sorting your contacts

Your contacts are displayed in the Contacts app in a certain order: alphabetically by first name, first name first. You can change that order if you like. Here's how:

1. **Start the Contacts app.**

2. **Touch the Menu button, and then choose the Settings command.**

3. **Choose the List By command and specify how contacts are sorted: by First Name or Last Name.**

   The Contacts app is configured to show contacts by first name.

4. **Choose Display Contacts By and specify how the contacts appear in the list: First Name First or Last Name First.**

   The Contacts app shows the contacts listed by first name first.

There's no right or wrong way to display your contacts — only whichever method you're used to. I prefer them sorted by last name and listed first name first.

Searching contacts

You may have a massive number of contacts. Although the Contacts app doesn't provide a running total, I'm certain that I have more than 500,000 contacts on my tablet. That number combines my Facebook, Gmail, Twitter, and other accounts. I have a lot of contacts, and not all of them owe me money.

Rather than endlessly scroll the Contacts list and run the risk of rubbing your finger to a nub, you can employ the tablet's powerful Search command. Type the name you want to locate in the Search text box at the top of the screen (labeled in Figure 5-1). The list of contacts quickly narrows to show only the contacts that contain the text you type.

✔ To clear a search, touch the X button, found on the right side of the Search text box.

✔ No, there's no correlation between the number of contacts you have and how popular you are in real life.

More Friends in Your Galaxy

Having friends is great. Having more friends is better. Keeping all those friends is best. In the Contacts app, myriad ways are available to add more friends or create contacts. This section lists a few of the more popular and useful methods.

Creating a contact from scratch

Sometimes it's necessary to create a contact when you actually meet another human being in the real world, or maybe you finally got around to transferring information to the tablet from your old paper address book. In either instance, you have information to input, and it starts like this:

1. **Open the Contacts app.**

2. **Touch the Add Contact icon.**

   Refer to Figure 5-1 for the icon's specific location. The icon may also look like a giant plus, as shown in the margin.

3. **Choose your Google account from the menu.**

   I recommend creating contacts by using Google because it synchronizes the information with the Internet and any other Android gizmos you may own.

   If you choose the Device item, the contact information is saved only on your Galaxy tablet. It won't be synchronized with other Android devices you may own.

4. **Fill in information on the New Contact screen as best you can.**

   Fill in the text fields with the information you know, as illustrated in Figure 5-2. When a contact has multiple phone numbers or e-mail addresses, use the + (plus) button to add another field. To remove an excess field, touch the – (minus) button.

5. **Touch the Save button to complete editing and add the contact.**

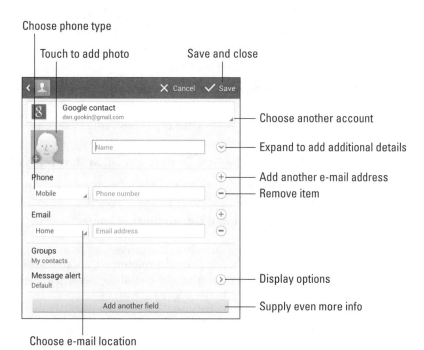

Figure 5-2: Creating a new contact.

Providing that you followed my advice in Step 3, the new contact is automatically synched with your Google account. That's one beauty of the Android operating system used by the Galaxy Note and Galaxy Tab: You have no need to duplicate your efforts; contacts you create on the tablet are instantly updated with your Google account on the Internet.

 ✔ It's also possible to use your Samsung account, should you have one, to synchronize contacts across multiple Samsung devices you may own. If so, choose that account in Step 3. (Refer to Figure 5-2 for the location to tap to choose another account.)

 ✔ Information from social networking sites is stirred into the Contacts list automatically, though sometimes the process creates duplicate entries. See the "Joining identical contacts" section to remedy such a situation.

Creating a contact from an e-mail message

Perhaps one of the easiest ways to build up the Contacts list is to create a contact from an e-mail message. Follow these steps when you receive a message from someone not already in the tablet's address book:

1. **Touch the picture by the contact's name at the top of the message.**

   The picture, whether it shows a generic image or the contact's actual visage, is a button. Touching that button displays a pop-up window with additional information and two buttons.

2. **Touch the Create Contact button.**

3. **Choose your Google account as the location to save the contact's information.**

   Refer to the preceding section for my reason why Google is a good choice.

4. **Fill in the blanks on the New Contact screen, as shown in Figure 5-2.**

   The name and e-mail address may already be entered for you. Smart tablet, smart. Fill in other fields if you know them.

5. **Touch the Save button to finish adding the contact.**

If the e-mail is from someone already in the tablet's address book, touch the Update Existing button in Step 2. Scroll through the Contacts list to select the person. The contact information from the e-mail message is automatically added to that person's entry in the address book.

Importing contacts from your computer

Your computer's e-mail program is doubtless a useful repository of contacts you've built up over the years. You can export these contacts from your computer's e-mail program and then import them to the tablet. It's not easy, but it's possible.

The key is to save or export your computer e-mail program's records in the *vCard* (.vcf) file format. These records can then be imported into the Contacts app. The method for exporting contacts varies depending on the e-mail program:

- ✔ **In the Windows Live Mail program,** choose Go⇨Contacts and then choose File⇨Export⇨Business Card (.VCF) to export the contacts.

- ✔ **In Windows Mail,** choose File⇨Export⇨Windows Contacts and then choose vCards (Folder of .VCF Files) from the Export Windows Contacts dialog box. Click the Export button.

- ✔ **On the Mac,** open the Address Book program and choose File⇨Export⇨ Export vCard.

After the vCard files are created on your computer, connect the tablet to the computer and transfer them. Transferring files from your computer to a Galaxy tablet is covered in Chapter 17.

After the vCard files have been copied over, follow these steps in the Contacts app to complete the process:

1. **Touch the Menu button.**

2. **Choose the Import/Export command.**

3. **Choose Import from USB Storage.**

   If you've copied the contacts to the SD Card, choose Import from SD Card instead.

4. **Choose your Google account.**

5. **Select the Import All vCard Files option.**

6. **Touch the OK button.**

   The contacts are not only saved in the tablet but are also synchronized to your Gmail account, which instantly creates a backup copy.

The importing process may create some duplicates. That's okay: You can join two entries for the same person in the Contacts app. See the "Joining identical contacts" section, later in this chapter.

Grabbing contacts from your social networking sites

You can pour your whole gang of friends and followers from your social networking sites into the tablet. The operation is automatic: Simply add the social networking site's app to the tablet's inventory of apps as described in Chapter 8. At that time, you'll be prompted to sync the contacts or the apps will be added instantly to the Contacts app's address book.

Manage Your Friends

Nothing is truly perfect the first time, especially when you create things on a Galaxy tablet while typing with your thumbs at 34,000 feet during turbulence. You can do a whole slate of things with (and to) your friends in the tablet's address book. This section covers the more interesting and useful things.

Editing contact information

To make minor touch-ups to any contact, start by locating and displaying the contact's information in the Contacts app. Touch the Edit icon (similar to the pencil icon shown in the margin), and start making changes.

Change or add information by touching a field and typing with the onscreen keyboard. You can edit information as well: Touch the field to edit and change whatever you want.

Some information cannot be edited. For example, fields pulled in from social networking sites can be edited only by that account holder on the social networking site.

When you've finished editing, touch the Save button.

Taking a picture of a contact

Nothing can be more delicious than snapping an inappropriate picture of someone you know and using the picture as his contact picture on your Galaxy tablet. Then, every time he contacts you, that embarrassing, potentially career-ending photo comes up.

I suppose you could use nice pictures as well, but what's the fun in that?

To use the tablet's camera to snap a contact picture, heed these directions:

1. **Locate and display the contact's information.**

2. **Touch the contact's picture.**

   This trick works even when the picture is one of the boring generic images.

3. **Choose the Take Picture command.**

4. **Use the tablet's camera to snap a picture.**

   Chapter 11 covers using the camera. Both the front and rear cameras can be used (but not both at the same time). Touch the Shutter icon to take the picture.

5. **Review the picture.**

   Nothing is set yet. If you want to try again, touch the Discard button and start over in Step 4.

6. **Touch the Save button to confirm the new image and prepare for cropping.**

7. **If you see a prompt asking you to choose an app, choose Gallery (Crop Picture) and touch the Just Once button.**

   Later, as you become more familiar with the tablet, you can touch the Always button, which speeds up the process.

8. **Crop the image, as shown in Figure 5-3.**

   Adjust the cropping box so that it surrounds only the portion of the image you want to keep.

9. **Touch the Done button to crop and save the image.**

   The image now appears whenever the contact is referenced on your tablet.

Portion discarded

Portion kept

Save the cropped image

Change cropping rectangle

Drag cropping rectangle

Figure 5-3: Cropping a contact's image.

To remove an image from a contact, you need to edit the contact as described in the preceding section. Touch the contact's picture while you're editing, and then choose the Remove command.

You can also use any image stored on the tablet as a contact's picture. In Step 3, choose the Image command to view the Gallery. Browse for and select an image, and then crop.

See Chapter 12 for more information on the Gallery app.

Building contact groups

It's possible to corral contacts into groups, which makes it easier to send that group an e-mail, to chat via voice or video, or to perform a number of interesting group activities. The variety of things you can do depends on the apps installed on your tablet.

To build a group of contacts, obey these steps while using the Contacts app:

1. **Touch the Groups tab.**

   You'll see any groups already created, such as those associated with your Gmail account.

2. **Add a new group.**

    If you see the New Group icon, as shown in the margin, touch it. Otherwise, touch the Menu button and choose the Create command.

3. **Type a name for the group.**

   For example, type **Friends Who Dislike Me.**

4. **Touch the Save button.**

   The group is created, but it's empty. The next step is to add members to the group.

5. **On the left side of the screen, select the group.**

6. **Add members.**

    Touch the Add icon atop the screen to add members. If you don't see that icon, touch the Menu button and choose the Add Member command.

   The tablet's address book is displayed. Next to each contact you find an empty check box.

7. **Scroll your Contacts list and touch the box next to the name of each person you want to add to the group.**

   A green check mark appears in the box next to each selected name.

8. **Touch the Done button.**

   You see the group displayed, along with all its members.

To perform an action with the group, first choose it from the list of groups shown in the Groups tab. Press the Menu button and choose Send Message or Send Email. Then follow along with the directions on the screen, as well as elsewhere in this book, for completing your group message or activity.

✔ To add members to an existing group, follow Steps 5 through 8 in this section.

✔ To remove people from the group, display the group and long-press the contact you want to remove. Choose the Remove command or the Remove Member command from the pop-up menu.

✔ Delete a group by long-pressing the group's name on the screen. Choose the Delete command, and then choose Group Only. Touch the OK button to zap the group. Deleting a group doesn't remove its members from the tablet's address book.

Making a favorite

A *favorite* is a special type of contact group that consists of people you frequently stay in touch with, which doesn't necessarily mean people you like. Making a contact a favorite places the person in the Favorites group, which isn't really a group. Favorite contacts have their own tab in the Contacts app (refer to Figure 5-1).

 To add a contact to the Favorites group, display the contact's information and touch the Favorite (star) icon by the contact's image. When the star is gold, the contact is one of your favorites and listed in the Favorites group.

To remove a favorite, touch the contact's star again, and it loses its color. Removing a favorite doesn't delete the contact.

By the way, a contact has no idea whether he's one of your favorites, so don't believe that you're hurting his feelings by not making him a favorite.

Joining identical contacts

The Galaxy Note and Galaxy Tab can pull in contacts from multiple sources (Facebook, Gmail, and Twitter), so you may discover duplicate contact entries in the Contacts app. Rather than fuss over which entry to use, you can join similar contacts. Here's how:

1. **Wildly scroll the Contacts list until you locate a duplicate.**

   Well, maybe not *wildly* scroll, but locate a duplicated entry. Because the address book is sorted, duplicates usually appear close together.

2. **Select one of the duplicate contacts.**

3. **Touch the Menu button.**

4. **Choose Join Contact or Link Contact.**

   The window that appears lists some contacts that the tablet guesses could be identical. It also displays the entire list of contacts in case the tablet guesses incorrectly. Your job is to find the duplicate contact.

5. **Select the duplicate contact from the list.**

   The accounts are merged, appearing as a single entry in the Contacts app.

 Joined contacts can be discovered by looking at the Connection area when viewing the contact's information. You'll see more than one icon when multiple contacts have been joined.

Separating contacts

The topic of separating contacts has little to do with parenting, though separating bickering children is the first step in avoiding a fight. Contacts in the address book might not be bickering, but occasionally the tablet may automatically join two contacts who aren't really the same person. When that happens, you can split them by following these steps:

1. **Display the contact that comes from two separate sources.**

   Sometimes it's difficult to spot such a contact. An easy way for me is to see two diverse e-mail addresses for the contact, which often indicates a mismatch.

2. **Touch the Menu button.**

3. **Choose the Separate Contact command.**

   You see a list of contact sources, each with a red minus icon to the right.

4. **Touch the red minus icon by the account you want to separate, and then touch the OK button to confirm.**

5. **Repeat Step 4 for each account you want to split off.**

6. **Touch the Back button when you're done.**

You don't need to actively look for improperly joined contacts as much as you'll just stumble across them. When you do, feel free to separate them, especially if you detect any bickering.

Removing a contact

Every so often, consider reviewing your contacts. Purge those folks whom you no longer recognize or have forgotten. It's simple: View the forlorn contacts and touch the Trash icon (shown in the margin and also labeled in Figure 5-1). Touch the OK button to confirm. Poof! They're gone.

- ✔ Because the Contacts list is synchronized with your Gmail contacts for your Google account, the contact is also removed there.

- ✔ For some linked accounts, the Contacts app won't let you delete the account. Instead, you need to remove the account from the linked source, such as Facebook.

- ✔ Removing a contact doesn't kill the person in real life.

Mail of the Electronic Kind

I'll bet it's been a long time since you've asked someone for his e-mail address and he didn't have one. Probably longer still since someone responded, "E-mail? What's that?" It would probably be odder still if people asked why there's a hyphen in "e-mail" now, when in my books published before 2010 there wasn't, but I'm getting sidetracked.

To help keep you electronically connected, the Galaxy Note and Galaxy Tab feature the capability to collect and send your electronic missives. You can read and compose missives just about anywhere you go, peruse attachments, forward messages, and do the entire e-mail e-nchilada all in one spot.

Galactic E-Mail

Electronic mail is handled by two apps on your tablet: Gmail and Email.

The Gmail app hooks directly into your Google Gmail account. It's a copy of all the Gmail you send, receive, and archive, just as you could access on the Internet by using a web browser.

You can also use the Email app to connect with non-Gmail electronic mail, such as the standard mail service provided by your ISP or a web-based e-mail system such as Yahoo! Mail or Windows Live Mail.

Regardless of the app, electronic mail on your tablet works just like it does on a computer: You can receive mail, create messages, forward e-mail, send messages to a group of contacts, and work with attachments, for example. As long as there's an Internet connection, e-mail works just peachy.

- ✔ Both the Gmail and Email apps are located on the Apps screen. The tablet may also come with app shortcuts on the Home screen.

- ✔ The Gmail app is updated frequently. To review any changes since this book went to press, visit my website at www.wambooli.com/help/android/gmail/.

- ✔ The Email app can be configured to handle multiple e-mail accounts, as discussed later in this section.

- ✔ Although you can use the tablet's web browser app to visit the Gmail website, you should use the Gmail app to pick up your Gmail.

- ✔ If you forget your Gmail password, visit www.google.com/accounts/ForgotPasswd.

Setting up an Email account

The Email app is used to access web-based e-mail, or *webmail*, such as Yahoo! and Windows Live. It also lets you read e-mail provided by your Internet service provider (ISP), office, or other large, intimidating organization. To get things set up regardless of the service, follow these steps:

1. Start the Email app.

Look for it on the Apps screen, along with all the other apps on your tablet. The first screen you see is Set Up Email. If you've already run the Email app, you're taken to the Email inbox and you can skip these steps.

2. Type your e-mail address.

For example, if you have a Comcast e-mail account, type your whoever@comcast.net e-mail address in the box. That's how you add your Comcast e-mail account to the tablet.

You'll find a .com key on the onscreen keyboard, which you can use to more efficiently type your e-mail address. Look for it in the lower-right corner of the screen.

3. Type the password for that account.

4. Touch the Done button on the onscreen keyboard or the Next button in the upper-right part of the screen.

If you're lucky, everything connects smoothly, and you see the Account Options screen. Move on to Step 5.

If you're unlucky, you have to specify some details, which include the incoming and outgoing server information, often known by the bewildering acronyms POP3 and SMTP. Plod through the fields shown on the screen, filling in the information as provided by your ISP, although you primarily need to specify only the incoming and outgoing server names.

Eventually, you'll end up at the Account Options screen.

5. **Set the account options on the aptly named Account Options screen.**

   You might want to reset the Inbox Checking Frequency to something other than 15 minutes.

6. **Touch the Next button.**

7. **Give the account a name and check your own name.**

   The account is given your e-mail address as a name. If you want to change the name, type something new in that field. For example, I name my ISP's e-mail account *Main* because it's my main account.

   The Your Name field lists your name as it's applied to outgoing messages. So if your name is really Wilma Flagstone and not wflag4457, you can make that change now.

8. **Touch the Done button.**

   You're done.

The next thing you'll see will be your e-mail account inbox. The tablet proceeds to synchronize any pending e-mail you have in your account, updating the screen as you watch. See the "You've Got E-Mail" section for what to do next.

Adding even more e-mail accounts

The Email app can be configured to collect mail from multiple sources. If you have a Yahoo! Mail, Windows Live, or corporate account, in addition to your ISP's account, you can add them. Follow through with these steps:

1. **Visit the Apps screen and start the Settings app.**

2. **Visit the Accounts area.**

   If you find category tabs across the top of the screen, tap the General tab to find the Accounts area. Otherwise, scroll down the items on the left side of the screen to find the Accounts area.

3. **Choose Add Account.**

4. **If the list displays your account type, such as Yahoo! Mail, select it. Otherwise, select Email.**

   For accessing your evil organization's Microsoft Outlook Exchange server, choose the Microsoft Exchange ActiveSync item. Be aware that this option requires a tad bit more setup than other types of e-mail accounts — but it can be done!

5. **Type the account's e-mail address.**

6. **Type the password for the account.**

7. **You can leave empty the box by the Send Email from This Account by Default option.**

   Select this box only when you're adding your primary e-mail account. You've probably already done that. And if not, you can always set the primary account later; see the later section "Setting the primary e-mail account" for details.

8. **Touch the Next button.**

   In a few magical moments, the e-mail account is configured and added to the account list.

   If you goofed up the account name or password, you're warned: Try again. Or if the account requires additional setup, use the information provided by the ISP or other source to fill in the appropriate fields.

9. **Set account options on the aptly named Account Options screen.**

   Most of the preset choices are fine for a web-based e-mail account.

   You might also consider a more frequent update interval, especially if you get a lot of mail or need to respond to it quickly.

10. **Touch the Next button.**

11. **Name the account.**

    Feel free to change the account name to something more descriptive than your e-mail address.

12. **Touch the Done button.**

    The account is added to the list on the Settings app screen, in the Accounts area.

You can repeat the steps in this section to add more e-mail accounts. E-mail from the accounts you configure is accessed by using the Email app.

For some corporate accounts, you may be prompted to activate the Device Administrator option. That's a fancy term for allowing your corporate IT humans access to your Galaxy Note or Galaxy Tab for the purpose of remotely controlling e-mail. If you're shackled to corporate e-mail, you've probably already agreed to such a thing when you signed up to be an employee. Otherwise, keep in mind that you can always get your corporate e-mail at work and you may not even need to use your tablet for that purpose.

You've Got E-Mail

Both the Galaxy Note and Galaxy Tab work flawlessly with Gmail. In fact, if Gmail is already set up to be your main e-mail address, you'll enjoy having access to your messages all the time by using your tablet.

Non-Gmail e-mail, handled by the Email app, must be set up before it can be used, as covered earlier in this chapter. After completing the quick and occasionally painless setup, you can receive e-mail on your tablet just as you can on a computer.

Getting a new message

You're alerted to the arrival of a new e-mail message in your tablet by a notification icon. The icon differs depending on the e-mail's source.

 For a new Gmail message, the New Gmail notification (shown in the margin) appears at the top of the touchscreen.

 For a new e-mail message, you see the New Email notification.

Pull down the notifications shade to review pending e-mail. You see either a single notification representing the most recent message or a running total of the number of pending messages. Touch the notification to visit either the Gmail app or the Email app to read the message.

Checking the inbox

To peruse your Gmail, start the Gmail app. You can find it on the main Home screen or on the Apps screen. A typical Gmail inbox is shown in Figure 6-1.

To check your Email inbox, open the Email app. You're taken to the inbox for your primary e-mail account.

When you have multiple e-mail accounts accessed through the Email app, you can view your universal inbox by choosing the Combined View command from the Account menu, as shown in Figure 6-2.

Don't bother looking for your Gmail inbox in the Combined View window (refer to Figure 6-2). Gmail is its own app; your Gmail messages don't show up in the universal inbox.

- ✔ Search your Gmail messages by touching the Search icon (labeled in Figure 6-1).

- ✔ Gmail is organized using labels, not folders. To see your Gmail labels, view the sidebar by touching the App icon (labeled in Figure 6-1).

- ✔ The Email app is used to access non-Gmail e-mail accounts.

- ✔ Multiple e-mail accounts gathered in the Email app are color-coded. When you view the combined inbox, you see the color codes to the left of each message.

Search

App icon Compose

Mark as unread

Delete Label

Sidebar   All Mail inbox   Message

Figure 6-1: The Gmail inbox.

Reading e-mail

As mail comes in, you can read it by choosing the new e-mail notification, as described earlier in this chapter. Reading and working with the message operate much the same whether you're using the Gmail or Email app.

Touch a message to read it. The message text appears on the right side of the window or full screen, depending on how the tablet is oriented. Scroll the message up or down by using your finger.

To work with the message, use the icons that appear above the message. These icons, which may not look exactly like those shown in the margin, cover common e-mail actions:

Reply: Touch this icon to reply to a message. A new message window appears (as covered in the next section), but the To and Subject fields are already filled out.

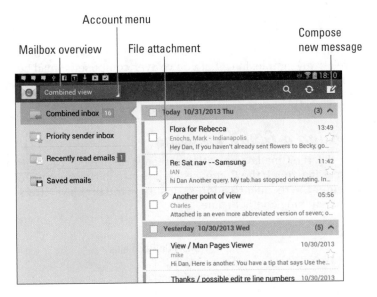

Figure 6-2: Messages in the Email app.

 Reply All: Touch this icon to respond to everyone who received the original message, including folks on the Cc line. Use this option only when everyone else must get a copy of your reply.

 Forward: Touch this icon to send a copy of the message to someone else.

 Delete: Touch this icon to delete a message in the Email app.

To access additional e-mail commands, touch the Menu button. The commands available depend on what you're doing in the Gmail or Email app at the time you touch the button.

✔ Use Reply All only when everyone else must get a copy of your reply. Because most people find endless Reply All e-mail threads annoying, use the Reply All option judiciously.

✔ Starred messages in Gmail can be viewed or searched separately, making them easier to locate later.

✔ If you properly configure the Email program, there's no need to delete messages you read. See the "Configuring the manual delete option" section, later in this chapter.

✔ I find it easier to delete (and manage) Gmail by using a computer.

Write That Message

To get mail you need to send mail. Doing so on your Galaxy Note or Galaxy Tab is relatively simple. In fact, if you've ever composed e-mail before, you'll find writing an electronic epistle on your tablet quite familiar. However, the process is subtly different between the Gmail and Email apps.

Composing a Gmail message

In Figure 6-3, the Gmail composition screen is displayed. To create a new Gmail message, touch the Compose icon, shown in the margin. Touch the To field to enter the recipient's address; just type the first few letters and then choose a matching contact name.

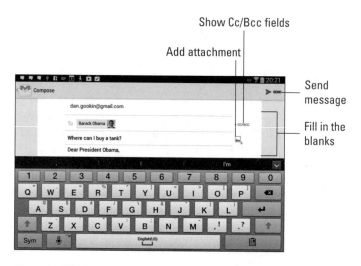

Figure 6-3: Writing a new Gmail message.

Continue the Gmail message by filling in the Subject field. Type the message. Touch the Send icon (shown in Figure 6-3) to whisk off the message. Or if you'd rather save it and work on it later, touch the Menu button and choose the Save Draft command.

✔ To cancel a message in Gmail, touch the Menu button and choose the Discard command. Touch the Discard button to continue.

✔ To work on a draft you've saved, touch the App icon (refer to Figure 6-1) and choose the Drafts folder. Touch the draft message in the list, and then touch the Edit (pencil) icon to continue editing.

✓ To summon the Cc and Bcc fields, touch the +CC/BCC icon, as shown in Figure 6-3. The Cc (Carbon Copy) and Bcc (Blind Carbon Copy) fields appear, eager for you to fill them in.

Crafting an Email message

 To create a message in the Email map, touch the Compose icon (shown in the margin). The new message composition screen appears, similar to what you see in Figure 6-4. Your main or primary account is shown, but you can choose another account from which to send the message.

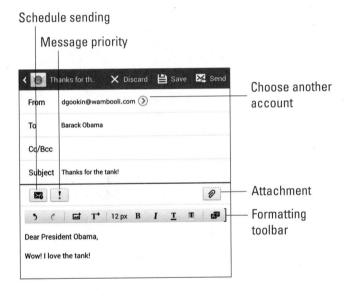

Figure 6-4: Composing an Email message.

Fill in the To field by typing a contact's name or e-mail address. You need only type the first few letters of the name and then choose the person from the list — providing that the person's account is in the tablet's address book.

Type a subject, and then type the message's contents.

To send the message, touch the Send button at the top of the composition window. Or you can touch the Save button to save the message in the Drafts folder to edit and send later.

✔ The Email app's composition window features a formatting toolbar (labeled in Figure 6-4). If you don't see it, touch the arrow icon on the right side of the composition window. Use the formatting icons as you type or select text and then apply a format. (Text selection is described in Chapter 4.)

✔ Use the Schedule Sending command to preset a time at which the Email app sends the e-mail. Normally, e-mail is sent right away. Or if an Internet connection isn't available, e-mail is sent the next time the tablet is connected. If you don't see the Schedule Sending icon (refer to Figure 6-4), touch the Menu button and choose the command from there.

✔ If the Priority icon doesn't appear on the screen as shown in Figure 6-4, touch the Menu button and choose the Priority command.

✔ Saved e-mail is found in the Drafts folder associated with the e-mail account you're using. Select the Drafts folder from the left side of the screen, and then select the draft from the right side of the screen to edit or send.

✔ To cancel a message, touch the Discard button (refer to Figure 6-4). Touch the Discard button in the Sending Canceled window to confirm.

Sending e-mail to a contact

A quick and easy way to compose a new message is to use the Contacts app to find a contact and then create a message using the contact's information. Heed these steps:

1. **Open the Contacts app.**

2. **Locate the contact to whom you want to send an electronic message.**

3. **Touch the contact's e-mail address.**

4. **Select Gmail or Email to use the related app to compose the message.**

5. **Touch Always to always use the app chosen in Step 4, or select Just Once to pick an app every time.**

   If you choose Always, the app you choose is always used to send e-mail to a contact; you won't see the prompt in Step 4 again.

At this point, creating the message works as described in the preceding sections.

Message Attachments

The key to understanding attachments in the Galactic e-mail apps is to look for the paperclip icon. After you find that icon, you can either deal with an attachment for incoming e-mail or add an attachment to outgoing e-mail.

Dealing with attachments

Attachments work differently between Gmail and Email. Either way, your goal is to either view or save the attachment. Sometimes you can do both!

Figure 6-5 shows both the Gmail app and Email app methods of dealing with an attachment. In the Gmail app, you can touch the paperclip icon to view the attachment, or touch the Menu button to choose whether to Preview or Save the attachment.

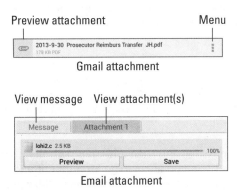

Figure 6-5: Attachment methods and madness.

In the Email app, touch the Attachment tab in the message, shown in Figure 6-5. You can then touch the Preview button or the Save button to view the attachment or save it to the tablet's storage, respectively. When multiple items are attached, touch the Save All button.

The only snag you may encounter is one you may have on a computer as well: When nothing exists with which to open the attachment. When an app can't be found, you'll either have to suffer through not viewing the attachment, or simply reply to the message and direct the person to resend the attachment in a common file format.

✔ Common file formats include PNG and JPEG for pictures, and HTML or RTF for documents. PDF, or Adobe Acrobat documents, are also common. Your Galaxy tablet should have no trouble opening them.

✔ Look for saved attachments by using the Downloads app. You can also use the My Files app to locate the attachments in the Download folder. Attachments you save may also generate a notification icon; choose that notification to view the attachment.

Sending an attachment

You have two methods to send an e-mail attachment from your Galaxy Note or Galaxy Tab. The first is to find the attachment and use a Share command to stick it in an e-mail message. The second is to create the message and then attach the item.

 Most apps that create or view information feature a Share command. Look for the Share icon, similar to what's shown in the margin. View the item you want to share — a picture, a video, music, a text message, or what-have-you — and then touch the Share icon. Choose the Gmail or Email app, and then compose your message. The item you chose to share is automatically attached to the message.

The second way to share is to compose a new message using the Gmail or Email app. When you compose the message, attach the message by using the Attach icon in the Gmail app (refer to Figure 6-3) or the paperclip icon in the Email app (refer to Figure 6-4). Follow the directions on the screen to hunt down the attachment.

✔ When you compose a message and then add an attachment, you start by choosing the app that lets you access the attachment and then find the attachment itself. For example, you choose the Gallery app and then look for the photo you want to attach. Unlike using a computer, you don't just hunt down a specific file.

✔ It's possible to attach multiple items to a single e-mail message. Just keep touching the attachment icon for the message to add additional goodies.

✔ The variety of items you can attach depends on which apps are installed on the tablet.

 ✔ The Gmail and Email apps sometimes accept different types of attachments. So if you can't attach something by using the Gmail app, try using the Email app instead.

E-Mail Configuration

You can have oodles of fun and waste oceans of time confirming and customizing the e-mail experience on your Galaxy tablet. The most interesting things you can do are to modify or create an e-mail signature, specify how mail you retrieve is deleted from the server, and assign a default e-mail account for the Email app.

Creating a signature

I highly recommend that you create a custom e-mail signature for sending messages from your tablet. Here's my signature:

```
DAN

This was sent from my Galaxy tablet.
Typos, no matter how hilarious, are unintentional.
```

To create a signature for Gmail, obey these directions:

1. **Start the Gmail app.**
2. **Touch the Menu button.**
3. **Choose Settings.**
4. **Choose your Gmail account.**
5. **Choose Signature.**
6. **Type or dictate your signature.**

   If the account already has a signature, you can delete or edit it.

7. **Touch OK.**

To set a signature for the Email app, heed these steps:

1. **While using the Email app, touch the Menu button.**
2. **Choose Settings.**
3. **On the left side of the screen, select an account.**

   Email app signatures are set by account. If you have multiple accounts, you need to select each one to set up a signature.

4. **Choose Signature.**
5. **Type or dictate your new outgoing e-mail signature.**
6. **Touch the Done button.**

Repeat Steps 3 through 6 for each of your Email accounts.

Configuring the manual delete option

Non-Gmail e-mail you fetch on your tablet is typically left on the e-mail server. That's because the Email app, unlike a computer's e-mail program, doesn't delete messages after it picks them up. The advantage is that you can retrieve the same messages later by using a computer. The disadvantage is that you end up retrieving mail you've already read and possibly replied to.

You can control whether the Email app removes messages after they're picked up. Follow these steps:

1. **Open the Email app.**

2. **Touch the Menu button and choose the Settings command.**

3. **On the left side of the screen, select a specific account.**

4. **Choose the More Settings command, and then choose the Incoming Settings command.**

   If you can't find an Incoming Settings command, you're dealing with a web-based e-mail account, in which case there's no need to worry about the manual delete option.

5. **Below the Delete Email from Server item, select the When I Delete from Inbox option.**

   The only other option besides When I Delete from Inbox is Never. If you see the Never option, choose the other one.

6. **Touch the Done button.**

Repeat Steps 3 through 6 for any additional e-mail accounts you have.

After configuring the Delete Email from Server option, any message you delete in the Email app is deleted also from the mail server. It isn't picked up again, not by the tablet, another mobile device, or any computer that fetches e-mail from that same account.

- ✔ Mail you retrieve using a computer's mail program is deleted from the mail server after it's picked up. That's normal behavior. Your tablet cannot pick up mail from the server if your computer has already deleted it.

- ✔ Deleting mail on the server isn't a problem for Gmail. No matter how you access your Gmail, from a mobile device or from a computer, the inbox lists the same messages.

Setting the primary e-mail account

When you have more than one e-mail account, the main account — the default — is the one used by the Email app to send messages. To change that primary mail account, follow these steps:

1. **Start the Email app.**

2. **On the Account menu, choose Combined View.**

3. Touch the Menu button and choose Settings.

4. On the left side of the screen, select the e-mail account you want to mark as your favorite.

5. On the right side of the screen, select the Default Account item.

The messages you compose and send using the Email app are sent from the account you specified in Step 4.

Web Browsing

In This Chapter

▶ Browsing the web

▶ Adding a bookmark

▶ Working with tabs

▶ Sharing web pages

▶ Downloading images and files

▶ Setting a new home page

▶ Configuring the Internet app

The World Wide Web was designed to be viewed on a computer. The monitor is big and roomy. Web pages are displayed amply, like Uncle Ron on the sofa watching a ballgame. The smaller the screen, the more difficult it is to view web pages designed for those roomy monitors. The web on a smartphone? Tragic. But on a Galaxy Note or a Galaxy Tab?

The Galaxy family of tablets comes in a variety of sizes. Even the smallest cousin sports a screen large enough to make viewing information on the web enjoyable. It's like seeing a younger, thinner version of Uncle Ron sitting on the Hepplewhite. The web on your tablet can be a pleasure to witness, especially when you've read the good information in this chapter.

Add to Dropbox   AK Notepad   Barcode Scanner   B

ChatON   Cloud Print   Email   Fa

     ✔ If you have a cellular tablet, activate the Wi-Fi connection before you venture out on the web. Although you can use the mobile data connection, the Wi-Fi connection incurs no data usage charges.

     ✔ Many places you visit on the web can instead be accessed directly and more effectively by using specific apps. Facebook, Gmail, Twitter, YouTube, and potentially other popular web destinations each have apps that are preinstalled or can be downloaded for free from the Google Play Store. Use those individual apps instead of the Internet app.

Mobile Web Browsing

Rare is the person these days who has had no experience with the World Wide Web. More common is someone who has used the web on a computer but has yet to taste the Internet waters on a mobile device. If that's you, consider this section your quick mobile web orientation.

Viewing the web

Your Galaxy tablet's web-browsing app is named Internet. Yeah, that's kind of generic, but it's the app you open when you desire to surf the 'net. Find that app on the Apps screen or perhaps as a shortcut icon affixed to the Home screen. Figure 7-1 illustrates the Internet app's interface.

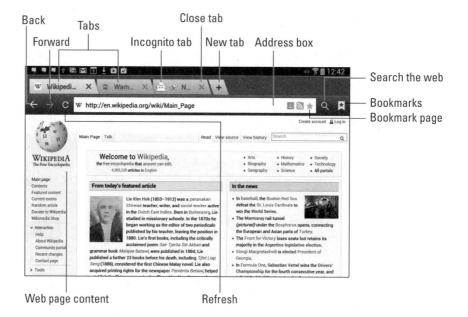

Figure 7-1: The Internet app.

Here are some handy tablet web-browsing tips:

- ✔ Pan the web page by dragging your finger across the touchscreen. You can pan up, down, left, or right when the page is larger than the tablet's screen.

- ✔ Pinch the screen to zoom out and spread two fingers to zoom in.

✔ The page you see may be the mobile page, or a customized version of the web page designed for small-screen devices. To see the non-mobile version, touch the Menu button and choose the Desktop View command.

✔ The Search icon (refer to Figure 7-1) may change to a Microphone icon. If so, touch that icon to give a voice command to the Internet app.

✔ Reorient the tablet between vertical and horizontal positions to improve the appearance of web pages. Sometimes it's easier to read a page in the vertical orientation, but the horizontal orientation may better present information.

The first time you fire up the Internet app on your tablet, you may see the Samsung Galaxy tablet registration page. Register your tablet to receive sundry Samsung bonus stuff — or not. Registration is optional.

Visiting a web page

To visit a web page, type its address into the Address box (refer to Figure 7-1). You can also type a search word or phrase if you don't know an exact web page address. Touch the Go button on the onscreen keyboard to search the web or visit a specific web page.

If you don't see the Address box, touch the web page's tab atop the screen. The Address box, along with the various buttons left and right, appears on the screen.

You "click" links on a page by touching them with your finger. If you have trouble stabbing the right link, zoom in on the page and try again.

✔ When typing a web page address, use the onscreen keyboard's www. key to instantly type those characters for the address. The www. key changes to the .com key to assist you in rapidly typing those characters as well.

✔ To reload a web page, touch the Refresh symbol on the left end of the Address bar.

✔ To stop a web page from loading, touch the X that appears to the left of the Address bar. The X replaces the Refresh button and appears only when a web page is loading.

✔ The Refresh icon may change to a menu icon (see the margin) as you type in the Address bar. Touch that icon to choose a search engine to use when looking up information.

Browsing back and forth

To return to a web page, you can touch the Internet app's Back icon (labeled in Figure 7-1) or touch the tablet's Back button (shown in the margin).

Touch the Internet app's Forward icon to go forward or to return to a page you were visiting before you touched the Back icon.

To review the long-term history of your web-browsing adventures, touch the Bookmark icon in the upper-right corner of the screen (refer to Figure 7-1). Select the History tab to view your web-browsing history. Select a web page from the History list to view a page you visited weeks or months ago.

To clear the History list, touch the Menu button and choose the Clear History command.

Working with bookmarks

Bookmarks are those electronic breadcrumbs you can drop as you wander the web. Need to revisit a website? Just look up its bookmark. This advice assumes, of course, that you bothered to create (I prefer *drop*) a bookmark when you first visited the site.

The cinchy way to bookmark a page is to touch the Favorite (star) icon on the right end of the Address bar. You see the Add Bookmark window, similar to what's shown in Figure 7-2. It's okay if not all the fields show up.

Add bookmark	
Name	Wambooli Mobile
Address	http://m.wambooli.com/
Account	My device
Folder	🔖 Bookmarks
Cancel	**OK**

Figure 7-2: Creating a bookmark.

I often edit the Name (or Title) field to something shorter and more descriptive, especially if the web page's title is long. Shorter names look better on the Bookmarks window. Touch the OK or Save button to add the bookmark.

 After the bookmark is set, it appears in the list of bookmarks. To see the list, touch the Bookmarks icon on the Internet app's main window (refer to Figure 7-1). Choose the Bookmarks tab to see a list of bookmark folders. Touch a folder to view web page thumbnails, complete with labels or titles. Swipe the list downward to see more bookmarks and thumbnails.

Touch a bookmark to visit that page.

✔ Remove a bookmark by long-pressing its entry in the Bookmarks list. Choose the Delete command or the Delete Bookmark command. Touch the OK button to confirm. The bookmark is gone.

✔ Bookmarked websites can also be placed on the Home screen: Long-press the bookmark thumbnail and choose the Add Shortcut command.

Managing web pages in multiple tabs

The Internet app uses a tabbed interface to display more than one web page at a time. Refer to Figure 7-1 to see various tabs marching across the Internet app's screen, just above the Address bar.

Here's how you work the tabbed interface:

✔ *To open a blank tab,* touch the plus button to the right of the last tab.

✔ *To open a link in a new tab,* long-press that link. Choose the Open in New Tab (or Open in New Window) command from the menu.

✔ *To open a bookmark in a new window,* long-press the bookmark and choose the Open in New Tab (or Open in New Window) command.

You switch between tabs by choosing one from the top of the screen.

Close a tab by touching its X (Close) button; you can close only the tab you're currently viewing.

✔ The tabs continue sprouting across the screen, left to right. You can scroll the tabs to view the ones that have scrolled off the screen.

✔ New tabs open using the home page that's set for the Internet application. See the "Setting a home page" section, later in this chapter, for information.

✔ For secure browsing, you can open an *incognito tab:* Touch the Menu button and choose the New Incognito Tab command. When you go incognito, the Internet app won't track your history, leave cookies, or provide other evidence of which web pages you've visited in the incognito tab. A short description appears on the incognito tab page, describing how it works.

Searching in and on the web

The handiest way to find things on the web is to use the Google Now app, covered in Chapter 14. You can also find a Google Search widget on the Primary Home screen. If not, refer to Chapter 19 for information on adding the Google Search widget.

While you're using the Internet app, you can touch either the Search icon or the Microphone icon to search the web. Refer to Figure 7-1 for its location.

To locate text on a web page, touch the Menu button and choose the Find on Page command. You'll see a new toolbar atop the screen, as shown in Figure 7-3.

Figure 7-3: Searching for text on a web page.

Type the search text in the Find on Page box, shown in Figure 7-3. As you type, found text is displayed on the screen. Use the up and down triangle buttons to page through the document. Touch the Back button to dismiss the toolbar after you've finished searching.

Sharing a page

There it is! That web page that you just *have* to talk about to everyone you know. The gauche way to share the page is to copy and paste it. Because you're reading this book, though, you know the better way to share a web page. Heed these steps:

1. **Go to the web page you want to share.**

2. **Touch the Menu button and choose the Share Via or Share Page command.**

The Share Via menu appears, listing apps and methods by which you can share the page, as shown in Figure 7-4. The variety and number of items on the Share Via menu depend on the apps installed on your tablet.

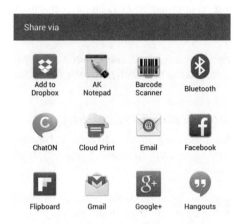

Figure 7-4: Apps available for sharing a web page.

3. **Choose a method to share the link.**

   For example, choose Email to send the link by e-mail, or Facebook to share the link with your friends.

4. **Do whatever happens next.**

   Whatever happens next depends on how you're sharing the link: Compose the e-mail, write a comment in Facebook, or whatever. Refer to various chapters in this book for specific directions.

You cannot share a page you're viewing on an incognito tab.

The Art of Downloading

There's nothing to downloading, other than understanding that most people use the term without knowing exactly what it means. Officially, a *download* is a transfer of information over a network from another source to your gizmo. For a Galaxy Note or a Galaxy Tab, that network is the Internet, and the other source is a web page.

✔ The download notification appears after the tablet has downloaded something. You can choose that notification to view the download.

✔ There's no need to download program files. New software for your tablet is obtained from the Google Play Store. See Chapter 15.

✔ Most people use the term *download* to refer to copying or transferring a file or other information. That's technically inaccurate, but the description passes for social discussion.

✔ The opposite of downloading is *uploading.* That's the process of sending information from your gizmo to another location on a network.

Grabbing an image from a web page

The simplest thing to download is an image from a web page. It's cinchy: Long-press the image. You see a pop-up menu, from which you choose the Save Image command.

To view images you download from the web, you use the Gallery app. Downloaded images are saved in the Download album.

✔ Refer to Chapter 12 for information on the Gallery app.

✔ Technically, the image is stored in the Download folder in the tablet's internal storage. You can read about tablet file storage in Chapter 17.

Downloading a file

The web is full of links that don't open in a web browser window. For example, some links automatically download, such as links to PDF files, Microsoft Word documents, and other types of files that can't be displayed by a web browser.

To save other types of links that aren't automatically downloaded, long-press the link and choose the Save Link command from the menu that appears. If the Save Link command doesn't appear, the file cannot be downloaded, either because the file is an unrecognized type or because there could be a security issue.

To review the items you've downloaded, open the Downloads app, which is found on the Apps screen. You'll see the list of downloads sorted by date, as shown in Figure 7-5.

Selected items   Share   Delete

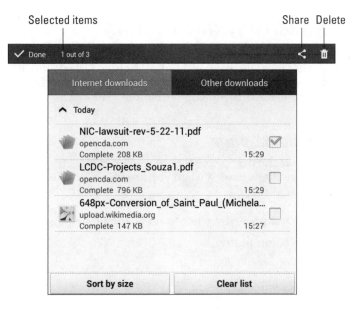

Figure 7-5: Download Manager.

To view a download, choose it from the list. The appropriate app is then opened so you can view the download.

Should your tablet not have a Downloads app, you can choose the download notification to view the file. If prompted, choose an app to use for viewing, such as Gallery or Polaris Office, and then touch the Just Once button.

 ✔ To remove an item from the Downloads list, select its box, as shown in Figure 7-5. Touch the Trash icon at the top of the screen to remove that download.

 ✔ Sharing a downloaded item is done by placing a green check mark by the downloaded file and choosing the Share icon at the top of the screen (refer to Figure 7-5).

 ✔ Downloads are stored in the Download folder on the tablet's internal storage device. Use the My Files app to locate that folder and peruse the files. The My Files app is found on the Apps screen. If you can't find it there, look in the Samsung app folder.

Internet App Controls and Settings

More options and settings and controls exist for the Internet app than just about any other app I've used on a Galaxy Note or Galaxy Tab. It's complex. Rather than bore you with every dangdoodle detail, I thought I'd present just a few of the options worthy of your attention.

Setting a home page

The *home page* is the first page you see when you start the Internet app, and it's the first page that's loaded when you fire up a new tab. To set a home page, heed these directions:

1. **Browse to the page you want to set as the home page.**

2. **Touch the Menu button.**

3. **Choose Settings.**

   The Settings screen appears.

4. **Choose Set Home Page.**

   If you don't see the Set Home Page item on the left side of the screen, choose General, and then choose Set Home Page.

5. **Choose the Current Page item.**

   Now you see why I had you browse to the page in Step 1.

The home page is set.

I changed the home page on my tablet because it was preset to my cellular provider's page, and that page took forever to load. Remember: You don't have to use your cellular provider's home page or the Samsung home page.

If you want your home page to be blank (not set to any particular web page), choose Blank Page in Step 5. If that option isn't available, choose Other, and then type **about:blank** in the box. Touch the OK button to set the page, and then touch the Done button at the top-right corner of the screen.

I prefer a blank home page because it's the fastest web page to load. It's also the web page with the most accurate information.

Changing the way the web looks

No matter which size Galactic tablet you own, you have several ways to improve the way the web looks. First and foremost, don't forget that you can orient the device horizontally and vertically, which rearranges the way a web page is displayed.

From the Settings screen, you can also adjust the zoom setting used to display a web page. Heed these steps when using the Internet app:

1. **Touch the Menu button, and then choose the Settings command.**

2. **On the left side of the screen, select Screen and Text.**

   If you don't see this item, refer to the next set of steps.

3. **Use the slider to adjust the text scaling.**

Older versions of the Internet app follow a different set of steps:

1. **Touch the Menu button, and then choose the Settings command.**

2. **Choose Advanced, and then choose Default Zoom.**

3. **Select a setting.**

   You have three options: Far, Medium, and Close for tiny, normal, and larger-sized web pages, respectively.

You can spread your fingers to zoom in on any web page.

Setting privacy and security options

As far as the Internet app's settings go, most of the security options are already enabled, including the blocking of pop-up windows (which normally spew ads).

If information retained on the tablet concerns you, you can clear it when you use the Internet app: Touch the Menu button and choose the Settings command. Then choose either the Privacy category or the Privacy and Security category, depending on which version of the Internet app is installed on your tablet.

If the screen says Privacy, choose the Delete Personal Data item. Place check marks by the items you want to remove from the tablet's storage, and then touch the Done button. Back on the Privacy screen, remove check marks next to all items to add the most security. Be aware that these settings do slow down the Internet app a tad.

If the screen says Privacy and Security, you'll find several commands that begin with the word *Clear*. These options vacuum away personal information and settings that may be of concern to you. For example, choose the Clear History command to remove browser history. Or touch the Clear Form Data item to remove any preset data from Internet forms you may have filled in the past.

As you use your Galaxy tablet, you may see various warnings regarding location data. What they mean is that the tablet can take advantage of your location on planet earth (using the GPS or satellite position system) to help locate businesses and people near you. I see no security problem in leaving the feature on, though you can disable location services. Refer to Chapter 10.

With regard to general online security, my advice is always to be smart and think before doing anything questionable on the web. Use common sense. One of the most effective ways that the Bad Guys win is by using *human engineering* to try to trick you into doing something you normally wouldn't do, such as click a link to see a cute animation or a racy picture of a celebrity or politician. As long as you use your noggin, you should be safe.

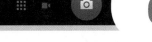

The Digital Social Life

In This Chapter

▶ Accessing social updates for your contacts

▶ Getting Facebook

▶ Sharing your life on Facebook

▶ Sending pictures to Facebook

▶ Tweeting on Twitter

▶ Exploring other social networking opportunities

*A*t the dawn of the Internet, there was no reason to use the Internet. Well, yes: It was a time-killer. Then came the glory of e-mail, the thrill of online shopping, the tedium of blogging. At the end of the first decade of the twenty-first century, another reason popped up: online social networking.

Armed with your Galaxy Note or Galaxy Tab, you can keep your digital social life up-to-date wherever you go. You can communicate with your friends, followers, and buddies; upload pictures and videos you take on the tablet; or just share your personal, private, intimate thoughts with the whole of humanity.

In Your Facebook

Of all the social networking sites, Facebook is the king. It's the online place to go to catch up with friends, send messages, express your thoughts, share pictures and videos, play games, and waste more time than you ever thought you had.

> ✔ Although you can access Facebook on the web by using the Internet app, I highly recommend that you use the Facebook app described in this section.

✔ You can access updates to your contacts' Facebook statuses from the Contacts app. See Chapter 5.

✔ Future software updates to your Galaxy tablet may include a Facebook app or another social networking app. If so, you can read an update on my website at `www.wambooli.com/help/android/facebook/`.

Setting up your Facebook account

The best way to use Facebook is to have a Facebook account, and the best way to do that is to sign up at `www.facebook.com` by using your computer. Register for a new account by setting up your username and password.

Don't forget your Facebook username and password!

Eventually, the Facebook robots send you a confirmation e-mail. You reply to that message, and the online social networking community braces itself for your long-awaited arrival.

After you're all set up, you're ready to access Facebook on your Galaxy tablet. To get the most from Facebook, however, you need the Facebook app. Keep reading in the next section.

Getting the Facebook app

As this book goes to press, neither the Galaxy Note nor Galaxy Tab come with a Facebook app. Fret not! You can get the Facebook app free from the Google Play Store. That app is your red carpet to the Facebook social networking kingdom.

To get the Facebook app, go to the Google Play Store and search for the Facebook for Android app. Download that app. If you need specific directions, see Chapter 15, which covers using the Play Store app.

After you install the Facebook app, you may see a Facebook notification icon. Touch that icon and complete the steps required to complete installation on your tablet.

Running Facebook on your tablet

You access Facebook by running the Facebook app. If you can't find the Facebook app, you need to install it; refer to the preceding section.

The first time you behold the Facebook app, you'll probably be asked to sign in. Do so: Type the e-mail address you used to sign up for Facebook and then type your Facebook password. Touch the Log In button.

If you're asked to sync your contacts, do so. I recommend choosing the Sync All option, which brings in all your Facebook friends to the tablet's Contacts list. Touch the Sync button in the upper-right corner of the screen to begin using Facebook.

Eventually, you see the Facebook News Feed, similar to what's shown in Figure 8-1.

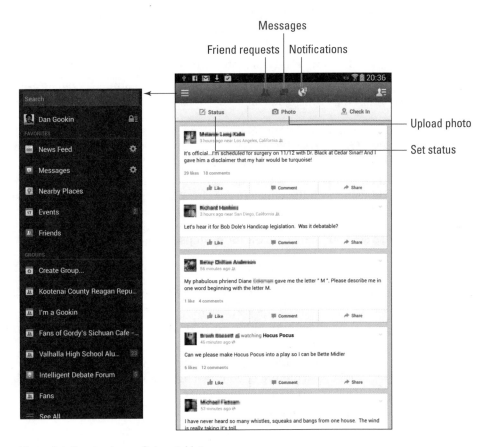

Figure 8-1: Facebook on a Galaxy tablet.

When you need a respite from Facebook, press the Home key to return to the Home screen.

The Facebook app continues to run until you either sign out or turn off the tablet. To sign out of Facebook, touch the Menu button and choose the Log Out command. Then touch the Confirm button.

- ✔ Display the sidebar by touching the Facebook app button. To hide the sidebar, touch that button again.

- ✔ Refer to Chapter 19 for information on placing a Facebook app or widget on the Home screen.

- ✔ Use the Comment, Like, or Share buttons below a News Feed item to comment, like, or share something, respectively. You can see the comments only when you choose the Comment item.

- ✔ The News Feed is updated when you swipe down on the screen.

- ✔ Notifications for Facebook appear in the notifications area of the screen. They look similar to what's shown in the margin.

Setting your status

The primary thing you live for on Facebook, besides having more friends than anyone else, is to update your status. It's the best way to share your thoughts with the universe, far cheaper than skywriting and far less offensive than a robocall.

To set your status, follow these steps in the Facebook app:

1. **Touch the Status button at the top of the screen.**

   You see the Write Post screen, where you can type your musing, similar to what's shown in Figure 8-2.

2. **Type something pithy, newsworthy, or typical of the stuff you read in Facebook.**

   When you can't think of anything to post, take off your shoes, sit down, and take a picture of your feet against something else in the background. That seems to be really popular.

3. **Touch the Post button.**

Share your location

Upload photo

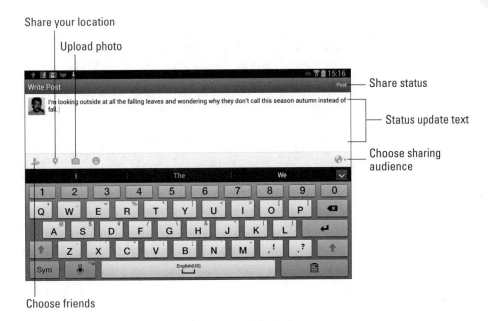

Share status

Status update text

Choose sharing audience

Choose friends

Figure 8-2: Updating your Facebook status.

You can also set your status by using the Facebook widget on the home page, if it's been installed. Touch the What's on Your Mind text box, type your important news tidbit, and then touch the Share button.

Uploading a picture to Facebook

One of the many things your Galaxy tablet can do is take pictures. Combine that feature with the Facebook app, and you have an all-in-one gizmo designed for sharing the various intimate and private moments of your life with the ogling throngs of the Internet.

The picture-posting process starts by touching a Photo icon in the Facebook app. Refer to Figures 8-1 and 8-2 for popular Photo icon locations on the main screen and the Write Post screen, respectively. After touching the Photo icon, you see the photo selection screen. You have two choices:

✔ First, you can select an image from pictures shown on the screen. Those are images found on the tablet. Touch an image, or touch several images to select a bunch, and then proceed with the steps listed later in this section.

✔ Second, you can take a picture by using the tablet's camera.

If you elect to use the tablet's camera to take a picture, touch the Camera icon on the photo selection screen. (It's in the lower-left corner.) You then find yourself thrust into Facebook's camera app, shown in Figure 8-3. This is not the same app as the Camera app, covered in Chapter 11.

Use the onscreen controls to take your picture, as shown in Figure 8-3. Or you can shoot a quick video. When you're done, touch the Gallery button.

To proceed with uploading your image, follow these steps:

1. **Touch an image in the gallery to select it.**

2. **(Optional) To add a tag, tap the image and type the person's name.**

   You can touch someone's face in the picture and then type her name. Choose from a list of your Facebook friends to apply a name tag to the image.

Switch cameras
(front/back)

Flash control (not on all tablets)

Take picture

Record video   Return to gallery

Figure 8-3: Snapping a pic for Facebook.

3. **Use the rotate button to reorient the image, if necessary.**

   The button's icon is shown in the margin.

4. **Touch the Compose button.**

   The compose button is shown in the margin.

5. **Add a message to the image.**

   At this point, posting the image works just like adding a status update, similar to what's shown in Figure 8-2.

6. **Touch the Post button.**

   The image is posted as soon as it's transferred over the Internet and digested by Facebook.

The image can be found as part of your status update or News Feed, and it's also saved to Facebook's Mobile Uploads album.

Facebook also appears on the various Share menus you find in other apps on the tablet. Choose that command to send to Facebook whatever it is you're looking at. (Other chapters in this book give you more information about the various Share menus and where they appear.)

Configuring the Facebook app

The commands that control Facebook are stored on the Settings screen, which you access by touching the Menu button while viewing the main Facebook screen and choosing the Settings command.

Choose Refresh Interval to specify how frequently the app checks for new Facebook activities. You might find the one-hour value to be too long for your frantic Facebook social life, so choose something quicker. Or, to disable Facebook notifications, choose Never.

The Notification Ringtone item sets the sound that plays when Facebook has a new update. Choose the Silent option when you don't want the app to make noise upon encountering a Facebook update.

Touch the Back button to close the Settings screen and return to the main Facebook screen.

Tweet Suite

Twitter is a social networking site, similar to Facebook but far briefer. On Twitter, you write short spurts of text that express your thoughts or observations, or you share links. Or you can just use Twitter to follow the thoughts and twitterings, or *tweets,* of other people.

> ✔ A message posted on Twitter is a *tweet.*

> ✔ A tweet can be no more than 140 characters long. That number includes spaces and punctuation.

> ✔ You can post messages on Twitter and follow others who post messages. Twitter is a good way to get updates and information quickly, from not only individuals but also news outlets and other organizations.

Setting up Twitter

The best way to use Twitter on your Galaxy tablet is to already have a Twitter account. Start by going to `http://twitter.com` on a computer and following the directions there for creating a new account.

After you've established a Twitter account, you can use the Twitter app on your tablet. Not all Galaxy tablets come with Twitter installed. If you don't find the app on the Apps screen, you can obtain the Twitter app from the Google Play Store. Search for the Twitter app from Twitter, Inc. Refer to Chapter 15 for information on downloading apps to your tablet.

When you start the Twitter app for the first time, touch the Sign In button. Type your Twitter username or e-mail address and then type your Twitter password. After that, you can use Twitter without having to log in again — until you turn off the tablet or exit the Twitter app.

Figure 8-4 shows the Twitter app's main screen, which shows the current tweet feed. The main screen may look subtly different on your tablet, depending on the Twitter app version.

New tweet notification

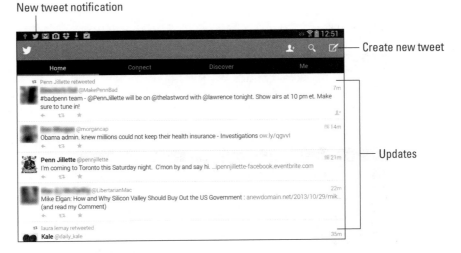

Create new tweet

Updates

Figure 8-4: The Twitter app.

See the next section for information on *tweeting,* or updating your status using the Twitter app.

TIP

The Twitter app comes with companion widgets you can affix to the Home screen. Use the widgets to peruse recent tweets or compose a new tweet. Refer to Chapter 19 for information on affixing widgets to the Home screen.

Tweeting

The Twitter app provides an excellent interface to the many wonderful and interesting things that Twitter does. Of course, the two most basic tasks are reading and writing tweets.

To read tweets, choose the Home category, as shown in Figure 8-4. Recent tweets are displayed in a list, with the most recent information at the top. Scroll the list by swiping it with your finger.

To tweet, touch the New Tweet icon. (Refer to Figure 8-4.) Use the New Tweet screen, shown in Figure 8-5, to compose your tweet.

Share the tweet

Twitter notification icon   Characters left

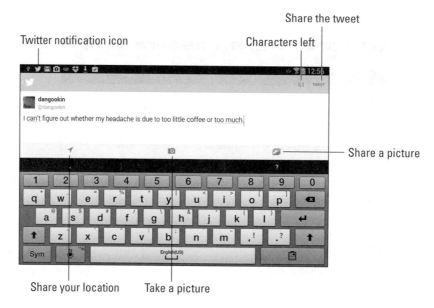

Share a picture

Share your location   Take a picture

Figure 8-5: Creating a tweet.

 The Galaxy Note features an extra icon on the New Tweet screen, Draw, which is shown in the margin. Touch that icon to use the S Pen to scribble something, which will be attached to the tweet.

 Touch the Tweet button to share your thoughts with the Twitterverse.

✔ You have only 140 characters for creating your tweet. That includes spaces.

✔ The character counter in the Twitter app lets you know how close you're getting to the 140-character limit.

✔ Twitter itself doesn't display pictures, other than your account picture. When you send a picture to Twitter, you use an image-hosting service and then share the link, or URL, to the image. All that complexity is handled by the Twitter app.

 ✔ The Twitter app appears on various Share menus in other apps. You use those Share menus to send to Twitter whatever you're looking at.

Even More Social Networking

The Internet is nuts over social networking. Facebook may be the king, but lots of landed gentry are out for that crown. It almost seems as though a new social networking site pops up every week. Beyond Facebook and Twitter, other social networking sites include, but are not limited to

- Google+
- LinkedIn
- Meebo
- Myspace

I recommend first setting up the social networking account on your computer, similar to the way I describe it earlier in this chapter for Facebook and Twitter. After that, obtain an app for the social networking site by using the Google Play Store. Set up and configure that app on your Galaxy tablet to connect the tablet with your existing account.

- See Chapter 15 for more information on the Google Play Store.
- Google+ is Google's social networking app, which is related to the Hangouts app. See Chapter 9 for information on using Hangouts.

- The HootSuite app can be used to share your thoughts on a multitude of social networking platforms. It can be obtained from the Play Store, as described in Chapter 15.
- As with Facebook and Twitter, you may find your social networking apps appearing on Share menus in various apps. That way, you can easily share your pictures and other types of media with your online social networking pals.

9

Text Chat, Video Chat, and Even Phone Calls

. . . .

In This Chapter

▶ Setting up Google+ Hangouts

▶ Chatting with friends

▶ Doing a video chat

▶ Typing to contacts on Skype

▶ Texting with Skype

▶ Using Skype to make phone calls

. . . .

*T*he cellular models of the Galaxy Note and Galaxy Tab do have a phone number. It's not a dial-up phone number; your cellular provider merely uses the number to bill you. So as far as phone calls are concerned, you're just as out-of-luck as owners of the Wi-Fi–only tablets. That's no cause for despair, however, because your Galactic tablet is more than capable of placing — and receiving — phone calls. All you need are the proper apps, which also provide tools for text chat, video chat, even text messaging. This chapter explains how it all works.

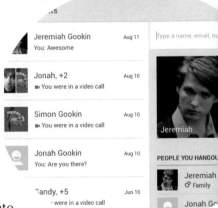

Let's Hang Out

One of the ways that you can fool your Galaxy tablet into acting more like a phone is to use the Hangouts app. It does text chat and video chat. The only downside to the app is that you can communicate only with your friends who have Google accounts.

The Hangouts app is a reincarnation of the old Google Talk app. Most of the things that could be done on Google Talk are now done by using the Hangouts app instead.

Using Hangouts

The Hangouts app can be found on the Apps screen. If you don't see it directly in the list of apps, look for it inside the Google folder. And if you still can't find it, you can obtain the app from the Google Play Store. It's free! See Chapter 15.

Hangouts hooks into your Google account. If you have any previous conversations, they're listed on left side the main screen, as shown in Figure 9-1. The right side of the screen shows frequent contacts. If you scroll down the right side, you'll see all your Google contacts.

App button   Add friends/view contacts

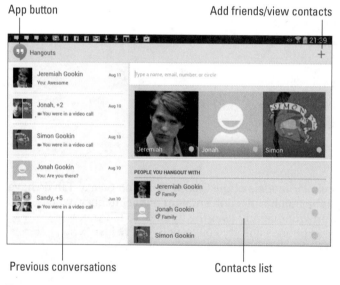

Previous conversations   Contacts list

Figure 9-1: Google Hangouts.

The Hangouts app listens for incoming conversation requests; you can also start your own. You can even do other things on the tablet — you'll be alerted via notification of an impending Hangout request.

To sign out of the app, which means you won't receive any notifications, touch the Menu button and choose the Settings command. Choose the Sign Out item. (Scroll down to find that item.) Touch OK to confirm.

✔ When using the tablet in the vertical orientation, you need to swipe the right side of the screen to see previous conversations or the Contacts list.

✔ Conversations are archived in the Hangouts app. To peruse a previous text chat, select it from the list on the left. Video calls aren't archived, but you can review when the call took place and with whom.

✔ To remove a previous conversation, long-press it. Touch the Trash icon that appears atop the screen.

✔ Your friends can be on a computer or a mobile device to use Hangouts; it doesn't matter which. But they must have a camera available to enable video chat.

Typing at your friends

The most basic form of communication in the Hangouts app — and one of the oldest forms of communications on the Internet — is text chatting, in which people type text back and forth at each other. It can be most tedious. I'll be brief.

You start text chatting by obeying these steps:

1. **Touch a contact in the Contacts list.**

   If you want to chat with several friends, keep selecting them. Selected friends have a check mark next to their account name or image.

   To deselect a contact, touch the contact's account icon again.

2. **Choose Message from the bottom of the screen.**

3. **Type your message, as shown in Figure 9-2.**

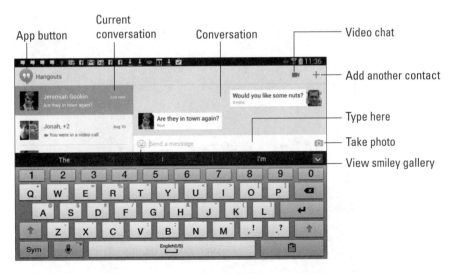

Figure 9-2: Text chatting.

4. **Touch the Send icon to send your comment.**

   The Send icon replaces the Photo icon when you type a message.

You type, your friend types, and so on until you grow tired or the tablet's battery dies.

When you're text chatting, or "hanging out," with a group, everyone in the group receives the message.

Resume any conversation by choosing that same contact from the Previous Conversations list.

Adding more people to the hangout is always possible: During a chat, touch the Menu button, and choose the New Group Hangout command. Touch a friend (only available friends are listed) to invite him in.

 When someone sends you a text message by using the Hangouts app, you'll see a notification, similar to what's shown in the margin. Select that notification to review the message and begin a conversation.

Talking and video chat

Take the conversation up a notch by touching the Video icon on the right side of the text chat window (labeled in Figure 9-2). When you do, your friend receives a pop-up invite, as shown in Figure 9-3. Touch the Accept button to begin talking.

Figure 9-3: Someone wants to video chat!

Figure 9-4 shows an ongoing video chat. The person you're talking with appears in the big window; you're in the smaller window. Other video chat participants appear at the bottom of the screen as well, as shown in the figure.

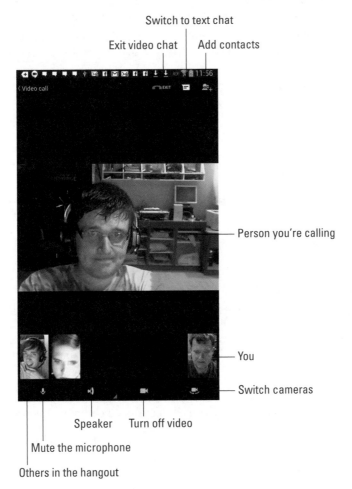

Figure 9-4: Video chat in the Hangouts app.

The onscreen controls (shown in Figure 9-4) may vanish after a second; touch the screen to see the controls again.

To end the conversation, touch the Exit button. Well, say "Goodbye" first, and then touch the button.

✔ When you're nude, touch the Decline button for the video chat invite. Then choose that contact and reply with a text message or voice chat instead.

✔ Use the Speaker icon to choose how to listen when you video chat. You can use the tablet's speaker, headphones, and so on.

✔ When video chatting with multiple contacts, select a contact from the bottom of the screen to see the person in a larger format in the center of the screen.

✔ The tablet's front-facing camera is at the top center of the tablet. If you want to make eye contact, look directly into the camera. When you do, however, you can't see the other video chat participants.

Connect to the World with Skype

When it comes time to turn your Galactic tablet into a phone, you need something called Skype. It's one of the most popular Internet communications tools, allowing you to text chat, voice chat, or video chat with others on the Internet as well as use the Internet to make real, honest-to-goodness phone calls.

Getting Skype for your tablet

The typical Galaxy tablet doesn't come with the Skype app preinstalled. To get Skype, slide your finger all over the touchscreen to get to the Google Play Store. (Refer to Chapter 15 if sliding your finger randomly doesn't work.) Obtain the Skype app. If you find multiple apps, get the one from the Skype company itself.

To use Skype, you need a Skype account. You can sign up for one using the app, or you can visit www.skype.com on a computer to complete the process.

When you start the Skype app for the first time, work through the start-up screens. You can even take the tour. Be sure to have Skype scour the tablet's address book (the Contacts app) for contacts you can Skype. This process may take a while, but if you're just starting out, it's a great help.

✔ Skype is free to use. Text chat is free. Voice and video chat with one other Skype user is also free. But if you want to call a real phone or video chat with a group, you need to boost your account with Skype Credit.

✔ You can use video chat with Google Hangouts without having to pay extra.

✔ Don't worry about getting a Skype number, which costs extra. It's necessary only if you expect to receive phone calls on your tablet by using Skype.

Chatting with another Skype user

Text chat with Skype works similarly to texting on a smartphone. The only difference is that the other person must be a Skype user. So in that respect, Skype text chat works a lot like Google Hangouts chat, covered elsewhere in this chapter.

To chat, follow these steps:

1. **Start the Skype app and sign in.**

   You don't need to sign in when you've previously run the Skype app. Like all other apps, Skype continues to run until you sign out or turn off the tablet.

2. **At the main Skype screen, touch the People icon and choose a contact.**

   Or you can choose one of the contact icons shown on the main screen.

3. **Type your text in the text box.**

   The box is found at the bottom of the screen. It says *Type a Message Here.*

4. **Touch the blue arrow to send the message.**

   As long as your Skype friend is online and eager, you'll be chatting in no time.

At the far right end of the text box, you find the Smiley icon. You can use this icon to insert a cute graphic into your text.

- ✔ The Skype Chat notification, shown in the margin, appears whenever someone wants to chat with you. It's handy to see, especially when you may have switched away from the Skype app to work in some other app. Choose that notification to get into the conversation.

- ✔ You can add more people to the conversation, if you like: Touch the Add People button in the upper-right corner of the screen. Select the contacts who you want to join with your chat session, and then touch the Add Selected button. It's a gang chat!

- ✔ To stop chatting, touch the Back navigation button. The conversation is kept in the Skype app, even after the other person has disconnected.

- ✔ For the chat to work, the other user must be online and available.

Seeing on Skype (video call)

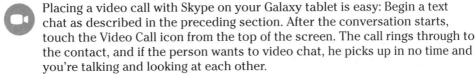

Placing a video call with Skype on your Galaxy tablet is easy: Begin a text chat as described in the preceding section. After the conversation starts, touch the Video Call icon from the top of the screen. The call rings through to the contact, and if the person wants to video chat, he picks up in no time and you're talking and looking at each other.

Placing a Skype phone call

Ah. The big enchilada: Skype can be used to turn your Galaxy tablet — be it cellular or Wi-Fi — into a smartphone. It's an amazing feat. And it works quite well, providing you have Skype Credit.

To ensure that you have Skype Credit, touch your Account icon on the main Skype screen, shown in Figure 9-5. Touch the Skype Credit item to see a summary of the credit and potentially get more, as illustrated in the figure.

Dial phones   Account icon

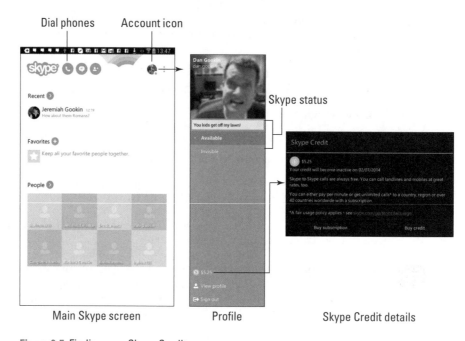

Skype status

Main Skype screen   Profile   Skype Credit details

Figure 9-5: Finding your Skype Credit.

After you have Skype Credit, you can use the tablet to make a "real" phone call, which is a call to any phone number on the planet (planet earth). Heed these steps:

1. Choose a contact to call.

Your Skype contact must have a phone number listed in his contact information. Otherwise you'll have to dial the number directly, which is described near the end of this section.

2. Touch the Phone icon, in the upper-right corner of the screen.

If you don't see the Phone icon, the contact's information doesn't include a real live phone number.

Mute Dialpad   End call

Figure 9-6: Calling a real phone by using Skype.

3. **Talk.**

   The Call screen looks similar to the one in Figure 9-6.

4. **To end the call, touch the red End Call button.**

   Refer to Figure 9-6 for the button's location.

To dial a number not associated with a contact, touch the Phone icon at the top of the main Skype screen (refer to Figure 9-5, left). Punch in the number to dial, starting with 1 (for the United States), then the area code, and then the number. Touch the green Dial icon to place the call.

Lamentably, you can't receive a phone call using Skype unless you pay for a Skype online number. In that case, you can use Skype to both send and receive regular phone calls. This book doesn't cover the Online Number option.

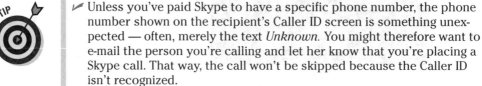

Chatting with your Samsung friends

One chatting app that does come with your Galaxy tablet is the ChatON app. It's from Samsung. As such, it's keyed into your Samsung account. Further, if you want to use the app to chat with others, they must also have Samsung accounts. As long as all your friends have Samsung mobile devices and have all signed up for Samsung accounts, and you know all those accounts, the ChatON app works marvelously. Until then, using Google Hangouts or Skype is probably a better option.

> ✒ I recommend getting a good headset if you plan to use Skype often to place phone calls.

> ✒ In addition to having to pay the per-minute cost, you may be charged a connection fee for making the call.

> ✒ You can check the Skype website (www.skype.com) for a current list of call rates, for both domestic and international calls.

> ✒ Unless you've paid Skype to have a specific phone number, the phone number shown on the recipient's Caller ID screen is something unexpected — often, merely the text *Unknown*. You might therefore want to e-mail the person you're calling and let her know that you're placing a Skype call. That way, the call won't be skipped because the Caller ID isn't recognized.

Part III
Everything in the Galaxy

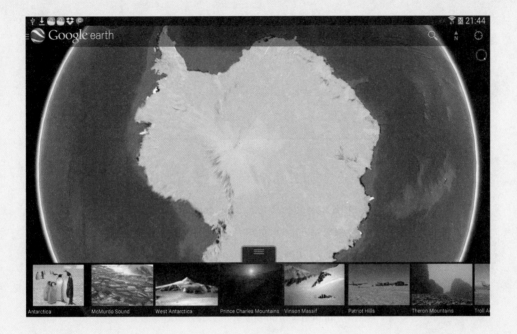

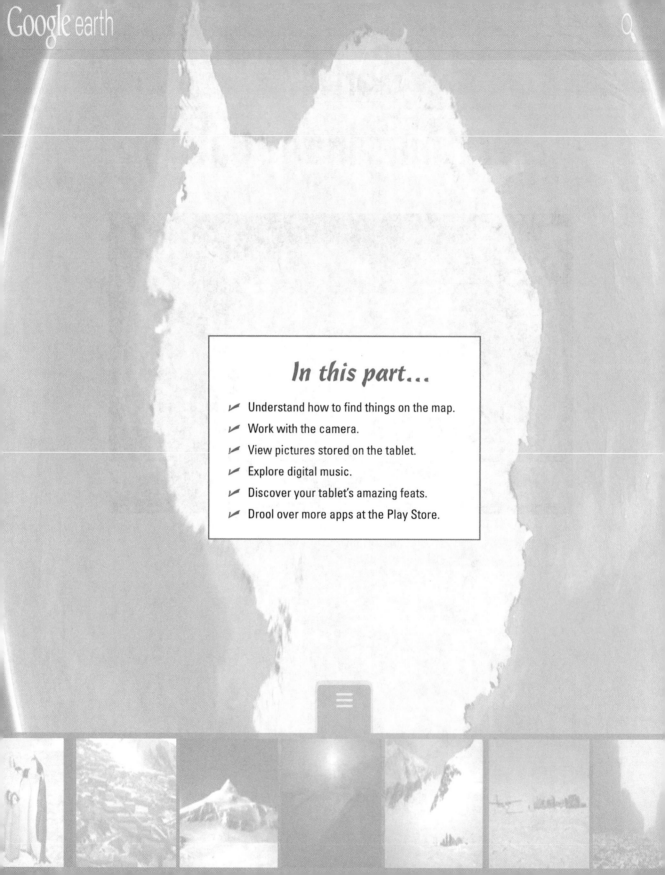

In this part...

- ✐ Understand how to find things on the map.
- ✐ Work with the camera.
- ✐ View pictures stored on the tablet.
- ✐ Explore digital music.
- ✐ Discover your tablet's amazing feats.
- ✐ Drool over more apps at the Play Store.

10

Getting from Here to There

In This Chapter

▶ Exploring your world with Maps

▶ Adding layers to the map

▶ Finding your location

▶ Sharing your location

▶ Searching for places

▶ Using your tablet as a navigator

▶ Adding a navigation Home screen shortcut

*S*tupid kidnappers. They frisked me for a phone but left the Galaxy tablet. I suppose they thought it might be a picture frame. Or perhaps they didn't even look inside the fine, imitation leatherette case, figuring it was portfolio. That was a mistake.

Even from inside the uncomfortable trunk, I could use the tablet. The screen was bright, the cellular signal was clear. The Maps app told me that I was somewhere in Seattle.

Seattle! Had they driven that far? It wasn't that important: Using the tablet, I knew not only where I was, but where a fancy Hungarian restaurant was nearby. I could send an e-mail with my location to the authorities and then be chowing down on a hot bowl of goulash in no time. Thank heavens for the Maps app!

There's a Map for That

Your location, as well as the location of things near and far, is found on your Galaxy tablet by using the Maps app. Good news: You run no risk of improperly folding the Maps app. Better news: The Maps app charts the entire country, including freeways, highways, roads, streets, avenues, drives, bike paths, addresses, businesses, and points of interest.

Using the Maps app

You start the Maps app by choosing Maps from the Apps screen. If you're starting the app for the first time or it has been recently updated, you must agree to the terms and conditions. Do so as directed on the touchscreen.

The tablet communicates with global positioning system (GPS) satellites to hone in on your current location. (See the later sidebar, "Activate your locations!") The position is accurate to within a given range, as shown by a blue circle around your location on the map, as shown in Figure 10-1. If the circle doesn't appear, your location is either pretty darn accurate or you need to zoom in.

Here are some fun things you can do when viewing the basic street map:

Zoom in: To make the map larger (to move it closer), spread your fingers on the touchscreen.

Zoom out: To make the map smaller (to see more), pinch your fingers on the touchscreen.

Figure 10-1: Your location on a map.

Pan and scroll: To see what's to the left or right or at the top or bottom of the map, drag your finger on the touchscreen; the map scrolls in the direction that you drag your finger.

Rotate: Using two fingers, rotate the map clockwise or counterclockwise. Touch the Compass Pointer (labeled in Figure 10-1) to reorient the map with north at the top of the screen.

Perspective: Touch the screen with two fingers and swipe up or down to view the map in perspective. You can also tap the Location button to switch to Perspective view, although this trick works only for your current location. To return to flat-map view, touch the Compass Pointer (refer to Figure 10-1).

The closer you zoom in to the map, the more detail you see, such as street names, address block numbers, businesses, and other sites — but no tiny people.

- ✔ The blue triangle (refer to Figure 10-1) shows in which general direction the tablet is pointing.
- ✔ When the tablet's direction is unavailable, you see a blue dot as your location on the map.
- ✔ Touch the App icon to view the sidebar, shown in Figure 10-1. To hide the sidebar, touch the App icon again.
- ✔ When all you want is a virtual compass, similar to the one you lost as a kid, get the Compass app from the Google Play Store. See Chapter 15 for more information about the Google Play Store.

Adding layers

You add details to the map by applying *layers:* A layer can enhance the map's visual appearance, provide more information, or add other fun features to the basic street map, such as Satellite view, shown in Figure 10-2.

The key to accessing layers is to touch the App icon in the upper-left corner of the screen. The sidebar displays several layers you can add, such as the Satellite layer shown in Figure 10-2. Another popular layer is Traffic, which lists updated travel conditions.

To remove a layer, choose it again from the Layers menu; any active layer appears highlighted in the sidebar. When a layer isn't applied, the Street view appears.

App icon   Main roads

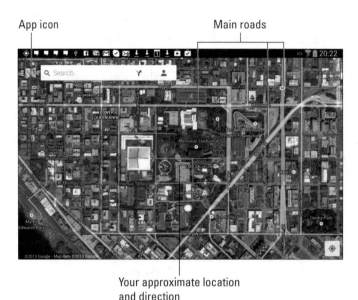

Your approximate location
and direction

Figure 10-2: The Satellite layer.

Activate your locations!

The Maps app works best when you activate all location technology in the tablet. From the Apps screen, open the Settings icon. Select the Connections tab, and then select Location Services from the left side of the screen. If the Settings app lacks a Connections tab, scroll down the left side of the screen and choose Location Services.

Ensure that all the items on the right side of the screen are activated. Here's what each means:

Access to My Location: Allows various apps to check in on the tablet's (and therefore your) location. That information is used by the app for some purpose, usually locating things nearby or marking your location for later reference. If you don't like that feature, turn it off.

Use GPS Satellites: Allows your tablet to access the GPS (global positioning system) satellites. But the tablet's GPS is not that accurate, which is why you need to activate more than this service to fully use your tablet's location capabilities.

Use Wireless Networks: Allows the tablet to use signals from cell towers to triangulate your position and refine the data received from GPS satellites.

Use Mobile Network Location: Allows cellular tables to triangulate your location based on nearby cell towers. (This setting may be combined with the Wi-Fi setting.)

The location services work best when you've activated the tablet's Wi-Fi networking. See Chapter 16 for information.

It Knows Where You Are

You can look at a physical map all day long, and unless you have a sextant or a GPS, how would you know where you are? Never fear! Your tablet knows where you are. Not only does it have a GPS, but by using the Maps app, it can instantly discover where you are, find what's nearby, and even send your location to someone else.

Finding out where you are

The Maps app shows your location as a blue dot on the screen. But *where* is that? I mean, if you need to phone a tow truck, you can't just say, "I'm the blue triangle on the orange slab by the green thing."

Well, you *can* say that, but it probably won't do any good.

To find your current street address, or any street address, long-press a location on the Maps screen. Up pops a card that gives your approximate address, similar to the one shown in Figure 10-3, left.

If you touch the card, you see a screen with more details and additional information, shown on the right in Figure 10-3.

✔ This trick works only when the tablet has Internet access. When Internet access isn't available, the Maps app is unable to communicate with the Google map servers.

✔ To make the card go away, touch anywhere else on the map.

Route

✔ The time under the Travel icon (the car in Figure 10-3) indicates how far away the address is from your current location. If the address is too far away, you'll see the Route icon, as shown in the margin.

✔ When you have *way* too much time on your hands, play with the Street View command. Choosing this option displays the location from a 360-degree perspective. In Street view, you can browse a locale, pan and tilt, or zoom in on details — whether you're familiarizing yourself with a location or planning a burglary.

Helping others find your location

It's possible to use the Maps app to send your current location to a friend. If your pal has a mobile device (phone or tablet) with smarts similar to a Galaxy tablet, he can use the coordinates to get directions to your location. Maybe he'll even bring some goulash!

Touch the card to see more info   Information about your current location

Mark the location as a favorite   Share this location

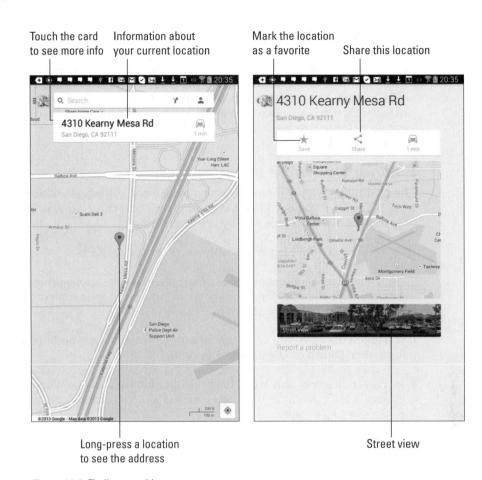

Long-press a location to see the address

Street view

Figure 10-3: Finding an address.

To send your current location in an e-mail message, obey these steps:

1. **Long-press your current location on the map.**

   To see your current location, touch the Location icon in the lower-right corner of the Maps app screen.

   After long-pressing your location (or any location), you see a card showing the approximate address.

2. **Touch the card.**

3. **Touch the Share icon.**

   Refer to Figure 10-3 for its location.

4. **Choose the Gmail item or the Email item from the Share Via menu.**

   The Gmail or Email app starts, with a preset subject and message. The subject is your street address or the address of the card you touched in Step 2. The message content is the address again, but it's also a link to the current location.

5. **In the To field, type one or more recipients.**

6. **Touch the Send button to whisk off the message.**

When the recipient receives the e-mail, he can touch the link to open your location in his Android mobile device's Maps app. When the location appears, he can follow my advice in the later section "Getting directions" for getting to your location. And don't loan him this book; have him buy his own copy — and bring goulash. Thanks.

Find Things

The Maps app can help you find places in the real world, just like the Internet app helps you find places on the Internet. Both operations work basically the same.

Open the Maps app and, in the Search text box, type something to find (refer to Figure 10-1). You can type a variety of terms in the Search box, as explained in this section.

Looking for a specific address

To locate an address, type it in the Search box; for example:

   1600 Pennsylvania Ave., Washington, D.C. 20006

Touch the Search button on the keyboard, and the location is shown on the map. The next step is getting directions, which you can read about in the later section "Getting directions."

   ✔ You don't need to type the entire address. Oftentimes, all you need is the street number and street name and then either the city name or zip code.

   ✔ If you omit the city name or zip code, the tablet looks for the closest matching address near your current location.

   ✔ Touch the X icon in the Search box to clear the previous search.

Finding a business, restaurant, or point of interest

You may not know an address, but you know when you crave sushi or Hungarian or perhaps the exotic flavors of Freedonia. Maybe you need a hotel or a gas station, or you have to find a place that buys old dentures. To find a business entity or a point of interest, type its name in the Search box; for example:

> Movie theater

This command flags movie theaters on the current Maps screen or nearby.

To find locations near you, have the Maps app jump to your current location, as described earlier in this chapter. Otherwise, the Maps app looks for places near the area you see on the screen.

Or you can be specific and look for businesses near a certain location. Specify the city name, district, or zip code, such as

> Hungarian 98001

After typing this command and touching the Search button, you see a smattering of Hungarian restaurants found near Seattle, similar to the ones shown on the left in Figure 10-4.

To see more information about a result, touch its card, such as the one for the Danube Bistro in Figure 10-4. Or choose Results List to see a whole swath of cards. After touching a card, you can view more details, similar to what's shown on the right in Figure 10-4.

Route

You can touch the Route button on the restaurant's (or any location's) details screen to get directions; see the later section "Getting directions."

- ✔ Every letter or dot on the screen represents a search result. (Refer to Figure 10-4, left.)

- ✔ Spread your fingers on the touchscreen to zoom in on the map.

- ✔ If you *really* like the location, touch the Favorite (star) icon. That directs the Map to keep the location as one of your favorite places. The location appears as a star on the Maps app screen. See the next section.

Figure 10-4: Finding Hungarian restaurants near Seattle, Washington.

Searching for favorite or recent places

Just as you can bookmark favorite websites on the Internet, you can mark favorite places in the real world by using the Maps app. The feature is called Saved Places.

 To visit your favorite places or browse your recent map searches, touch the Saved Places icon at the top of the Maps app screen. If you don't see the icon, touch the X button in the Search box.

The Saved Places window sports various categories of places you've starred (marked as favorites), locations you've recently searched for, or places you've been.

✐ Mark a location as a favorite by touching the Favorite (star) icon when you view the location's details.

 ✐ The Recently Accessed Places list allows you to peruse items you've located or searched for recently.

 ✐ Touch the App icon to return to the Maps app when you've finished looking at saved places.

Locating a contact

You can hone in on where your contacts are located by using the Maps app. This trick works when you've specified an address for the contact — home, work, bathhouse, or another location. If so, the Galaxy tablet can easily help you find that location and might even give you directions.

The secret to finding a contact's location is the little Place icon by the contact's address, shown in the margin. Anytime you see this icon, you can touch it to view that location by using the Maps app.

The Galaxy Navigator

Finding something is only half the job. The other half is getting there. Your Galaxy tablet is ever-ready, thanks to the various direction and navigation features nestled in the Maps app.

I don't believe that the Galaxy tablet has a car mount, at least the larger models don't. It's not a smartphone, after all. Therefore, I strongly recommend that if you use your tablet in your auto, have someone else hold it and read the directions. Or use voice navigation and, for goodness' sake, don't look at the tablet while you're driving!

Getting directions

One command associated with locations on the map is getting directions. In the Maps app, the command is called Route. Here's how to use it:

1. **Touch the Route icon in a location's card.**

Route

 The Route icon appears as a set of split arrows, as shown in the margin. When a location is found on the same screen as your current location, you may see a car icon instead. Such an icon is shown in Figure 10-3.

 After touching the Route icon, you see a screen similar to what's shown in Figure 10-5.

2. **Choose a method of transportation.**

 The available options vary, depending on your location. In Figure 10-5, the items are (from left to right) Car, Public Transportation, Bicycle, and On Foot.

Starting location

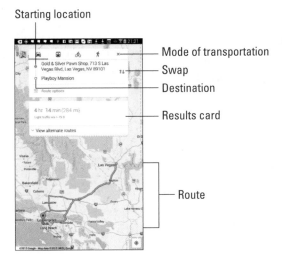

Mode of transportation

Swap

Destination

Results card

Route

Figure 10-5: Planning your trip.

3. **Set a starting location.**

   You can type a location or select one of the locations shown on the screen, such as your current location, your home location, or any location you've previously searched. Touch the Starting Location item to choose another location.

4. **Ensure that the starting location and destination are what you want.**

   To reverse them, touch the Swap icon (labeled in Figure 10-5).

5. **Peruse the results.**

The map shows your route, highlighted as a blue line on the screen, as shown in Figure 10-5.

To see a list of directions, touch the Results card (refer to Figure 10-5). A scrolling list appears on the screen, similar to what's shown in Figure 10-6.

To interactively follow your journey, touch the Preview icon (labeled in Figure 10-6).

   ✔ The Maps app alerts you to any toll roads on the specified route. As you travel, you can choose alternative, non-toll routes if available. You're prompted to switch routes during navigation; see the next section.

   ✔ You may not get perfect directions from the Maps app, but it's a useful tool for finding places you've never visited.

Trip overview   Travel details

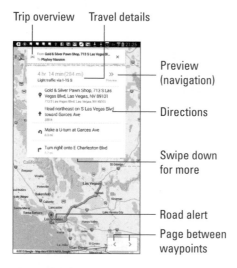

Preview
(navigation)

Directions

Swipe down
for more

Road alert

Page between
waypoints

Figure 10-6: The Maps app gives directions.

Adding a navigation Home screen widget

When you visit certain places often — such as the liquor store or the parole office — you can save yourself the time you would spend repeatedly inputting navigation information. All you need to do is create a navigation shortcut on the Home screen. Here's how:

1. **Touch the Apps button to visit the Apps screen.**

2. **Select the Widgets tab from the top of the Apps screen.**

3. **Long-press the Directions widget and, keeping your finger down, drag it to a spot on the Home screen.**

   See Chapter 19 for complete information on adding widgets to the Home screen.

4. **Choose a traveling method.**

   Your options are car, public transportation, bicycle, and on foot.

5. **In the Choose Destination text box, type a destination, a contact name, an address, or a business.**

6. **Type a shortcut name.**

   The name appears below the icon on the Home screen.

7. **Touch the Save button.**

   The navigation shortcut is placed on the Home screen.

To use the shortcut, simply touch it on the Home screen. Instantly, the Maps app starts and enters Navigation mode, steering you from wherever you are to the location referenced by the shortcut.

The Whole Google Earth

The Google Earth map is similar to the Maps app, except it covers the entire planet. And while you can get around and explore your locale or destination using the Maps app, Google Earth is more of a look-and-see, interactive world atlas.

To run Google Earth, start the Earth app, found on the All Apps screen. You can also find a shortcut on the Maps app sidebar (refer to Figure 10-1).

If Google Earth isn't installed on your tablet, then you can obtain the app from the Google Play Store. Refer to Chapter 15.

The Google Earth interface, shown in Figure 10-7, has features similar to those in the Maps app but is customized for viewing the globe.

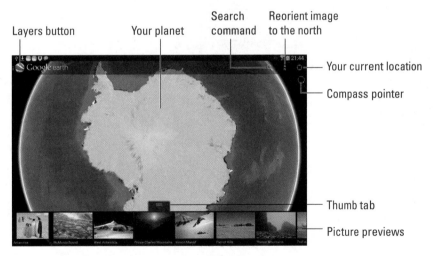

Figure 10-7: Google Earth, once known as Planet Earth.

The best advice for using the Earth app is to explore: Drag your finger around the screen to pan and tilt the globe; pinch and spread your fingers to zoom out and zoom in, respectively.

  ✔ You can use the Search command to find things.

  ✔ Items on the Layers sidebar are used to show or hide map details.

  ✔ Use the thumb tab to slide the picture previews up or down.

> ✏ If you enjoy looking up as much as you enjoy looking down, consider getting the Sky Map app. Search the Google Play Store for the Sky Map app from Sky Map Devs. (It was once known as Google Sky Map.) Refer to Chapter 15 for details on getting new apps for your Galaxy Note or Galaxy Tab.

It's a Big, Flat Camera

Cameras have come a long way since Nicéphore Niépce took a daylong exposure of his backyard using a *camera obscura*. Photography was an analog, real-world thing until the 1990s. Then technology went digital. In a few years, no one will be around who remembers what a roll of film was.

What's also changed is the camera. No longer do you hold the thing up to your face. Instead, you hold the device at arm's length and peer at an LCD screen. What's even stranger is holding up a large, flat object such as the Galaxy Note or Galaxy Tab and using it to take a picture. Sure, it works. It's handy. But it's just unusual and different enough that I present to you an entire chapter on using your tablet as a camera.

Your Galactic Camera

I admit that a Samsung Galaxy tablet isn't the world's best camera. And I'm sure that Mr. Spock's tricorder wasn't the best camera in the *Star Trek* universe, either. That comparison is kind of the whole point: Your tablet is an incredible gizmo that does many things. Two of those things are taking pictures and recording video, as described in this section.

Capturing the moment

Picture-taking and video-recording duties on your Galaxy tablet are handled by the same app, the Camera app. You may be able to find a shortcut to that app on the Home screen, and it also dwells with all its app buddies on the Apps screen.

The Camera app controls both the main camera, which is on the tablet's butt, and the front-facing camera, which is not on the tablet's butt. The app also takes still images as well as records videos, depending on how it's used.

After starting the Camera app, you see the main Camera screen, as illustrated in Figure 11-1.

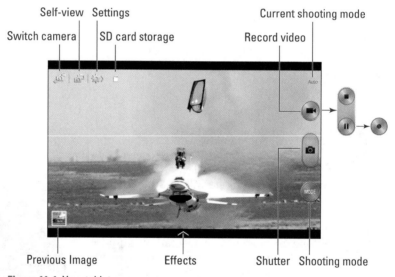

Figure 11-1: Your tablet as a camera.

To take a still picture, touch the Shutter icon. The camera focuses, you may hear a mechanical shutter sound, and the flash may go off. You're ready to take the next picture.

To record video, touch the Video Camera icon (labeled in Figure 11-1). As video is being recorded, two new icons appear: Stop and Pause. Touch the Stop icon to end the recording; touch Pause to suspend recording; touch that same icon again, which is now the Record icon, to continue. Then, finally, touch the Stop icon to end the video.

To preview the image or video, touch the Previous Image icon, which appears in the lower-left corner of the screen (labeled in Figure 11-1). After viewing the preview, touch the Back button to return to the Camera app.

✔ The tablet can be used as a camera in either landscape or portrait orientation.

✔ The camera focuses automatically. However, you can touch the screen to drag around a focus square to bring a certain part of the image into focus.

✔ Use the Volume key to zoom in or out. Once the Zoom gizmo appears on the touchscreen, you can manipulate it by using your finger.

✔ You can take as many pictures or record as much video with your tablet as you like, as long as you don't run out of space in the tablet's internal storage or external storage. Speaking of which:

✔ The SD Card icon in Figure 11-1 indicates that images and recordings are saved to the tablet's microSD card. To change storage locations, see the later section "Choosing the storage device."

✔ Hold the tablet steady when recording video! The camera still works when you whip the tablet around, but wild gyrations render the video unwatchable.

✔ If your pictures appear blurry, ensure that the camera lens on the back of the tablet isn't dirty.

✔ Use the Gallery app to preview and manage your pictures. See Chapter 12 for more information.

✔ The Galaxy tablet stores pictures in the JPEG image file format, using the .jpg filename extension. Video is stored in the MPEG4 file format, using the .mp4 filename extension. Images and videos are stored in the DCIM/ Camera folder in either internal storage or on the microSD card.

Doing a self-portrait

Who needs to pay all that money for a mirror when you have the Galaxy tablet? Well, forget the mirror. Instead, think about taking all those selfies without having to second-guess whether the camera is pointed at your face.

To take your own mug shot, follow these steps:

1. **Start the Camera app.**

2. **Touch the Switch Camera icon.**

   When you see yourself on the screen, you're doing it properly.

3. **Touch the Camera icon to snap a still, or the Video icon to record something longer than a snap.**

   That's it, although if you're recording a video, touch the Stop button when you're done.

Touch the Switch Camera icon again to direct the Galaxy tablet to go back to using the main camera.

 You can use the Self View icon (shown in the margin and in Figure 11-1) to take a picture or record a video using both the front and rear cameras at the same time.

Taking in a panorama

No, it's not an exotic new alcoholic drink: A *panorama* is a wide shot, like a landscape, a beautiful vista, or a family photograph after a garlic feast. To take a panoramic shot using your Galaxy tablet, you need to switch the camera to Panorama mode and then capture several pictures in sequence. Obey these steps:

1. **Start the Camera app.**

2. **Touch the Mode button.**

3. **Choose Panorama.**

   Scroll the list of modes with your finger, and then touch Panorama.

4. **Hold your arms steady.**

5. **Touch the Shutter icon.**

   You see a frame and a guide on the screen, which approximates the current shot and the extent (left-right or up-down) for the panorama. Arrows point in the directions in which you can pan.

6. **Pivot slightly to your right (or in whatever direction, but you must continue in the same direction).**

   As you move the camera, the onscreen frame adjusts to your new position. The tablet beeps as the next image in the panorama is snapped automatically. All you need to do is keep moving.

7. **Continue pivoting as subsequent shots are taken, or touch the Shutter icon again to finish the panorama.**

   After the last image is snapped, wait while the panorama is assembled.

The Camera app sticks the different shots together, creating a panoramic image.

 ✔ To exit Panorama mode, repeat Steps 1 and 2, but in Step 3 choose Auto as the shooting mode.

✔ See the later section "Adjusting the camera" for more details on various modes and effects available in the Camera app.

✔ The Camera app automatically captures the panoramic shot. You touch the Shutter icon only when you're done.

Doing a screen shot

A _screen shot,_ also called a _screen cap_ (for capture), is a picture of your tablet's touchscreen. So if you see something interesting on the screen, or just want to take a quick pic of your tablet life, you take a screen shot.

For the Galaxy Note, the fastest way to take a screen shot is to press and hold the S Pen button and then long-press the screen by using the S Pen. You hear a shutter sound, and then the screen shot is presented in the Screen Write app for saving or scribbling.

For the Galaxy Tab, as well as the Galaxy Note, you can enable a screen capture motion setting. Heed these directions:

1. **Open the Settings app.**

2. **Touch the Controls tab, and then select the Palm Motion item.**

   If your tablet doesn't have a Controls tab, scroll down the categories on the left side of the screen and select the Motion item.

3. **Ensure that the Capture Screen item is active or that the Palm Swipe to Capture item is selected.**

   An active item features a green button or check mark to its right.

Once the setting is enabled, you capture a screen shot by swiping left or right across the touchscreen with the side of your open palm. Upon success, you'll hear a clicking sound. The screen has been captured.

✔ As a bonus, the captured screen is saved to the Clipboard, where you can paste it into an app that accepts graphic input. See Chapter 4 for information on cut, copy, and paste.

✔ You can view the screen shots by using the Gallery app. You'll find the shots in the Screenshots album.

✔ Screen shots are kept in the Pictures/Screenshots folder in the tablet's internal storage. They're saved in the PNG graphics file format.

Camera Settings and Options

The Galaxy tablet's camera is much more than just a hole in the case. Taking a picture or shooting a video can involve more than just touching an icon. To help you get the most from the tablet's camera, various settings, options, and effects eagerly lurk beneath the Camera app's interface. This section describes some common features, the handy ones, and even the oddballs.

Deleting an image immediately after you take it

Sometimes, you just can't wait to delete an image. Either an irritated person is standing next to you, begging that the photo be deleted, or you're just not happy and you feel the urge to smash into digital shards the picture you just took. Hastily follow these steps:

1. **Touch the Previous Image rectangle that appears on the Camera app's screen (refer to Figure 11-1).**

   After touching the preview, you see the full-screen image. Videos appear with a Play icon center screen.

2. **Touch the Trash icon.**

   If you don't see the Trash icon, briefly touch the screen.

3. **Touch the OK button to remove the image or video.**

4. **Touch the Back button to return to the Camera app.**

When you desire destruction of more than just the last image you took (or video you recorded), visit the Gallery app. See Chapter 12.

Setting the flash

Not all Galaxy tablets feature a flash on the rear camera. If your tablet does, you can set the flash's behavior, as shown in Table 11-1.

Table 11-1	Galaxy Tablet Camera Flash Settings	
Setting	**Icon**	**Description**
Auto	⚡Ⓐ	The flash activates during low-light situations but not when it's bright out.
On	⚡	The flash always activates.
Off	⚡⊘	The flash never activates, even in low-light situations.

To change or check the flash setting, touch the Settings icon on the Camera app screen. (The icon is shown in the margin. For its location on the screen, refer to Figure 11-1.) After touching the Settings icon, you see the Quick Settings, as shown in Figure 11-2.

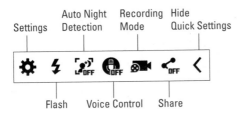

Figure 11-2: Quick Settings in the Camera app.

The icon for the current flash setting is shown in the lineup, similar to the flash icon listed in Table 11-1. Touch that icon repeatedly to cycle through the three available options.

✔ When the Auto or On flash option is set, that icon appears on the Camera app's screen. When the flash setting is Off, no icon appears.

✔ To illuminate the subject when shooting video, choose the On setting. The On setting uses a lot of battery power, so use it sparingly.

✔ A good time to turn on the flash is when taking pictures of people or objects in front of something bright, such as a fuzzy brown kitten playing with a ball of white yarn in front of an exploding gasoline truck.

✔ The icons shown in Figure 11-2 are called the Quick Settings. You can add or remove icons to the list by touching the Menu button and choosing the Quick Settings command. Because the Quick Settings can be modified, the ones you see on the Camera app's screen may not be identical to what's shown in Figure 11-2.

Changing the resolution

A useful Camera app setting that most people ignore is the image resolution. That setting is routinely ignored on digital cameras as well, mostly because people don't understand resolution. I'll be blunt:

You don't always need to use the highest resolution.

High-resolution images are great for printing photos and for photo editing. They're not required for images you plan on sharing with Facebook or sending as an e-mail attachment. Plus, the higher the resolution, the more storage space each image consumes.

Another problem with resolution is remembering to set it *before* you snap the photo or shoot the video. Here's how image resolution is set in the Camera app:

1. **Touch the Menu button.**

2. **Choose Settings.**

   The Settings window appears, as shown in Figure 11-3. You can also get there by choosing the Settings icon shown in Figure 11-2, which is why the Settings icon in Figure 11-3 is the third settings icon.

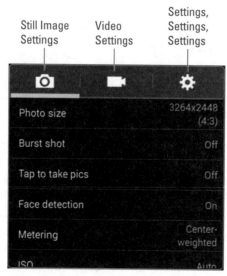

Figure 11-3: The window with the third Settings icon.

3. **Touch the Camera icon.**

4. **Choose Photo Size.**

5. **Select a resolution.**

   The numbers in the white circles represent megapixels. The other numbers are the horizontal-by-vertical image resolution in pixels. The final numbers (in parentheses) are the aspect ratio, width to height.

   The list of resolutions can be scrolled up and down.

6. **Tap the Back button to return to the Camera app's main screen.**

   All the images you take from this point on are at the resolution you set in Step 5.

To choose a new resolution, repeat these steps.

To set the resolution for recording video, work through the same steps, but touch the Video icon in Step 3 and choose Video Size in Step 4.

✔ Check the video quality before you shoot!

✔ The tablet's front-facing camera has different resolutions than the rear camera. You must first switch to the front camera to set its resolution.

✔ Yes, low resolutions are just fine for uploading to Facebook. The resolution of the output device (a computer monitor or tablet screen) is low; therefore, you don't need to waste storage and upload time sending high-resolution images or videos to Facebook.

✔ *Megapixel* is a measurement of the amount of information stored in an image. A megapixel is approximately 1 million pixels, or individual dots that compose an image. It's often abbreviated MP.

Setting the image's location

Your Galactic tablet's camera not only takes a picture but also keeps track of where you're located on planet earth when you take the picture — if you've turned on that option. The feature is commonly called Geo-Tag, but in the Camera app it's known as the Location Tag or GPS Tag. Here's how to ensure that it's on — or off if you'd rather not let people know where you caught that fish:

1. **While using the Camera app, touch the Menu button.**

   Refer to Figure 11-1 for the button's location.

2. **Choose Settings.**

   The Settings window appears (refer to Figure 11-3).

3. **Touch the Settings tab.**

   In Figure 11-3, it's called the Settings, Settings, Settings tab. Read the preceding section for why that is so.

4. **Choose Location Tag or GPS Tag.**

   Different versions of the Camera app call it different things. In fact, it's rumored that the Galaxy Tab 4 will call it the WhereU@ tag.

5. **Choose On to enable this feature; Off to disable.**

   You may see an Attention box, explaining the potential peril you face when activating the GPS Tag feature. Touch the OK button after you skip reading the information.

6. **Touch the Back icon to return to the Camera app's main screen.**

When the GPS Tag feature is activated, the GPS icon appears on the Camera's screen. The icon is shown in the margin.

See Chapter 12 for information on perusing a photograph's location.

Choosing the storage device

Images you take and videos you record on your tablet are stored on the primary storage device, also known as internal storage. You can change that location to the microSD card, or external storage. To do so, follow these steps while using the Camera app:

1. **Press the Menu button, and then choose the Settings command.**

2. **Touch the Settings tab.**

    Refer to Figure 11-3 for its location.

3. **Scroll down to choose the Storage item.**

4. **Choose Memory Card to direct the Camera app to use the microSD card for storing images and videos, or choose Device to use internal storage.**

When Memory Card is chosen, a memory (SD) card icon appears on the Camera app screen, as shown in Figure 11-1. When internal storage is chosen, the SD card icon doesn't appear.

Adjusting the camera

Two items you can adjust in the Camera app are the shooting mode and visual effects. The shooting mode is handled by the Mode icon (labeled in Figure 11-1). The array of visual effects appears at the bottom of the screen when you touch the Effects chevron shown in Figure 11-1.

Shooting mode sets the camera's behavior. It provides handy shortcuts to solve some typical photo-taking problems. To view the various modes, touch the Mode icon. They appear similar to what's shown in Figure 11-4.

The standard shooting mode is Auto, which also has a shortcut, as illustrated in Figure 11-4. The Panorama mode is covered earlier in this chapter. The other modes feature a pop-up description, as shown in the figure.

Reset to Auto mode

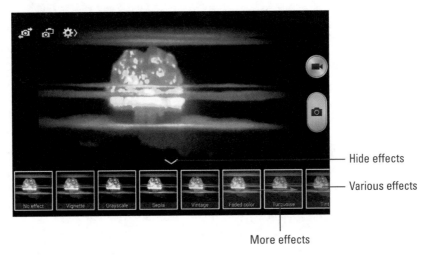

Swipe through
the modes

Display all modes
in a grid

Figure 11-4: Shooting modes.

When you've finished using a specific shooting mode, remember to change
the mode back to Auto.

Effects are a series of filters you can apply to the image before you shoot.
Touch the chevron at the bottom of the screen to peruse the options, several
of which are shown in Figure 11-5. (Your tablet's Camera app may not feature
the same variety of effects shown in the figure.)

Hide effects

Various effects

More effects

Figure 11-5: Various interesting visual effects.

Each effect has its own wee preview window, as shown in Figure 11-5. Choose an effect, and then take the picture. For example, to capture a grayscale (black-and-white) shot, choose that effect, and then touch the Shutter icon. The effects also apply to shooting video.

To cancel an effect, choose the No Effect option.

12

Image Madness and Management

In This Chapter

▶ Viewing images and videos

▶ Finding an image's location

▶ Setting an image as wallpaper

▶ Editing images

▶ Deleting pictures and videos

▶ Saving pictures to the Internet

▶ Printing an image

▶ Publishing a video on YouTube

▶ Sharing images and videos

There's no point in the Galaxy Note or Galaxy Tab having a camera unless it also has a place to store pictures and videos. That location is a digital Louvre of sorts called the Gallery. It's more than just a point-at-the-Picasso type of gallery because, in addition to looking at the painting of the woman with the weird eyeballs, you can use the Gallery app to fix those eyes. Hey, make her look normal again! That kind of useful image management and editing is covered in this chapter.

Where Your Pictures Lurk

Some people hang their pictures on the wall. Some put pictures on a piano or maybe on a mantle. In the digital realm, pictures are stored electronically, compressed and squeezed into a series of ones and zeroes that means nothing unless you have an app that lets you view those images. On your Galactic tablet, that app is the *Gallery*.

Visiting the Gallery

Start the Gallery app by choosing its icon from the Apps screen, or you may find a shortcut lurking on the Home screen. When the Gallery app opens, you see pictures organized into albums, similar to what's shown in Figure 12-1.

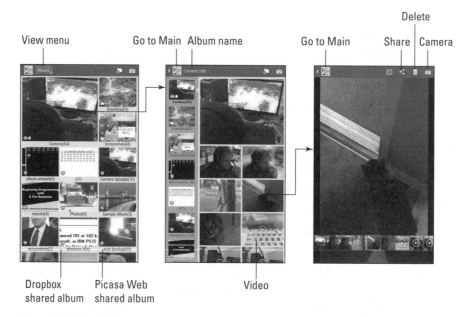

Figure 12-1: The Gallery app.

 If you see the Camera app when you start the Gallery, touch the Back button to return to the Gallery. (The Camera and Gallery apps are linked and sometimes one starts instead of the other.)

The number and variety of albums (refer to Figure 12-1) depend on how you synchronize your tablet with your computer, which apps you use for collecting media, and which photo-sharing services you use on the Internet and have synchronized with the tablet.

Touch an album to display that album's contents; the pictures appear in a grid of thumbnail previews. Swipe the screen left and right to peruse them all.

Touch an individual thumbnail in the album to view that item full size on the screen, similar to what's shown in Figure 12-1, right. You can rotate the tablet horizontally (or vertically) to see the image in another orientation. Spread your fingers or pinch on the touchscreen to zoom in or out, respectively. Swipe the screen to page through images in an album.

If any videos are stored in an album, they appear with a Play button on the screen. Touch that button to play the video. As the video is playing, touch the screen again to see the control to pause the video.

 You back up from an image or a video to an album by touching the Back icon. Touch the Back icon again to return to the main Gallery screen.

✔ The Camera album contains pictures you've shot using the tablet's camera.

✔ The Download album contains images downloaded from the Internet.

✔ Albums labeled with special icons, such as the Dropbox and Picasa Web icons shown in Figure 12-1, have been synchronized between your tablet and the Internet.

✔ Use the View menu to choose how images appear in the Gallery. The Albums view is shown in Figure 12-1, left.

✔ Other albums in the Gallery represent images synchronized between the tablet and a computer. See Chapter 17 for information on swapping images between your Galaxy tablet and a computer.

✔ Various apps may also create their own albums in the Gallery app.

✔ Touch an image (far right in Figure 12-1) to see the onscreen controls and other information. If weather and location information is saved with the image, it appears on the screen as well (albeit briefly).

 ✔ To view all the images in an album, touch the Menu button and choose the Slideshow command. Playing a slide show turns your expensive tablet into a less-expensive digital picture frame.

Finding a picture's location

Your tablet can be configured to save additional information with each picture you snap. Details are offered in Chapter 11. What you can do with that information is display it while viewing a picture, and even locate the exact spot where you took a picture, right on the Maps app.

To view location and weather information for a photo, touch the photo's image when it's displayed full screen in the Gallery app. The first time you touch the screen, you may see the onscreen controls. That's fine; touch the screen again to see any stored weather or location information, as shown in Figure 12-2.

Figure 12-2: Image location and weather information.

To use the Maps app to view the displayed location, touch the Menu button and choose the Get Directions command. The Maps app starts, showing the location where the image was taken. It also lists directions, plus a Start icon to begin navigating to that location.

If you'd rather just view the map location, touch the X button in the Search box on the Maps app screen. When you do so, the pin icon marking the photo's location disappears, but you can still view the general area.

- Not every image stores location information. In some cases, the tablet cannot read its GPS radio to store the information. When this happens, location information is unavailable.

- You can sort images in the Gallery based on their location. Touch the View menu and choose the Locations command.

- Refer to Chapter 11 for information on how to turn location information on or off when taking pictures.

Setting an image as wallpaper

You can choose any picture that's viewable in the Gallery as the tablet's Home screen wallpaper. You can assign a different image for use as the lock screen wallpaper. Or you can use the same image for both! Follow these steps:

1. **View an image in the Gallery.**

2. **Touch the Menu button and choose the Set As command.**

   If the Set As command doesn't appear, you can't use that image; not every album allows its images to be set as wallpaper.

3. **Choose Home Screen, Lock Screen, or Home and Lock Screens.**

   When you choose the Home and Lock Screens command, you set both screen wallpapers at once.

4. **Crop the image.**

   You may be prompted to choose an app before you crop. If so, choose the Gallery app, shown as Crop Picture. Then touch the Always button to always use that app. You'll never be bothered with the prompt again!

   You need to crop the image to match the tablet's frame. A guide appears when the tablet is oriented differently from the picture's orientation, such as when cropping a horizontal image to match a vertical screen. Refer to Figure 12-3 for a visual guide.

Figure 12-3: Cropping a wallpaper image.

5. **Touch the Done button.**

   The image is set as the wallpaper you selected.

To see the wallpaper, touch the Home button or lock the tablet.

> ✔ You can use these steps to assign an image to a contact. In Step 3, choose Contact. Then select the contact and crop the image. See Chapter 5 for additional information on assigning pictures to contacts.

> ✔ The Home and Lock screen wallpapers can be set also from the Home screen directly. See Chapter 19 for information.

Image Editing

The best tool for image editing is a computer armed with photo-editing software, such as Photoshop or one of its less expensive alternatives. Even so, it's possible to use the Gallery app to perform some minor photo surgery. This section highlights some of the more useful things you can do.

Cropping a picture

One of the few true image-editing commands available in the Gallery app is Crop. You can use Crop to slice out portions of an image, such as when removing ex-spouses and convicts from a family portrait. To crop an image, obey these directions:

1. **Summon the image you want to crop.**

2. **Touch the Menu button and choose the Crop command.**

   If the Crop command is unavailable, you have to choose another image; not every image in the Gallery can be modified.

3. **Work the crop thing.**

   You can drag the rectangle around to choose which part of the image to crop. Drag an edge of the rectangle to resize the left and right or top and bottom sides. Or drag a corner of the rectangle to change the rectangle's size proportionally. Use Figure 12-4 as your guide.

4. **Touch the Done button when you're finished cropping.**

   Only the portion of the image within the rectangle is saved; the rest is discarded.

The cropped image is saved as a new picture in the Gallery. So if you don't like the crop, delete the cropped image and start over again with the original. See the later section "Deleting pictures and videos" for image destruction information.

Figure 12-4: Working the crop-thing.

Trimming a video

The process of *trimming* a video involves snipping off the head or tail from the recording. It works like this:

1. **Display the video in the Gallery.**

   Do not play the video; just have it loitering on the screen.

2. **Touch the Trim icon.**

   The icon looks like a pair of scissors, similar to what's shown in the margin. If you can't see the icon, touch the screen. If it still doesn't show up, the video is being shared from another source and cannot be edited.

3. **Adjust the video's start and end points.**

   Figure 12-5 illustrates how to trim a typical video: Adjust the Start and End markers to trim the video's length. Touch the Play button on the screen to preview how the shortened video looks. Adjust the Start and End markers further, if needed.
   You cannot trim a video so that it's less than one second in duration.

4. **Touch the Done button to save the edited video.**

   An Enter New File Name box appears.

5. **Type a new name for the video or edit the existing name.**

6. **Touch the OK button.**

   The trimmed video is saved under the new name specified in Step 5.

Figure 12-5: Film Editing 101.

The new video can be found in the Gallery's Output album.

Rotating pictures

Which way is up? Well, the answer depends on your situation. For taking pictures with your tablet, sometimes images just don't appear up, no matter how you turn the screen. To fix that situation, heed these steps:

1. **Choose an image to rotate.**

2. **Touch the Menu button.**

3. **Choose Rotate Left to rotate the image counterclockwise; choose Rotate Right to rotate the image clockwise.**

You can rotate a slew of images at one time: Select all the images as described in the later section "Selecting multiple pictures and videos." Then touch the Menu button and choose Rotate Left or Rotate Right. All the images are rotated at once.

✔ You cannot rotate videos.

✔ You cannot rotate certain images, such as images shared from your Picasa Web albums.

Deleting pictures and videos

It's entirely possible, and often desirable, to remove unwanted, embarrassing, or questionably legal images and videos from the Gallery.

To zap a single image or a video, summon the image or video and touch the Trash icon that appears atop the screen. Touch the OK button to confirm. It's gone.

- ✔ You can delete a swath of images by selecting a group at a time. See the next section.

- ✔ You can't undelete an image or a video you've deleted. There's no way to recover such an image using available tools on your Samsung Galaxy tablet.

- ✔ Some images can't be edited, such as images brought in from social networking sites or from online photo-sharing albums.

Selecting multiple pictures and videos

You can apply certain commands, such as Delete and Rotate, to an entire collection of items in the Gallery at once. To do so, you must select a group of images or videos. Here's how:

1. **Open the album (pile) you want to mess with.**

2. **Long-press an image to select it.**

   Instantly, you activate image selection mode. (That's my name for it.) The screen changes to look like Figure 12-6.

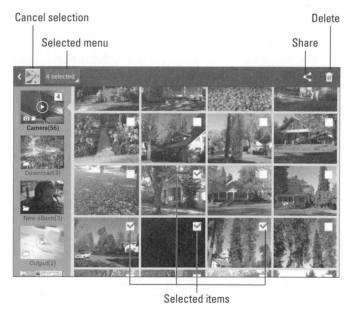

Figure 12-6: Choosing images to mess with.

3. **Continue touching images and videos to select them.**

   Or you can choose the Select All command from the Selected menu (labeled in Figure 12-6).

4. **Perform an action on the group of images or videos.**

   To remove the images, touch the Delete icon (labeled in Figure 12-6). To share the images with other sources, touch the Share icon. If you tap the Menu button, you'll see commands to Copy and Move the images to another album in the Gallery.

To deselect items, touch them again. To deselect everything, choose the Unselect All command from the Selected menu. Or if you want to cancel deselecting items, touch the App icon button in the upper-left corner of the screen.

The type of commands you can use on a group of items in an album depends on the group. Some commands, such as Delete and Share, can be performed on any old group. Other commands, such as the image rotation commands, work only with pictures, not with videos.

Set Your Pics and Vids Free

Keeping your precious moments and memories by themselves in the tablet is an elegant solution to the problem of lugging around photo albums and a video projector. When you want to show your pictures to the widest possible audience, however, you need a bigger stage. That stage is the Internet, and you have many ways to send and save your pictures and videos online, as covered in this section.

Refer to Chapter 17 for information on synchronizing and sharing information between the Galaxy tablet and your computer.

Accessing your Picasa Web account

Part of your Google account includes access to the online photo-sharing website, Picasa Web. If you haven't yet been to the Picasa Web site on the Internet, use your computer to visit `http://picasaweb.google.com`.

Configure things by logging into your Google account on that website.

The Picasa Web account should be synchronized and configured automatically with your Galaxy tablet. So if you've saved pictures on the Picasa Web site, you can find them on the tablet, similar to those shown in Figure 12-1. If not, follow these steps to ensure that Picasa Web is being property synced:

1. **On the Home screen, touch the Apps icon.**

2. **Touch the Settings icon.**

3. **View the list of installed accounts.**

   Touch the General tab and choose the Accounts item from the left side of the screen. If the Settings app doesn't display a General tab, scroll down the screen until you locate the Accounts area.

4. **Choose Google.**

5. **Choose your Google account.**

   It's on the right side of the screen.

6. **Ensure that there's a check mark by the Sync Picasa Web Albums item.**

   That's pretty much it.

Any images you have on Picasa Web are automatically copied to your Galaxy tablet from now on.

If you want to share on the Internet with Picasa Web the pictures you take with the Camera app, you need to select and share the images. See the later section "Sharing images with other apps."

 ✔ Picasa Web albums feature the Picasa Web logo on them, as shown in the margin.

 ✔ Images copied from your Picasa Web account to the tablet cannot be edited or deleted. You might find other restrictions on the images.

 ✔ The best way to manage Picasa Web images is to go to the Picasa Web site on the Internet.

Uploading to Dropbox

Another way to share images on the Internet is to use your Dropbox account. As this book goes to press, the Dropbox app is included with your Galaxy tablet, and signing up for Dropbox is part of the tablet's setup and configuration. Even if that's no longer the case, you can still obtain and use Dropbox to save and share photos. In fact, sharing photos is automatic. Obey these steps:

1. **Open the Dropbox app.**

2. **Press the Menu button and choose the Settings command.**

3. **Touch the Turn On Camera Upload text.**

   The text is found below the Camera Upload heading. If it instead reads Turn Off Camera Upload, you're all set. Unless you have a cellular tablet, in which case I recommend that you:

4. **Select the Upload Using item.**

5. **Select Wi-Fi Only.**

   By setting this item, you ensure that the tablet uploads images only when connected to a Wi-Fi network. That means you won't use precious megabytes from your monthly mobile data allocation.

With camera upload on, any image you snap is instantly copied to the Camera Uploads folder in your Dropbox account. If you use Dropbox on a computer, you can immediately access those pictures and videos. That's handy.

Printing your pictures

Yes, it's wireless. Yes, it's mobile. No, it shouldn't have a printer attached, but golly, it's almost a crime not to be able to print some of those images in your Galaxy tablet. So rather than break the law, you can instead print from your tablet. You have several options. Two of the most popular are Bluetooth and Google Cloud Print, described in the following subsections.

Bluetooth

To print an image to a Bluetooth printer, follow these steps:

1. **Ensure that the Bluetooth printer has been paired with the computer, is on, and is ready to print.**

   The pairing process is discussed in Chapter 16.

2. **Locate the image you want to print in the Gallery.**

   Show the image full screen, not in an album.

3. **Touch the Bluetooth icon.**

   If you don't see that icon, tap the touchscreen. If you still don't see it, tap the Share icon (shown in the margin) and choose Bluetooth.

4. **Select the Bluetooth printer from the list.**

5. **If prompted by the printer, confirm that the image upload is okay.**

   Not every Bluetooth printer has such a prompt; some just go ahead and print the image.

Google Cloud Print

The Google Cloud Print option is perhaps the easiest way to print from your Galaxy tablet. The problem is that you need four things to make it work:

- ✔ A desktop computer or access to one
- ✔ A printer connected to that computer, either directly or over a network
- ✔ The Google Chrome web browser on that computer
- ✔ The Google Cloud Print app on your tablet

Providing you can wrangle those four items, the next step is to configure everything. It works like this:

1. **Log into Chrome by using your Google account, the same one you use for your tablet.**

   Google insists that you do this when you first obtain the Chrome program for your computer.

2. **In Chrome (on your computer), click the Menu icon in the upper-right corner of the window.**

3. **Still on your computer, choose the Settings command.**

   A new browser tab opens, listing Chrome Settings.

4. **Click the Show Advanced Settings link.**

   The link is at the bottom of the page. After clicking the link, the page grows longer with more options and settings.

5. **In the Google Cloud Print section, click the Sign in to Google Cloud Print button.**

   That's it.

With the computer set up for Google Cloud Print, the next step is to download the Google Cloud Print app from the Play Store. General app-downloading directions are found in Chapter 15.

After the Cloud Print app is installed on your tablet, you can print from any app (not just the Gallery) by following these steps:

1. **Touch the Share icon.**

2. **Choose the Cloud Print item.**

3. **Select a local printer or device from the list.**

   The document prints.

The unusual thing with Google Cloud Print is that you don't need to be in the same place as the printer. I've printed from the library and other states. I could even print a document on my home computer while flying cross-country, although I'm too cheap to pay $20 for in-flight Wi-Fi.

Posting a video to YouTube

The best way to share a video is to upload it to YouTube. As a Google account holder, you also have a YouTube account. You can use the tablet's YouTube app to upload your videos to the Internet, where everyone can see them and make rude comments. Here's how:

1. **Ensure that the Wi-Fi connection is activated.**

   The best way to upload a video is to turn on the Wi-Fi connection, which doesn't incur data surcharges like the digital cellular network does. In fact, if you opt to use the 4G LTE network for uploading a YouTube video, you'll see a suitable onscreen reminder about data surcharges.

2. **Start the Gallery app.**

3. **Open the video you want to upload.**

   You do not need to play the video. Just have it on the screen.

 4. **Touch the Share icon.**

   If you don't see the Share icon, tap the screen.

5. **Choose YouTube.**

   The Upload Video window appears, listing all sorts of options and settings for sending the video to YouTube.

6. **Type the video's title.**

   Feel free to replace the timestamp title with something more descriptive.

7. **Type a description.**

   The description appears on YouTube when people go to view the video.

8. **Set whether the video is Private, Public, or Unlisted.**

9. **Touch the Upload button.**

   You return to the gallery, and the video is uploaded. The video continues to upload even if the tablet falls asleep.

 The uploading notification appears while the video is being sent to YouTube. When the upload has completed, the notification stops animating and becomes the Video Uploaded Successfully icon, as shown in the margin.

To view your video, open the YouTube app. It's found on the Apps screen and discussed in detail in Chapter 14.

> ✐ YouTube often takes awhile to process a video after it's uploaded. Allow a few minutes to pass (longer for larger videos) before expecting the video to be available for viewing.

> ✐ *Upload* is the official term to describe sending a file from the Galaxy tablet to the Internet.

Sharing images with other apps

Just about every app wants to get in on the sharing bit, especially when it comes to sharing pictures and videos. The key is to view something in the Gallery and then touch the Share icon atop the screen (and shown in the margin). From the Share menu, choose an app and that image or video is instantly sent to that app.

What happens next?

That depends on the app. For Facebook, Twitter, and other social networking apps, the image is attached to a new post. For Email or Gmail, the image or video becomes an attachment. Other apps treat the image in a similar manner: It's made available to the app for sharing, posting, sending, or what have you. The key is to look for that Share icon.

Music, Music, Music

In This Chapter

▶ Finding music on the tablet

▶ Enjoying a tune

▶ Turning the tablet into a deejay

▶ Transferring music from your computer

▶ Buying music online

▶ Organizing your tunes into a playlist

▶ Listening to streaming music

our Galactic tablet's amazing arsenal of features includes its capability to play music. So it effectively replaces any gramophone that you've been lugging around, which is the whole idea behind such an all-in-one gizmo like a Galaxy Note or Galaxy Tab. You can cheerfully and adeptly transfer all your old Edison cylinders and 78 LPs over to the tablet for your listening enjoyment. This chapter tells you how.

Your Hit Parade

The source of your musical joy on the Galaxy tablet is an app aptly named Play Music. You can find that app on the Apps screen. If you don't see it there directly, look inside the Google folder. You may also find a handy Play Music shortcut right on the main Home screen.

The first time you start the Play Music app, you may be asked whether you'd like to try Google Play Music All Access. It's an all-the-time music service from Google, available for a monthly fee. You do not have to subscribe to the service to use the Play Music app on your tablet.

Browsing your music library

After you start the Play Music app, you see a screen similar to Figure 13-1. If you're displeased with the quantity of available music, refer to the later section "Add Some Music to Your Life." It explains how to get more tunes.

Library menu   Categories   Album menu

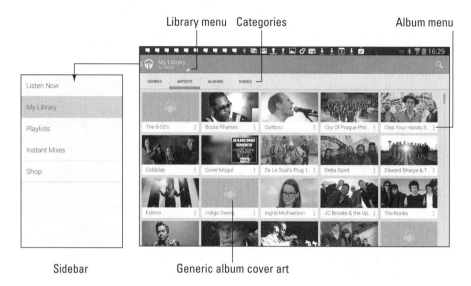

Sidebar   Generic album cover art

Figure 13-1: The Music library.

The music stored on your tablet is presented in the Play Music app by category. Each category appears as a tab atop the screen, as shown in Figure 13-1. Change categories by swiping the screen left or right, or touch a category tab directly.

The categories are merely ways the music is organized — ways to make the music easier to find when you may know, say, an artist's name but not an album title. The Genres category is for those times when you're in the mood for a certain type of music but don't know, or don't mind, who recorded it.

✔ Music is stored on the tablet's internal memory but is available also from your Google Play account on the Internet. Use the Library menu (labeled in Figure 13-1) to choose which music to view: The All Music item shows all music available to you, on the tablet as well as on the Internet. The On Device item shows only the music stored directly on the tablet.

✔ The size of internal memory limits the amount of music that can be stored on your tablet. Also, consider that storing pictures and videos horns in on some of the space that can be used to store music.

✔ Two types of album artwork are used by the Play Music app. For purchased music, the album artwork represents the original album. That may also happen for music copied (imported) from your computer. Otherwise, the Play Music app slaps down a generic album cover, as shown in Figure 13-1.

✔ When the tablet can't recognize an artist, it uses the title Unknown Artist. This usually happens with music you copy manually to your tablet, but it can apply also to audio recordings you make.

Figure 13-2: A song is playing.

Playing a tune

You listen to music by locating a song in the Play Music app library. From the Genres, Artists, or Albums categories, choose an item to open and then select a song to listen to. Touching the song title plays the song, as shown in Figure 13-2.

While the song plays, you're free to do anything else on the tablet. In fact, the song continues to play even when the tablet is locked or goes to sleep.

After the song has finished playing, the next song in the list plays. The list order depends on how you start the song. For example, if you start a song from the album view, all songs in that album play in the order listed.

The next song in the list doesn't play if you have the Shuffle button activated (refer to Figure 13-2). In that case, the Play Music app randomly chooses another song from the same list. Who knows which one will be next?

The next song also might not play when you have the Repeat option on: The three Repeat settings, as well as the Shuffle Settings, are listed in Table 13-1. To change settings, simply touch the Shuffle button or the Repeat button.

Table 13-1		Shuffle and Repeat Icons
Icon	*Setting*	*What Happens When You Touch the Icon*
⤬	No Shuffle	Songs play one after the other.
⤭	Shuffle	Songs are played in random order.
⮂	No Repeat	Songs don't repeat.
⮂①	Single Repeat	The same song plays over and over.
⮂	List Repeat	All songs in the list play over and over.

To stop a song from playing, touch the Pause button (labeled in Figure 13-2).

 A notification icon shown in the margin appears while music is playing on the Galaxy tablet. To quickly summon the Play Music app and see which song is playing, or to pause the song, touch that notification or pop up the notifications list. You can use the controls in the notification to pause the song or to skip forward or backward.

✔ You set the volume by using the Volume key on the side of the tablet.

✔ While browsing the Music library, you see the currently playing song at the bottom of the screen.

✔ Determining which song plays next depends on how you chose the song that's playing. If you choose a song by artist, all songs from that artist play, one after the other. When you choose a song by album, that album plays. Choosing a song from the entire song list causes all songs in your Galaxy tablet's Music library to play.

✔ You can arrange the playlist on-the-fly by touching the Show Song Queue icon (labeled in Figure 13-2). Drag the tab at the left end of each item in the list to rearrange the order. Also see the "Organize Your Music" section, later in this chapter.

✔ After the last song in the list plays, the Play Music app stops playing songs — unless you have the List Repeat option set, in which case the list plays again.

✔ You can use the Galaxy tablet's search capabilities to help locate tunes in your Music library. You can search by artist name, song title, or album. The key is to touch the Search icon when you're using the Play Music app. Type all or part of the text you're searching for, and then touch the Search button on the onscreen keyboard. Choose the song you want to hear from the list that's displayed.

Pinning your music

Most of the music you have in your Google Play Music library, especially music obtained from the Play Store, is stored on the Internet, not on the tablet. As long as you have an Internet connection, your tablet can play the music, but when you don't have an Internet connection . . . silence.

To make your music available offline, you need to pin it to the tablet's storage. That sounds weird, but you use a virtual pin. Here's how it works:

1. **Display the sidebar in the Play Music app, and then choose My Library.**

   Behold your music library.

2. **Locate the song, artist, or album you want to keep stored on the tablet.**

3. **Touch the Menu icon by the song, artist, or album.**

   The menu icon is shown in the margin. Touch that icon to see a pop-up menu.

4. **Choose the Keep on Device command.**

The music is downloaded to the tablet, keeping it on the device. It's available to play all the time.

✔ Music that's been kept on the tablet features a Pin icon, similar to what's shown in the margin. That icon can be used also when viewing an album; when you see it, touch the icon to keep the entire album on the device.

✔ When you copy music to the tablet from a computer, described in the later section "Borrowing music from a PC," the music is always kept on the tablet.

✔ To review the music already on the tablet, go to the main Play Music app screen. Touch the Library menu and choose the On Device command.

"What's this song?"

You might consider getting a handy, music-oriented widget called Sound Search for Google Play. You can obtain it from the Google Play Store and then add it to the Home screen, as described in Chapter 15. From the Home screen, you can use the widget to identify music playing within earshot of your tablet.

To use the widget, touch it on the Home screen. The widget immediately starts listening to your surroundings, as shown in the middle sidebar figure. After a few seconds, the song is recognized and displayed. You can choose to either buy the song at the Google Play Store or touch the Cancel button and start over.

The What's This Song widget works best (exclusively, I would argue) with recorded music. Try as you might, you can't sing into the thing and have it recognize a song. Humming doesn't work, either. I've tried playing the guitar and piano and — nope — those didn't work either. But for listening to ambient music, it's a good tool for discovering what you're listening to.

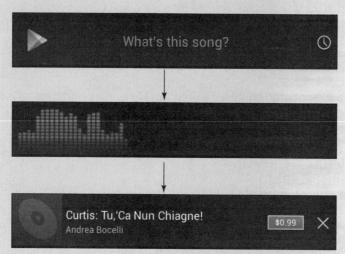

Being the life of the party

You need to do four things to make your Galaxy tablet the soul of your next shindig or soirée:

- ✔ Connect it to external speakers.
- ✔ Use the Shuffle command.

✔ Set the Repeat command.

✔ Provide plenty of drinks and snacks.

The external speakers can be provided by anything from a custom media dock, a stereo, or the sound system on the Times Square Jumbotron. As long as the device has a standard line input, you're good.

Oh, and you need an audio cable. On one end it needs a mini-headphone jack for the tablet. On the other end it needs an audio jack that matches the output device. Look for such a cable at Radio Shack or any store where the employees wear name tags.

After you connect your tablet, start the Play Music app and choose the party playlist you've created. If you want the songs to play in random order, touch the Shuffle button.

You might also consider choosing the List Repeat command (see Table 13-1) so that all songs in the list repeat.

✔ To play all songs saved on your Galaxy tablet, choose the Songs category and touch the first song in the list.

✔ Also see the later section "Organize Your Music" for information on creating playlists. Build one playlist for your book club and another one for your theater friends.

✔ Enjoy your party, and please drink responsibly.

Add Some Music to Your Life

Odds are good that your Note or Tab came without preinstalled music. You may find some tunes available, which are typically a generic sampling of the Google Play Music library. To add music, buy music, or steal it from somewhere else, read this section.

Borrowing music from a PC

Your computer is the equivalent of the 20th-century stereo system — a combination tuner, amplifier, and turntable, plus all your records and CDs. If you've already copied your music collection to your computer, or if you use your computer as your main music storage system, you can share that music with your tablet.

Many music-playing, or jukebox, programs are available. On Windows, the most common program is Windows Media Player. You can use this program to synchronize music between a PC and a tablet. Here's how it works:

1. **Connect the tablet to your PC.**

   Use the USB cable that comes with the tablet.

   Over on the PC, an AutoPlay dialog box appears in Windows, prompting you to choose how best to mount the Galaxy tablet onto the Windows storage system.

2. **Close the AutoPlay dialog box.**

3. **Start Windows Media Player.**

4. **Click the Sync tab or the Sync toolbar button.**

   The Galaxy tablet appears in the Sync list on the right side of Windows Media Player, as shown in Figure 13-3.

5. **Drag to the Sync area the music you want to transfer to your tablet (refer to Figure 13-3).**

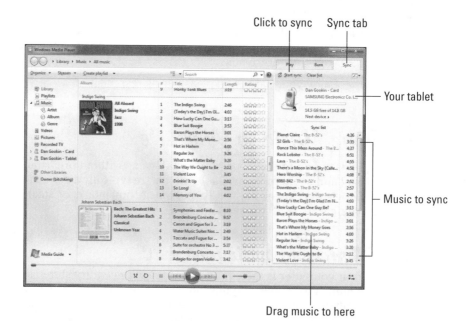

Figure 13-3: Windows Media Player meets Galaxy tablet.

6. **Click the Start Sync button to transfer the music from your PC to the tablet.**

   The Sync button may be located atop the list, as shown in Figure 13-3, or it might be found on the bottom.

7. **Close the Windows Media Player when you're done transferring music.**

   Or you can keep it open — whatever.

8. **Unplug the USB cable.**

   Or you can leave the tablet plugged in.

The steps for synchronizing music with other media jukebox programs work similarly to those outlined in the preceding list.

- ✔ The process of connecting your tablet to a PC is covered in more detail in Chapter 17.

- ✔ The Galaxy tablet can store only so much music! Don't be overzealous when copying your tunes. In Windows Media Player (refer to Figure 13-3), a capacity thermometer-thing shows you how much storage space is used and how much is available on your tablet. Pay heed to the indicator!

- ✔ Windows Media Player complains when you try to sync the Galaxy tablet to more than one PC. If you do, you're warned after Step 6 in this section. It's not a big issue: Just inform Windows Media Player that you intend to sync with the computer for only this session.

Buying music at the Google Play Store

It's possible to get your music from the same source where you buy your apps — the Google Play Store. Getting apps is covered in Chapter 15. Getting music is covered right here:

1. **Touch the Play Music app button to view the sidebar.**

   The sidebar is shown in Figure 13-1.

2. **Choose Shop.**

   The Play Store app starts, immediately whisking you to the Music part of the store.

3. **Use the Search icon to help you locate music, or just browse the categories.**

   Keep an eye out for special offers at the Play Store. It's a great way to pick up some free tunes.

   Eventually you'll see a page showing details about the song or album. Choose a song from the list to hear a preview. The button next to the song or album indicates the purchase price, or it says Free for free music.

4. **Touch the Free button to get a free song, or touch the price button to purchase a song or an album.**

   Don't worry, you're not buying anything yet.

5. **To buy music, choose your credit card or payment source.**

   If a credit card or payment source doesn't appear, choose the Add Card option to add a payment method. Sign up with Google Checkout and submit your credit card or other payment information.

6. **Touch the Buy or Confirm button.**

   The song or album is added to the music library.

The music you buy at the Play Store isn't downloaded to your tablet. It shows up, but it plays over the Internet. That means you can hear it only when the tablet has an Internet connection. To ensure that the music is always available, see the earlier section "Pinning your music."

- You'll eventually receive a Gmail message listing a summary of your purchase.

- All music sales are final. Don't blame me; I'm just writing down Google's current policy for music purchases.

- If you plan on downloading an album or multiple songs, connect to a Wi-Fi network. That way, you won't run the risk of a data surcharge on your cellular plan. See Chapter 16 for information on activating the tablet's Wi-Fi.

- Music you purchase from the Google Play Music store is available on any Android device with the Play Music app installed, providing you use the same Google account on that device. You can also listen to your tunes by visiting the `music.google.com` site on any computer connected to the Internet.

Organize Your Music

The Play Music app categorizes your music by album, artist, song, and so forth, but unless you have only one album and enjoy all the songs on it, that configuration probably won't do. To better organize your music, you can create *playlists*. That way, you can hear the music you want to hear, in the order you want, for whatever mood hits you.

Reviewing your playlists

To view any playlists that you've already created, or that have been preset on the tablet, display the Play Music app's sidebar and choose Playlists. You'll see the playlists displayed on the screen, as shown in Figure 13-4.

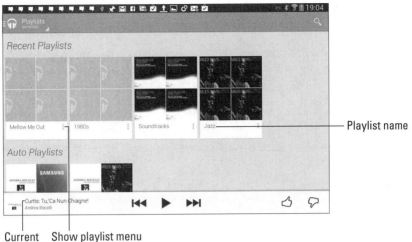

Playlist name

Current song

Show playlist menu

Figure 13-4: Playlists in the Play Music app.

To see which songs are in a playlist, touch the playlist album icon. To play the songs in the playlist, touch the first song in the list.

 A playlist is a helpful way to organize music when a song's information may not have been completely imported into the tablet. For example, if you're like me, you probably have a lot of songs labeled Unknown. A quick way to remedy that situation is to name a playlist after the artist and then add those unknown songs to the playlist. The next section describes how it's done.

Creating your own playlists

Making a new playlist is easy, and adding songs to the playlist is even easier. Follow these steps:

1. **Find an album or song in the library.**

    Locate music you want to add to a playlist.

 2. **Touch the Menu icon by the album or song.**

    The menu icon is shown in the margin.

3. **Choose the Add to Playlist command.**

4. **Choose New Playlist.**

5. **Type a name for the playlist and then touch the OK button.**

    The new playlist is created and the song or entire album is added to the playlist.

To add additional songs, or to build upon an existing playlist, repeat Steps 1 through 3, choosing the existing playlist in Step 3.

You can have as many playlists as you like on the tablet and stick as many songs as you like into them. Adding songs to a playlist doesn't noticeably affect the tablet's storage capacity.

- ✔ To remove a song from a playlist, open the playlist and touch the Menu icon by the song. Choose Remove from Playlist.

- ✔ Removing a song from a playlist doesn't delete the song from the Music library.

- ✔ Songs in a playlist can be rearranged: While viewing the playlist, use the tab on the far-left end of a song title to drag that song up or down in the list.

- ✔ To delete a playlist, touch the Menu icon in the playlist icon's lower-right corner (refer to Figure 13-4). Choose the Delete command. Touch OK to confirm.

Removing unwanted music

Depending on the source, you have two ways to deal with unwanted music in the Play Music app's library. The different ways depend on whether or not the song is stored directly on the tablet.

 For music stored on the device, locate the song or album and touch the Menu icon. Choose the Delete command. Touch the OK button to remove the song.

If you don't see a Delete command on the menu, the song is available only through Google Play Music. To remove the song, visit Google Play on the Internet at music.google.com. View your library to locate the song. Click the Menu icon by a song and then choose the Delete command. Click the Delete Song button to confirm.

Soap, No Soap, Galaxy Radio

Although they're not broadcast radio stations, some sources on the Internet — *Internet radio* sites — play music. Lamentably, your Galaxy tablet doesn't come with any Internet radio apps, but that doesn't stop you from finding a few good ones at the Google Play Store. Two free services that I can recommend are

- ✔ TuneIn Radio
- ✔ Pandora Radio

The TuneIn Radio app gives you access to hundreds of Internet radio stations broadcasting around the world. They're organized by category, so you can find just about whatever you want. Many of the radio stations are also broadcast radio stations, so odds are good you can find a local station or two, which you can listen to on your Galaxy tablet.

Pandora Radio lets you select music based on your mood and customizes, according to your feedback, the tunes you listen to. The app works like the Internet site www.pandora.com, in case you're familiar with it. The nifty thing about Pandora is that the more you listen, the better the app gets at finding music you like.

These apps are available at the Google Play Store. They're free, though paid versions might also be available.

✔ It's best to listen to Internet radio when your tablet is connected to the Internet via a Wi-Fi connection. Streaming music can use a lot of your cellular data plan's data allotment.

✔ See Chapter 15 for more information about the Google Play Store.

✔ Internet music of the type delivered by the apps mentioned in this section is referred to by the nerds as *streaming music*. That's because the music arrives on your Galaxy tablet as a continuous download from the source. Unlike music you download and save, streaming music is played as it comes in and is not stored long-term.

Wake up
T W T F S   S M T W T F S

Airport
S M T W T F S

Nap
S M

14

e up
W T F S

Airport
S M T W T F S

Nap
S M T W T F S

Wake up
S M T W T

What Else Does It Do?

In This Chapter

▶ Waking up to your tablet

▶ Making tablet calculations

▶ Keeping your appointments

▶ Scheduling new events

▶ Playing games

▶ Reading electronic books

▶ Watching junk on YouTube

▶ Buying or renting films and TV shows

Most gizmos are designed to solve a single problem. The food processor slices, grates, or chops food, but it doesn't play music (though I'm sure John Cage would argue that point). The lawn mower is good at cutting the grass but terrible at telling time. And if you have a tuba, it can play music, but it's a poor substitute for a hair dryer. That's all well and good because people accept limitations on devices designed with a specific purpose.

The Samsung Galaxy tablet is a gizmo with many purposes. Its capabilities are limited only by the apps you get for it. To help you grasp this concept, the tablet comes with a slate of apps preinstalled. They can give you an idea of what the tablet is capable of, or you can simply use those apps to make the Galaxy tablet a more versatile and useful device.

It's an Alarm Clock

Your Galaxy tablet keeps constant, accurate track of the time, which is displayed at the top of the Home screen as well as on the lock screen. The display is lovely and informative, but it can't actually wake you up. You need to choose a specific time and apply a noise to that time. This process turns the tablet into an alarm clock.

Alarm clock duties are the responsibility of the Alarm app, which you'll find on the Apps screen. Its main screen looks similar to what's shown on the left in Figure 14-1. The right side of the figure shows the alarm creation and editing screen.

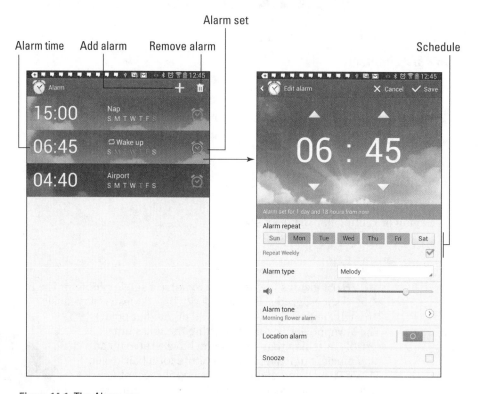

Figure 14-1: The Alarm app.

You create alarms for the Alarm app by touching the Add (+) icon, shown in Figure 14-1. Use the next screen to edit details about the alarm. Set the schedule, sound, name, and other details that appear on the screen. The most important thing to set is the date and time. Touch the Save button to save the alarm.

As an example, to set an alarm that wakes you up at 6:45 every morning, touch the day icons, Mon through Fri (see Figure 14-1), and then place a check mark by Repeat Weekly. Scroll down to the bottom of the screen and type a name, such as "Get Outta Bed." Touch the Save button and the alarm is created and set.

The alarm you create appears on the Alarm app's screen, similar to what's shown in Figure 14-1, left. Any new alarm you create is automatically set — it goes off when the proper time approaches. To disable an alarm, touch the Alarm Set icon (labeled in Figure 14-1).

Alarms must be set or else they don't trigger. If you've turned off an alarm, remember to set it again; touch the Alarm Set icon, as shown in Figure 14-1.

- ✔ When an alarm is set, the tablet shows an Alarm status icon atop the screen, similar to what appears in the margin.
- ✔ Turning off an alarm doesn't delete the alarm.
- ✔ To remove an alarm, long-press it and choose the Delete command from the menu. The alarm is deleted.
- ✔ The alarm doesn't work when you turn off the tablet. The alarm does work, however, when the tablet is locked.
- ✔ The Location Alarm feature, found on the Create Alarm and Edit Alarm screens, can be used to disable the alarm when you're at or near certain places. Touch the button to activate that feature, and then use the map to specify a location. As long as you're at that location, the alarm will not go off. I've had mixed results with this feature, mostly because the tablet can be iffy about knowing its exact location.
- ✔ Consider getting a docking station so you can use your tablet as a nighttime music station and clock.

It's a Very Big Calculator

The Calculator is perhaps the oldest of all computer programs. Even my stupid cellphone back in the 1990s had a calculator program. (I won't dignify it by calling it an "app.")

Sleep more soundly with Blocking Mode

The tablet makes an excellent bedside clock. It functions even better as a bedside clock when you activate the Blocking Mode feature, which allows you to set a time of day when notifications and alarms can be disabled or silenced.

To access the Blocking Mode feature, open the Settings app. Choose Blocking Mode from the left side of the screen to activate that feature. (If you can't find it, touch the Device category

atop the screen.) On the right side of the screen, select which items you want blocked, such as notifications or alarms. You can set the specific times that Blocking Mode is active in the Set Time area.

Remember that Blocking Mode does stifle any alarms you've set. So if you *really* need to be up by 4:00 AM, disable Blocking Mode so that you'll hear that alarm.

Start the Calculator app by choosing its icon from the Apps screen. The Calculator appears, as shown in Figure 14-2. When used in a vertical orientation, the app loses the scary math buttons.

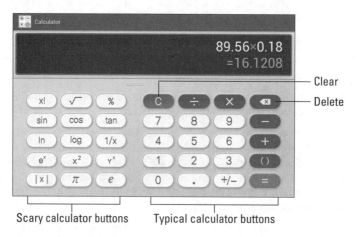

Figure 14-2: The Calculator.

Type your equations using the various buttons on the screen. The parentheses button can help you determine which part of a long equation gets calculated first. Use the C button to clear input.

- ✔ Long-press the calculator's text (or results) to cut or copy the results.

- ✔ I use the Calculator most often to determine my tip at a restaurant. In Figure 14-2, a calculation is being made for an 18 percent tip on an $89.56 tab.

- ✔ If your tablet doesn't have a Calculator app, you can obtain one from the Play Store.

It's a Calendar

Feel free to take out any datebook you have and throw it away. You never need to buy another one again. That's because your tablet is the ideal datebook and appointment calendar. Thanks to the Calendar app and the Google Calendar feature on the Internet, you can manage all your scheduling right on your Galaxy tablet. It's almost cinchy.

- ✔ Google Calendar works with your Google account to keep track of your schedule and appointments. You can visit Google Calendar on the web at http://calendar.google.com.

✔ You automatically have a Google Calendar; it comes with your Google account.

✔ I recommend that you use the Calendar app on your tablet to access Google Calendar. It's a better way to access your schedule than using the Internet app to reach Google Calendar on the web.

✔ Before you throw away your datebook, copy into the Calendar app some future appointments and info, such as birthdays and anniversaries.

✔ The Calendar app may be called the S Planner app on some tablets. They're both the same thing.

Browsing your schedule

To see what's happening next, to peruse upcoming important events, or just to know which day of the month it is, summon the Calendar (or S Planner) app. It's located on the Apps screen along with all the other apps that dwell on your Galactic tablet.

Figure 14-3 shows the Calendar app's three views: Month, Week, and Day. They look subtly different in horizontal orientation but provide the same information. There's also Agenda view, which displays only upcoming events. Each view is chosen from the View menu (labeled in the figure).

✔ Use Month view to see an overview of what's going on, and use Week or Day view to see your appointments.

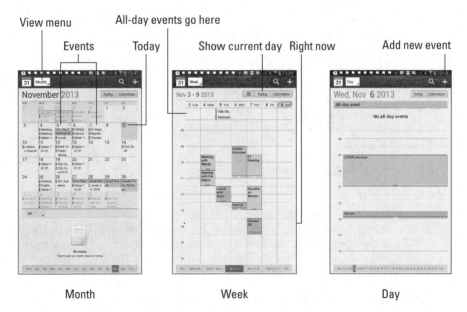

Figure 14-3: The Calendar app.

TIP

✔ I check Week view at the start of the week to remind me of what's coming up.

✔ To scroll from month to month, swipe the screen up or down. In Week view and Day view, scroll from left to right.

✔ Touch the Today button to be instantly whisked back to the current day.

✔ The current date, if it's visible on the screen, is circled in blue, as shown in Figure 14-3. A horizontal red bar marks the current time.

✔ Different colors flag your events, as seen by the teensy squares next to event names in Figure 14-3, left. The colors represent a calendar category to which the events are assigned. See the later section "Creating an event" for information on calendars.

Reviewing appointments

To see more detail about an event, touch it. When you're using Month view, touch the event's date to see the Week view. Then choose the event again to see its details, similar to the event shown in Figure 14-4.

Event menu

Touch to see event
location on the
Maps app

Remove reminder

Change to Gmail
reminder

Figure 14-4: Event details.

The details you see depend on how much information was recorded when the event was created. Some events have only a minimum of information; others may have details, such as a location for the event. When the event's location is listed, you can touch that location, and the Maps app pops up to show you where the event is being held.

 Touch the Back button to dismiss the event's details.

✔ Birthdays and a few other events on the calendar may be pulled from the Contacts app or even from some social networking apps. That probably explains why some events are listed twice — they're pulled in from two sources.

✔ The best way to review upcoming appointments is to choose the List item from the View menu or from atop the screen when the tablet is held horizontally.

✔ To quickly view upcoming events from the Home screen, slap down the Calendar widget. As in List view, the widget displays only a list of your upcoming appointments. See Chapter 19 for information on applying widgets to the tablet's Home screen.

✔ Google Now also lists any immediate appointments or events. See the later section "It's Google Now."

Creating an event

The key to making the Calendar app work is to add events: appointments, things to do, or meetings, or full-day events such as birthdays or colonoscopies. To create an event, follow these steps in the Calendar app:

1. Select the day for the event.

Or if you like, you can switch to Day view, where you can touch the starting time for the new event.

2. Touch the Add (+) icon.

The Add Event screen appears. Your job is to fill in the blanks to create the event.

The more information you supply, the more detailed the event and the more you can do with it on your tablet as well as on Google Calendar on the Internet.

3. Type an event title.

Sometimes I simply write the name of the person I'm meeting.

4. Choose a calendar category for the event.

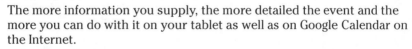

Calendar categories are handy because they let you organize and color-code your events. They're confusing because Google calls them "calendars." I think of them more as categories. So I have different calendars (categories) for my personal and work schedules, government duties, clubs, and so on.

5. Set the meeting duration by using the From and To buttons.

Because you followed Step 1, you don't have to set the date (unless the event is longer than a day). Touch the time buttons, if necessary, to adjust when the event starts and stops.

When the event lasts all day, such as a birthday or your mother-in-law's visit that was supposed to last for an hour, touch All Day to add a check mark.

6. **Specify whether the event repeats.**

Touch the Repeat menu to set up a recurring schedule. For example, if your meeting is held every month on the third Wednesday, choose the item Monthly (Every Third Wednesday).

When you have events that repeat twice a month — say, on the first and third Mondays — you need to create two separate events, one for the first Monday and another for the third. Then have each event repeat monthly.

7. **Type a location for the event.**

My advice is to type information in the event's Location field just as though you're typing information to search for in the Maps app. When the event is displayed, the location is a link; touch the link to see where it is on a map.

8. **Fill in other fields if you like.**

9. **Touch the Save button (in the upper-right corner of the Add Event window) to create the new event.**

The Save button now has a check mark by it.

You can change an event at any time: Simply touch the event to bring up more information, similar to what's shown in Figure 14-4. Touch the Menu icon and choose the Edit command to modify the event.

To remove an event, touch the event to bring up more information, touch the Menu icon, and choose the Delete command. Touch the OK button to confirm.

✔ It's necessary to set an event's time zone only when that event takes place in another time zone or when an event spans time zones, such as an airline flight. In that case, the Calendar app automatically adjusts the starting and stopping times for events, depending on where you are.

✔ If you forget to set the time zone and you end up hopping around the world, your events are set according to the time zone in which they were created, not the local time.

✔ Reminders can be set so that the tablet alerts you before an event takes place. The alert can show up as a notification icon (shown in the margin), as an audio alert, or as a vibrating alert. Pull down the notifications and choose the calendar alert. You can then peruse pending events.

It's a Game Machine

One of the best ways to put expensive, high-tech gizmos to work is to play games. Don't even sweat the thought that you have too much business or work or other important stuff you can do on your Galaxy Note or Galaxy Tab. The more advanced the mind, the more the need for play, right? So indulge yourself.

Lamentably, no sample games ship with your tablet. That may change in the future, but for now you're left to hunt down games at the Play Store just like everyone else in the Android Kingdom.

Just to be a tease, Figure 14-5 shows a game on the Galaxy tablet. It's one of many, so don't think I'm recommending anything, though I did play Jet Car Stunts on my Galaxy Tab 3 for hours on end during an intercontinental flight.

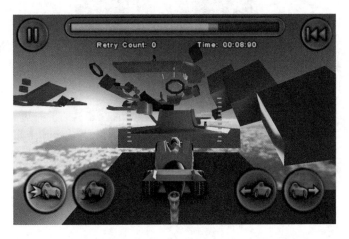

Figure 14-5: A game on a tablet.

- ✔ See Chapter 15 for information on using the Google Play Store to hunt down some exciting games. You can also use the Play Games app on the Apps screen. (The Play Games app may be in the Google folder.)

- ✔ Free or "lite" versions of popular games exist. Before plunking down your hard-earned 99 cents, consider testing the free version.

It's an E-Book Reader

Your Galactic tablet comes with Google's own e-book reader app. It has the clever name Play Books, and it can be found on the Apps screen either by its lonesome or in the Google apps folder.

Begin your reading experience by opening the Play Books app. If you're prompted to turn on synchronization, touch the Turn On Sync button.

The Play Books app organizes the books into a library and displays them for reading, similar to the way they're shown in Figure 14-6. The library lists any titles you've obtained for your Google Books account. Or when you're returning to the Play Books app after a break, you see the current page of the e-book you were last reading. You can choose either mode from the sidebar, as shown in the figure.

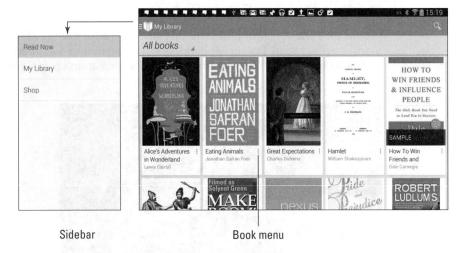

Sidebar   Book menu

Figure 14-6: The Play Books library.

Scroll through the library by swiping the screen.

Touch a book in the Play Books app library to open it. If you've opened the book previously, you're returned to the page you last read. Otherwise, the first page you see is the book's first page.

To begin reading, touch a book to open it.

Figure 14-7 illustrates the basic book-reading operation in the Play Books app. You turn pages by swiping left or right, but probably mostly left. You can turn pages also by touching the far left or right side of the screen.

The Play Books app also works in a vertical orientation, though when you turn the tablet that way, only one page is shown at a time.

✐ If you don't see a book in the library, touch the Menu button and choose the Refresh command.

Display library   Page progress   Search the book

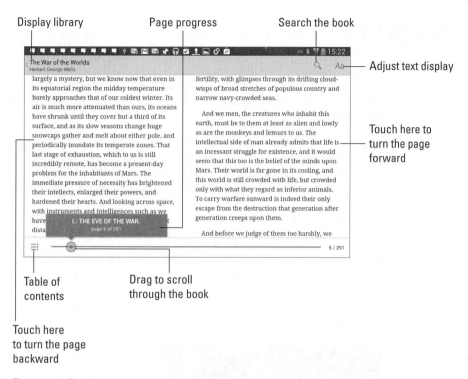

Adjust text display

Touch here to
turn the page
forward

Table of
contents

Drag to scroll
through the book

Touch here
to turn the page
backward

Figure 14-7: Reading an e-book in the Play Books app.

- ✔ To ensure that your reading material is always available, touch the Menu icon on a book's cover and choose the Keep on Device command. That way, the tablet doesn't need Internet access to synchronize and download books to the library. I choose this command specifically before I leave on a trip where an Internet signal may not be available (such as in an airplane).

- ✔ To remove a book from the library, touch the Menu icon on the book's cover and then choose the Delete from Library command.

- ✔ If the onscreen controls (refer to Figure 14-7) disappear, touch the screen to see them again.

- ✔ Touch the *Aa* icon to display a menu of options for adjusting the text on the screen and the brightness.

- ✔ To return to the library, touch the Play Books app button in the upper-left corner of the screen or touch the Back button.

- ✔ Synchronization allows you to keep copies of your Google Books on all your Android devices as well as on the `books.google.com` website.

- ✔ If you have a Kindle (and for that I must ask, "Why?" but I digress), you can obtain the Amazon Kindle app for your tablet. Use the app to access books you've purchased for the Kindle or just as a replacement or supplement to Google Books.

It's Google Now

Don't worry about your Galaxy tablet controlling too much of your life: The tablet harbors no insidious intelligence, and the Robot Revolution is still years away. Until then, you can use your tablet's listening capabilities to enjoy a feature called Google Now. It's not quite like having your own personal Jeeves, but it's on its way.

Google Now must be activated on your Galaxy Note or Galaxy Tab. To do so, start the Google app, found directly on the Apps screen or in the Google folder on the Apps screen. Obey the prompts on the screen to obtain Google Now. You might have to touch the Get Google Now link first.

Touch the Google app to start Google Now, or perform a Google search by using the Google Search widget on the Home screen. A typical Google Now screen is shown in Figure 14-8. Below the Search text box, you'll find cards. The variety and number of cards depend on how often you use Google Now. The more the app learns about you, the more cards appear.

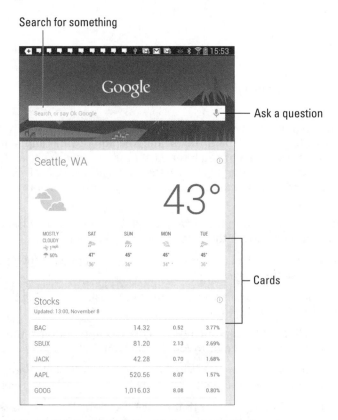

Search for something

Ask a question

Cards

Figure 14-8: Google Now is ready for business. Or play.

TIP

You can use Google Now to search the Internet, just as you'd use Google's main web page. More interesting than that, you can ask Google Now questions; see the sidebar, "Barking orders to Google Now."

✔ You can use Google Now features also by touching the Google Search widget. That widget normally comes preinstalled on the Home screen. If not, you can add it there; see Chapter 19.

✔ You cannot manually add cards to the Google Now screen. The only way to get more cards to show up is to use Google Now.

It's Your Video Entertainment

It's not possible to watch "real" TV on your tablet, but a few apps come close. The YouTube app is handy for watching random, meaningless drivel, which I suppose makes it a lot like TV. Then there's the Play Movies & TV app, which lets you buy and rent real movies and TV shows from the Google Play Store. And when you tire of those apps, you can use the Camera app with the front-facing camera to pretend that you're the star of your own reality TV show.

Enjoying YouTube

YouTube is the Internet phenomenon that proves that real life is indeed too boring and random for television. Or is that the other way around? Regardless, you can view the latest videos on YouTube — or contribute your own — by using the YouTube app on your Galactic tablet.

Search for videos in the YouTube app by touching the Search icon. Type the video name, a topic, or any search terms to locate videos. Zillions of videos are available.

The YouTube app displays suggestions for any channels you're subscribed to, which allows you to follow favorite topics or YouTube content providers.

✔ Use the YouTube app to view YouTube videos, rather than use the Chrome app to visit the YouTube website.

✔ Ensure that the tablet is oriented horizontally to view the video in a larger size.

✔ Because you have a Google account, you also have a YouTube account. I recommend that you log in to your YouTube account when using the YouTube app: Touch the Menu button and choose the Sign In command. Log in if you don't see your account information.

✔ Not all YouTube videos are available for viewing on mobile devices.

Buying and renting movies

You can use the Google Play Store to not only buy apps and books for your tablet but also to rent movies. Open the Play Movies & TV app, found on the Apps screen.

Renting or purchasing a movie is done at the Play Store, and it works just like purchasing an app (covered in Chapter 15). Choose a movie or TV show to rent or buy. Touch the price button, and then choose your method of payment.

Movies and shows rented at the Play Store are available for viewing up to 30 days after you pay the rental fee. After you start the movie, you can pause and watch it again and again during a 24-hour period.

15

A Galaxy of Apps

In This Chapter

▶ Shopping at the Play Store

▶ Downloading apps

▶ Using a computer to install apps

▶ Sending an app suggestion to a friend

▶ Updating your apps

▶ Removing apps

*W*ithout apps, your Samsung Galaxy tablet would be nothing more than a pricey frame without a picture. There must be apps!

A moderate assortment of apps was preinstalled on your tablet, first by Google and then by Samsung. Perhaps a smattering was installed by the cellular provider as well. Beyond that, you can add more apps to your tablet, which extends the list of things you can do in the mobile universe. Adding apps and managing all your tablet's apps are this chapter's topics.

Welcome to the Play Store

People love to shop when they're buying something they want or when they're spending someone else's money. You can go shopping for your Galaxy Note or Galaxy Tab, and I'm not talking about going to your local Phone Store to buy overpriced accessories. I'm talking apps, games, music, magazines, movies, TV shows, and books.

The Google Play Store may sound like the place where you can go buy outerwear for children, but it's really an online place where you go to pick up new goodies for your tablet. You can browse, you can get free stuff, you can pay. It all happens at the Play Store.

- Officially, it's the Google Play Store. It may also be referenced as Google Play. The app, however, is named Play Store.

- The Google Play Store was once known as Android Market, and you may still see it referred to as the Market.

- This section talks about getting apps for your tablet. For information on getting music, see Chapter 13. Chapter 14 mentions renting movies and TV shows. As well as buying books.

- *App* is short for application. It's a program, or software, you can add to your tablet to make it do new, wondrous, or useful things.

- All apps you download can be found on the Apps screen. Further, apps you download have shortcut icons placed on the Home screen. See Chapter 19 for information on moving apps on the Home screen.

- You obtain items from the Google Play Store by *downloading* them to your tablet. That file transfer works best at top speeds; therefore:

- I highly recommend that you connect your cellular tablet to a Wi-Fi network if you plan to obtain apps, books, or movies at the Play Store. Not only does Wi-Fi give you speed, but it also helps avoid data surcharges. See Chapter 16 for details on connecting your tablet to a Wi-Fi network.

- The Play Store app is frequently updated, so its look may change from what you see in this chapter. Updated information on the Google Play Store is available on my website at `www.wambooli.com/help/android/google-play/`.

Browsing the Google Play Store

You access the Google Play Store by opening the Play Store app, found on the Apps Menu screen but also on the main Home screen.

After opening the Play Store app, you see the main screen, similar to the one shown in Figure 15-1. You can browse for apps, games, books, or movie rentals. The categories are listed on the top-left part of the screen, with the other parts of the screen showcasing popular or recommended items.

Find apps by choosing the Apps category from the main screen (refer to Figure 15-1). The next screen lists popular and featured items plus categories you can browse by swiping the screen right to left. The category titles appear toward the top of the screen.

When you have an idea of what you want, such as an app's name or even what it does, searching works fastest: Touch the Search icon at the top of the Play Store screen (refer to Figure 15-1). Type all or part of the app's name or perhaps a description.

To see more information about an item, touch it. Touching something doesn't buy it but instead displays a more detailed description, screen shots, a video preview, comments, plus links to similar items, as shown in Figure 15-2.

Categories

App button

Search

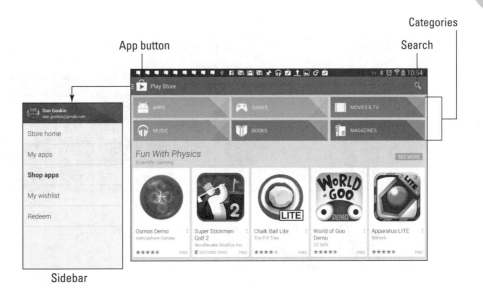

Sidebar

Figure 15-1: The Google Play Store.

Return to the main Google Play Store screen at any time by touching the Google Play app icon in the upper-left corner of the screen.

- The first time you enter the Google Play Store, you have to accept the terms of service; touch the Accept button.

- You can be assured that all apps that appear in the Google Play Store can be used with your tablet. There's no way to download or buy something that's incompatible.

- Pay attention to an app's ratings. Ratings are added by people who use the apps — people like you and me. Having more stars is better. You can see additional information, including individual user reviews, by selecting the app.

- Another good indicator of an app's success is how many times it's been downloaded. Some apps have been downloaded over ten million times. That's a good sign.

- In addition to getting apps, you can download widgets for the Home screen as well as wallpapers for the Galaxy tablet. Just search the Play Store for *widget* or *live wallpaper*. Some apps automatically come with their own widgets, such as Facebook and Twitter.

- See Chapter 19 for more information on widgets and live wallpapers.

Share app

App icon   Scroll categories   Add to wish list

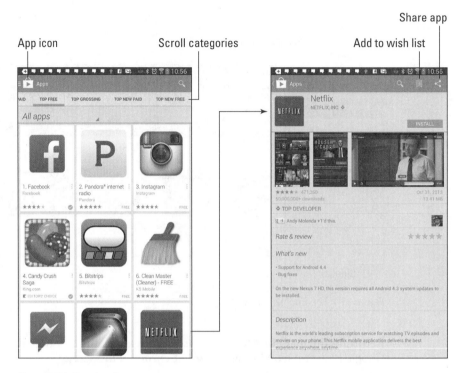

Figure 15-2: Hunting down an app.

Obtaining a new app

After you locate an app you want, the next step is to download it, by copying it from the Google Play Store on the Internet to your Galactic tablet. The app is installed automatically, building up your collection of apps and expanding what the tablet can do.

Good news: Most apps are available for free. Better news: Even the apps you pay for don't cost dearly. In fact, it seems odd to sit and stew over whether paying 99 cents for a game is "worth it."

I recommend that you download a free app first, to familiarize yourself with the process. Then try your hand at a paid app.

Free or not, the process of obtaining an app works pretty much the same. Follow these steps:

1. **Open the Play Store app.**

2. **Find the app you want and open its description.**

   The app's description screen looks similar to the one shown on the right side in Figure 15-2.

The difference between a free app and a paid app is found on the button used to obtain the app. For a free app, the button says Install. For a paid app, the button shows the price.

You may find three other buttons on an app's description screen: Open, Update, and Uninstall. The Open button opens an app that's already installed on your tablet; the Update button updates an already installed app; and the Uninstall button removes an installed app. See the later sections "Updating an app" and "Uninstalling apps" for more information on using the Update and Uninstall buttons.

3. **Touch the Install button to get a free app; for a paid app, touch the button with the price on it.**

   Don't fret! You're not buying anything yet.

   You see a screen describing the app's permissions. The list isn't a warning, and it doesn't mean anything bad. It's just that the Play Store is informing you which of your tablet's features the app will have access to.

4. **Touch the Accept button.**

   For a paid app, you may have to touch the I Agree to the Payments for Google Play item. Only after you do this does the Buy button become available.

   If you're obtaining a free app, skip up to Step 6.

5. **For a paid app:**

   a. Select your payment method.

   Select a credit card, if you have one set up with Google Wallet. If not, you can input credit card information per the directions on the screen.

   If you have any Google Credit, choose your Google Play balance from the credit card list.

   b. Touch the Buy button to purchase the app.

   c. If you're asked to confirm your Google account password, do so and then touch the Confirm button.

   The Downloading notification appears atop the screen as the app is downloaded. You're free to do other things on your Galaxy tablet while the app is downloaded and installed.

6. **Touch the Open button to run the app.**

   Or if you were doing something else while the app was downloading and installing, choose the Successfully Installed notification, as shown in the margin. The notification features the app's name with the text Successfully Installed below it.

Never buy an app twice

Any apps you've already purchased in the Google Play Store, say for an Android phone or other mobile device, are available for download on your Galaxy Note or Galaxy Tab at no charge. Simply find the app and touch the Install button.

You can review any already purchased apps in the Play Store: Choose the My Apps item from the sidebar (refer to Figure 15-1, left). Choose the All tab from the top of the screen. You'll see all the apps you've ever obtained at the Google Play Store, including apps you've previously paid for. Those apps are flagged with the text Purchased. Select that item to reinstall the paid app.

At this point, what happens next depends on the app you've downloaded. For example, you may have to agree to a license agreement. If so, touch the I Agree button. Additional setup may involve setting your location, signing in to an account, or creating a profile, for example.

After you complete the initial app setup, or if no setup is necessary, you can start using the app.

- ✔ Apps you download are added to the Apps screen, made available like any other app on your tablet.

- ✔ When you dither over getting an app, consider adding it to your wish list. Touch the Wish List icon when viewing the app (the icon is shown in the margin). You can review your wish list by choosing the My Wishlist item from the Play Store app's sidebar (refer to Figure 15-1, left).

- ✔ Some apps may install shortcut icons on the Home screen after they're installed. See Chapter 19 for information on removing the icon from the Home screen, if that is your desire.

- ✔ For a paid app, you'll receive an e-mail message from the Google Play Store, confirming your purchase. The message contains a link you can select to review the refund policy in case you change your mind about the purchase.

- ✔ Be quick on that refund: Some apps allow you only 15 minutes to get your money back. You know when the time limit is up because the Refund button on the app's description screen changes to Uninstall.

- ✔ Also see the "Uninstalling apps" section, later in this chapter.

Installing apps from a computer

You don't need to use the Play Store app on your tablet to install apps. Using a computer, you can visit the Google Play website, choose software, and have the app installed remotely. It's kind of cool, yet kind of mysterious. Here's how it works:

1. **Use your computer's web browser to visit the Google Play store on the Internet.**

   The address is `https://play.google.com/store`.

   Bookmark this site in the computer's web browser.

2. **If necessary, click the Sign In link to log in to your Google account.**

   Use the same Google account that you used when setting up your tablet. You need to have access to that account so that Google can remotely update your various Android gizmos.

3. **Browse for something.**

   You can hunt down apps, books, music — the whole gamut. It works just like browsing the Play Store on your tablet.

4. **After clicking the Install or Buy button to obtain the item, choose your Galaxy Note or Galaxy Tab from the Device menu.**

   The menu lists all your Android devices, or at least those compatible with what you're getting.

   Your tablet may be listed by its technical name, such as Samsung SM-P600 or Samsung SM-T310. If the name starts with the text *Samsung* and your tablet is the only Samsung gizmo you own, that's the one to choose.

5. **For a free app, click the Install button; for a paid app, click the Continue button.**

   If you're getting a free app, installation proceeds. Otherwise, for a paid app, you need select your payment source.

6. **For a paid app, select your payment type, such as a credit card, and then click the Buy button.**

As if by magic, the app is installed on your tablet — even though you used a computer to do it.

App Management 101

The apps you install on your Galactic tablet originate from the Play Store. That's also the app you can return to for app management. That task includes reviewing apps you've downloaded, updating apps, organizing apps, and removing apps you no longer want or that you severely hate.

Reviewing your apps

To peruse the apps you've downloaded from the Google Play Store, follow these steps:

1. **Start the Play Store app.**

2. **Select My Apps from the sidebar.**

   Touch the Play Store app button, illustrated in Figure 15-1, to view the sidebar.

3. **Peruse your apps.**

Your Play Store apps are in two categories: Installed and All, as shown in Figure 15-3. Installed apps are found on your tablet; All apps includes apps you've downloaded but which may not currently be installed.

App in need
of an update

Update button

Installed apps   All your apps

Figure 15-3: The My Apps list.

Touch an app to see details. Touch the Open button to run the app, the Update button to update to the latest version, or the Uninstall button to remove the app. Later sections in this chapter describe the details on updating and uninstalling apps.

 ✔ You can place a check mark by the Allow Automatic Updating option, which assists in keeping your apps current. Not every app features automatic updating.

 ✔ Uninstalled apps remain on the All list because you did, at one time, download the app. To reinstall them (without paying a second time for paid apps), choose the app from the All list and touch the Install button.

Sharing an app

When you love an app so much that you just can't contain your glee, feel free to share that app with your friends. You can easily share a link to the app in the Google Play Store by obeying these steps:

1. **In the Play Store, select the app to share.**

   You can select any app, but you need to be at the app's details screen, the one with the Free or price button.

2. **Touch the Share icon.**

   A menu appears listing various apps and methods for sharing the app's Play Store link with your pals.

3. **Choose a sharing method.**

   For example, choose Gmail to send a link to the app in an e-mail message.

4. **Use the chosen app to send the link.**

   What happens next depends on which sharing method you've chosen.

The end result of these steps is that your friend receives a link. That person can touch the link on his mobile Android device and be whisked instantly to the Google Play Store, where the app can be viewed and installed.

Methods for using the various items on the Share menu are found throughout this book.

Updating an app

The Play Store notifies you of new versions of your apps. Whenever a new version is available, you see it flagged for updating, as shown in Figure 15-3. Updating the app to get the latest version is cinchy.

Some apps are updated automatically; there's no need for you to do anything. Other apps must be updated individually. You can update a group of apps by touching the Update All button (labeled in Figure 15-3).

The updating process often involves downloading and installing a new version of the app. That's perfectly fine; your settings and options aren't changed by the update process.

Uninstalling apps

I can think of a few reasons to remove an app. It's with eager relish that I remove apps that don't work or somehow annoy me. It's also perfectly okay to remove redundant apps, such as when you have multiple e-book readers that you don't use. And if you're desperate for an excuse, removing apps frees up a modicum of storage.

Whatever the reason, remove an app by following these directions:

1. **Start the Play Store app.**

2. **Select My Apps from the sidebar.**

    Figure 15-1 illustrates the sidebar; touch the App icon to view it.

3. **In the Installed list, touch the app that offends you.**

4. **Touch the Uninstall button.**

5. **Touch the OK button to confirm.**

    The app is removed.

The app continues to appear on the All list even after it's been removed. After all, you downloaded it once. That doesn't mean that the app is installed.

✔ You can always reinstall paid apps that you've uninstalled. You aren't charged twice for doing so.

✔ You can't remove apps that are preinstalled on the tablet by either Samsung or your cellular service provider. I'm sure there's probably a technical way to uninstall the apps, but seriously: Just don't use the apps if you want to remove them and discover that you can't.

Part IV
Nuts and Bolts

Discover how to use the Google Drive online file-sharing service at www.dummies.com/extras/samsunggalaxytabs.

In this part...

- ✔ Understand networking.
- ✔ Work with a computer to share files.
- ✔ Explore taking your tablet on the road
- ✔ Discover how to customize the tablet.
- ✔ Maintain and troubleshoot your tablet.

It's a Wireless Life

*W*hat exactly is *portable?* Back in the olden days, the boys in Marketing would say that bolting a handle to just about anything made it portable. Even a rhinoceros would be portable if he had a handle. Well, and the legs, they kind of make the rhino portable, I suppose. But my point is that to be portable requires more than just a handle; it requires a complete lack of wires.

Your Samsung Galaxy tablet's battery keeps it away from a wall socket. The digital cellular signal keeps your gizmo away from a phone line. (Other types of wireless communications are available, including Wi-Fi and Bluetooth.) Both features ensure portability and both are covered in this chapter.

Wireless Networking Wizardry

You know that wireless networking has hit the big-time when you see people asking Santa Claus for a wireless router at Christmas. Such a thing would have been unheard of years ago because back then routers were used primarily for woodworking. Today, wireless networking is what keeps gizmos such as your Galaxy Note or Galaxy Tab connected to the Internet.

The primary reason for wireless networking on the Galaxy tablet is to connect to the Internet. For exchanging and synchronizing files, refer to Chapter 17.

Using the cellular data network

The cellular Galaxy tablet is designed to connect to the Internet by using the digital cellular network. This network is the same type used by smartphones and cellular modems to wirelessly connect to the Internet.

Several types of digital cellular networks are available:

- ✔ **4G LTE:** The fourth generation of wide-area data networks is up to ten times faster than the 3G network and is the latest craze in cellular networking. Many major carriers are busily covering the country in a coat of 4G LTE paint; if the signal isn't available in your area now, it will be soon.

- ✔ **3G:** The third generation of wide-area data networks is several times faster than the previous generation of data networks.

- ✔ **1X:** Several types of the original, slower cellular data signals are still available. They all fall under the 1X banner. It's slow.

Your tablet always uses the best network available. So, if the 4G LTE network is within reach, that network is used for Internet communications. Otherwise, the 3G network is chosen, and then 1X in an act of last-ditch desperation.

- ✔ A notification icon for the type of network being used appears in the status area, right next to the Signal Strength icon.

- ✔ Accessing the digital cellular network isn't free. Your tablet most likely has some form of subscription plan for a certain quantity of data. When you exceed that quantity, the costs can become prohibitive.

- ✔ See Chapter 18 for information on how to avoid cellular data overcharges when taking your Galaxy tablet out and about.

- ✔ Also see Chapter 21 for information on monitoring your mobile data usage.

- ✔ A better way to connect your Galaxy tablet to the Internet is to use the Wi-Fi signal, covered in the next section. The digital cellular network signal makes for a great fallback because it's available in more places than Wi-Fi is.

Understanding Wi-Fi

The digital cellular connection is nice, and it's available pretty much all over, but it costs you moolah. A better option, and one you should seek out when it's available, is *Wi-Fi,* or the same wireless networking standard used by computers for communicating with each other and the Internet.

Making Wi-Fi work on your Galactic tablet requires two steps. First, you must activate Wi-Fi, by turning on the tablet's wireless radio. The second step, covered in the following section, is connecting to a specific wireless network.

Wi-Fi stands for *wireless fidelity.* It's brought to you by the numbers 802.11 and the letters *b, n, g,* and *ac.*

Activating and deactivating Wi-Fi

Follow these carefully written directions to activate Wi-Fi networking on your tablet:

1. **Touch the Apps icon.**

2. **Open the Settings app.**

3. **If necessary, select the Connections tab.**

   Not every version of the Settings app features tabs across the top, shown in Figure 16-1.

4. **Ensure that the button by the Wi-Fi setting is green.**

   Green is on.

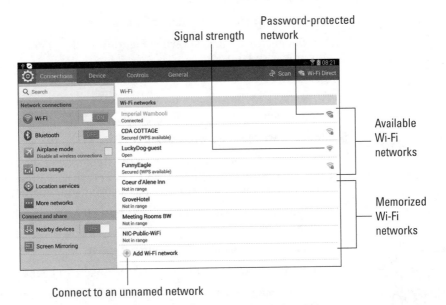

Figure 16-1: Finding a wireless network.

The tablet's Wi-Fi radio is activated. If you've already configured your tablet to connect to an available wireless network, it's connected automatically.

Otherwise, you have to connect to an available network, which is covered in the next section.

To turn off Wi-Fi, repeat the steps in this section but turn the Wi-Fi setting off. Turning off Wi-Fi disconnects the tablet from any wireless networks.

And now, the shortcut: Pull down the notifications shade and use the Wi-Fi Quick Setting to turn Wi-Fi on or off. If the button is green, Wi-Fi is on.

✔ Using Wi-Fi to connect to the Internet doesn't incur data usage charges.

✔ Wi-Fi does place an extra drain on the battery, but it's truly negligible. If you want to save a modicum of juice, especially if you're out and about and don't plan to be near a Wi-Fi access point for any length of time, turn off the Wi-Fi radio as described in this section.

Connecting to a Wi-Fi network

After you've activated the tablet's Wi-Fi radio, you can connect to an available wireless network. Heed these steps:

1. **Touch the Apps icon on the Home screen.**

2. **Open the Settings app.**

3. **If necessary, select the Connections tab.**

   The Connections tab is shown in Figure 16-1. If you don't see it, just continue with Step 4.

4. **Choose Wi-Fi.**

   The Wi-Fi radio must be on for you to find a network. If the button isn't green, touch it.

5. **Choose a wireless network from the list.**

   Available Wi-Fi networks appear on the right side of the screen, as shown in Figure 16-1. When no wireless networks are listed, you're sort of out of luck regarding wireless access from your current location.

   In Figure 16-1, I chose the Imperial Wambooli network, which is my office network.

6. **If the network requires a password, type it.**

   Touch the Password text box to see the onscreen keyboard.

   Touch the Show Password check box so that you can see what you're typing; some of those network passwords can be *long*.

7. **Touch the Connect button.**

   You should be immediately connected to the network. If not, try the password again.

When the tablet is connected to a wireless network, you see the Wi-Fi status icon, shown in the margin. This icon means that the tablet's Wi-Fi is on, connected, and communicating with a Wi-Fi network.

Some wireless networks don't broadcast their names, which adds security but also makes connecting more difficult. In these cases, select the Add Wi-Fi Network option (refer to Figure 16-1) to manually add the network. You need to type the network name, or *SSID,* and choose the type of security. You also need the password if one is used. You can obtain this information from the girl with the pink hair who sold you coffee or from the person in charge of the wireless network at your location.

  ✔ Not every wireless network has a password. They should! Generally speaking, I don't avoid connecting to any public network that lacks a password, but I don't use that network for shopping, banking, or any other secure online activity.

  ✔ Some public networks are open to anyone, but you have to use the Internet app to find a login page that lets you access the network: Simply browse to any page on the Internet, and the login page shows up.

  ✔ Your tablet automatically remembers every Wi-Fi network it has ever been connected to and automatically reconnects upon finding the same network again.

  ✔ To disconnect from a Wi-Fi network, simply turn off Wi-Fi. See the preceding section.

  ✔ Unlike a cellular data network, a Wi-Fi network's broadcast signal goes only so far. My advice is to use Wi-Fi whenever you plan to remain in one location for a while. If you wander too far, your tablet loses the signal and is disconnected.

Using Wi-Fi Direct

The Wi-Fi Direct feature is used to connect your tablet with another Wi-Fi Direct device. It's not necessarily about connecting to the Internet, but rather more about sharing with other mobile devices.

Heed these directions to use Wi-Fi Direct to connect your Samsung Galactic tablet to another Wi-Fi Direct device:

1. **Open the Settings app.**

2. **On the left side of the screen, select Wi-Fi.**

   If necessary, touch the Connections tab to view the Wi-Fi item.

3. **Touch Wi-Fi Direct.**

Your tablet begins to scan for another Wi-Fi Direct device.

4. **On the other device, choose the Wi-Fi Direct command, and then select the Galaxy Tablet from the list of available devices.**

For example, on an Android mobile device, choose the Wi-Fi Direct command and look for the Galaxy tablet's name and ID on the list of available networks.

If scanning stops while you're readying the other device, touch the Scan button atop the screen to start scanning again.

5. **On your Galaxy tablet, touch the Accept button.**

The connection is made.

On both devices, in their respective Wi-Fi Direct screens, you see the other device listed and flagged as connected.

 The key to working with Wi-Fi Direct on your tablet is to use the Share icon. For example, to share a photo, view the photo in the Gallery app and then touch the Share icon. Choose Wi-Fi Direct as the sharing method. Choose the other device from the list of Wi-Fi Direct connected gizmos, and then touch the Done button. On the other device, accept the transfer request, however that works. A notification should appear on the screen.

✔ A better way to share files from your tablet with a computer is by using the USB connection. See Chapter 17.

✔ Your tablet's name was set when you first configured it. You can reset it by choosing the About Device item in the Settings app. (Select the General tab, if necessary.) Select the Device Name item from the right side of the screen, and then type a new name.

A Connection Shared

Your Galaxy tablet has no trouble sniffing out a digital cellular signal, so it can access the Internet just about anywhere. Your laptop might not be so lucky. But hey: You're already paying for the digital cellular signal, right? So why should you bother getting a digital cellular modem for the laptop, as well as buying into another cellular contract, when you could just use your Galactic tablet as a portable modem?

Sharing the tablet's Internet connection is not only possible but also relatively easy. You can go about sharing in one of two ways: The wireless way is to create a mobile hotspot; the wired way is to use the *tethering* technique. Both methods are covered in this section.

Creating a mobile hotspot

You can direct your Galaxy tablet to share its digital cellular connection with as many as five other wireless gizmos. This process is referred to as *creating a mobile wireless hotspot,* though no heat or fire is involved.

To set up a mobile hotspot with your Galaxy tablet, heed these steps:

1. **Turn off the Galaxy tablet's Wi-Fi radio.**

   You can't be using a Wi-Fi connection when you create a Wi-Fi hotspot. Actually, the notion is kind of silly: If the tablet can get a Wi-Fi signal, other gizmos can too, so why bother creating a Wi-Fi hotspot in the first place?

   See the earlier section "Activating and deactivating Wi-Fi" for information on disabling Wi-Fi.

2. **If you can, plug in the tablet.**

   It's okay if you don't find a power outlet, but running a mobile hotspot draws a lot of power. The tablet's battery power drains quickly if you can't plug in.

3. **From the Apps screen, open the Settings app.**

4. **Choose Wi-Fi.**

   If you don't see the Wi-Fi item on the left side of the screen, touch the Connections tab.

5. **Touch the button by Mobile Hotspot.**

   When the button is green, the Mobile Hotspot feature is on.

Additional settings may appear after the Mobile Hotspot feature is activated. For example, you may be able to assign a password or change the network's name. Touch the Menu button to view additional items, just in case they aren't displayed directly on the screen.

While the mobile data signal is being shared, other devices can access it via their Wi-Fi connections. You can continue to use the tablet while it's sharing the digital cellular connection.

To turn off the mobile hotspot, repeat the steps in this section but disable the Mobile Hotspot feature.

✔ The Mobile Hotspot item might also be lurking in the More Networks or More Settings category, or you might have to first choose a Mobile Networks category. The reason for the variety is that different cellular providers may change its location.

✔ The range for the mobile hotspot is about 30 feet.

✔ Some cellular providers allow you to create a mobile hotspot only if you pay a surcharge on your account.

✔ Don't forget to turn off the mobile hotspot when you're done using it. Those data rates can add up!

Sharing the Internet via tethering

Another more personal way to share your Galaxy tablet's digital cellular connection and to get one other device on the Internet is *tethering*. This operation is carried out by connecting the tablet to another gizmo, such as a laptop computer, via a USB cable. Then you activate USB tethering, and the other gizmo is suddenly using the Galaxy tablet like a modem.

To set up tethering on your tablet, heed these directions:

1. **Turn off the tablet's Wi-Fi radio.**

   You can't share a connection with the Wi-Fi radio on; you can share only the digital cellular connection.

2. **Connect the tablet to a PC by using its USB cable.**

   Specifically, the PC must be running a current version of Windows (not Windows XP) or some flavor of the Linux operating system.

3. **Open the Settings app.**

4. **Touch the Connections tab (if necessary).**

5. **Choose More Networks or More Settings.**

6. **Activate the USB Tethering option.**

7. **On the PC, when prompted to specify the type of network to which you've just connected, choose Public.**

To disable the tethering option, repeat these steps but disable the USB Tethering feature in Step 6.

✔ Sharing the digital network connection incurs data usage charges against your cellular data plan. Be careful with your data usage when you're sharing a connection.

✔ You may be prompted on the PC to locate and install software for the tablet. Do so: Accept the installation of new software when prompted by Windows.

The Bluetooth Experience

Computer nerds have long had the desire to connect high-tech gizmos to one another. The Bluetooth standard was developed to sate this desire in a wireless way. Although Bluetooth is wireless *communication,* it's not the same as wireless networking. It's more about connecting peripheral devices, such as keyboards, mice, printers, headphones, and other gear. It all happens in a wireless way, as described in this section.

Understanding Bluetooth

Bluetooth is a peculiar name for a wireless communications standard. Unlike Wi-Fi networking, with Bluetooth you simply connect two gizmos. One would be your Galaxy tablet, and the other would be some type of peripheral, such as a keyboard, a printer, or speakers. Here's how the operation works:

1. **Turn on the Bluetooth wireless radio on both gizmos.**

2. **Make the gizmo you're trying to connect to discoverable.**

3. **On your tablet, choose the peripheral gizmo from the list of Bluetooth devices.**

4. **If necessary, confirm the connection on the peripheral device.**

    For example, you may be asked to input a code or press a button.

5. **Use the device.**

When you're done using the device, you simply turn it off. Because the Bluetooth gizmo is paired with your tablet, it's automatically reconnected the next time you turn it on (that is, if you have Bluetooth activated on the tablet).

Bluetooth devices are marked with the Bluetooth logo, shown in the margin. It's your assurance that the gizmo can work with other Bluetooth devices.

Bluetooth was developed as a wireless version of the old RS-232 standard, the serial port on early personal computers. Essentially, Bluetooth is wireless RS-232, and the variety of devices you can connect to and the things you can do with Bluetooth are similar to what you could do with the old serial port standard.

Activating Bluetooth

To make the Bluetooth connection, you turn on your tablet's Bluetooth radio. Obey these directions:

1. **On the Apps screen, touch the Settings icon.**

2. **Choose the Connection tab.**

   Not all versions of the Settings app feature a Connections tab. If you don't see the tab, don't worry.

3. **Touch the button by the Bluetooth item.**

   When the button is green, Bluetooth is activated.

 When Bluetooth is on, the Bluetooth status icon appears, as shown in the margin.

To turn off Bluetooth, repeat the steps in this section: Touch the button in Step 3 to turn off Bluetooth radio.

 From the And-Now-He-Tells-Us Department, you can quickly activate Bluetooth by using the Quick Actions on the notifications shade. Touch the Bluetooth icon to turn Bluetooth on or off. As a bonus, when you turn Bluetooth on by using the Quick Actions, you're immediately taken to a device-scanning screen. See the next section for more information.

Pairing with a Bluetooth device

To make the Bluetooth connection between your Galaxy tablet and some other gizmo, follow these steps:

1. **Ensure that Bluetooth is on.**

   Refer to the preceding section.

2. **Turn on the Bluetooth gizmo or ensure that its Bluetooth radio is on.**

   Some Bluetooth devices have separate power and Bluetooth switches.

3. **On your tablet, touch the Apps icon on the Home screen and open the Settings app.**

4. **Choose the Connections tab.**

   Not every Settings app has a Connections tab.

5. **Choose Bluetooth.**

Touch the Bluetooth item, not the green button. You'll see a list of available and paired devices shown in the right side of the screen, similar to Figure 16-2. Don't fret if the device you want doesn't yet appear in the list.

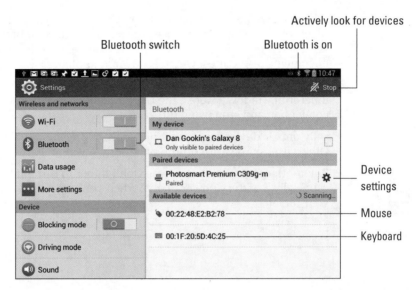

Figure 16-2: Finding Bluetooth gizmos.

6. **If the other device has an option to become visible, select it.**

   For example, some Bluetooth gizmos have a tiny button to press that makes the device visible to other Bluetooth gizmos. (You don't need to make the Galaxy tablet visible unless you're accessing it from another Bluetooth gizmo.)

7. **Touch the Scan button.**

   Eventually, the other device should appear on the Bluetooth window, as shown in Figure 16-2.

8. **Select the device.**

9. **If necessary, type the device's passcode or otherwise acknowledge the connection.**

   Not every device has a passcode. If prompted, acknowledge the passcode on the tablet or the other device.

After you acknowledge the passcode (or not), the Bluetooth gizmo and your tablet are connected and communicating. You can begin using the device.

Connected devices appear at the bottom of the Bluetooth Settings window, under the Paired Devices heading, such as the Photosmart Premium C309g-m printer shown in Figure 16-2.

To break the connection, you can either turn off the gizmo or disable the Bluetooth radio on your tablet. Because the devices are paired, when you turn on Bluetooth and reactivate the device, the connection is instantly reestablished.

- How you use the device depends on what it does. For example, a Bluetooth keyboard can be used for text input, a computer can be accessed for sharing files, and a printer can be used for printing documents or pictures, which is covered in Chapter 12.

- To unpair a device, touch the Settings icon by the device in the Bluetooth window. Choose the Unpair command to break the Bluetooth connection and stop using the device.

- Only unpair devices you don't plan on using again in the future. Otherwise, simply turn off the Bluetooth device.

- Bluetooth can use a lot of power. Don't forget to turn off the device, especially a battery-powered one, when you're no longer using it with your tablet.

17

Connect, Share, and Store

In This Chapter

▶ Making the USB connection

▶ Moving files between a PC and the tablet

▶ Transferring files with Bluetooth

▶ Synchronizing media with doubleTwist

▶ Performing basic file management

▶ Connecting to an HDMI TV

Despite its wireless nature, your Galactic tablet came with a USB cable. That cable not only serves to charge the tablet but can also be used for good old-fashioned wire-based communications. No, you cannot use the USB cable to connect the tablet to the couch, or the toaster, or a particle beam weapon. You can, however, use the USB cable to connect the Galaxy Note or Galaxy Tab to a computer. This chapter describes all the wonderful things that can happen after that connection is made.

The USB Connection

The most direct way to connect a Samsung Galaxy tablet to a computer is by using a wire — specifically, the wire nestled cozily in the heart of a USB cable. You can do lots of things after making the USB connection. Before doing those things, however, you need to connect the cable.

Connecting the tablet to a computer

The USB connection between the Galaxy tablet and your computer works fastest when both devices are physically connected. You make this connection happen by using the USB cable that comes with the tablet. Like nearly every computer cable in the Third Dimension, the USB cable has two ends:

- One end of the USB cable plugs into the computer.

- The other end of the cable plugs into the bottom of the tablet.

The connectors are shaped differently and cannot be plugged in backward or upside down.

After you understand how the cable works, plug the USB cable into one of the computer's USB ports. Then plug the USB cable into the Galaxy tablet. What happens next is described in the following sections.

- By connecting the tablet to your PC, you are adding, or *mounting,* its storage to your computer's storage system. The tablet's internal storage appears under the name Tablet. If a microSD card is installed, its storage shows up as Card. This mounting process allows file transfers to take place.

- Even if you don't use the USB cable to communicate with the computer, the tablet's battery charges when it's connected to a computer's USB port — as long as the computer is turned on, of course.

Dealing with the USB connection in Windows

Upon making the USB connection between the Galaxy Note or Galaxy Tab and a PC, a number of things happen. Don't let any of these things cause you undue alarm.

First, you may see some activity on the PC: some drivers being installed and such. That's normal behavior any time you first connect a new USB gizmo to a Windows computer.

Second, you may see one of two AutoPlay dialog boxes, as shown in Figure 17-1, depending on how the tablet's USB connection is configured. Both are pretty similar.

In Windows 8, things work differently. This prompt appears on the screen: Tap to Choose What Happens with This Device. Click or touch the prompt to view suggestions similar to those found in the AutoPlay dialog boxes (refer to Figure 17-1).

The tablet as   The tablet as
media player   digital camera

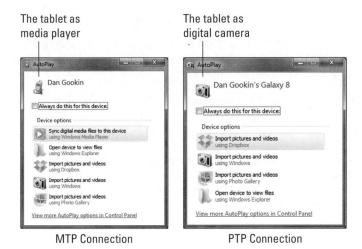

MTP Connection   PTP Connection

Figure 17-1: Windows AutoPlay dialog boxes.

Finally, choose an option from the AutoPlay dialog box or just close the dialog box. From that point on, you'll use Windows or a program on your computer to work with the files on your tablet. Later sections in this chapter provide the details.

✔ See the later section "Configuring the USB connection" for information on the difference between MTP and PTP, the two connection types shown in Figure 17-1.

✔ The AutoPlay dialog box may not appear when you connect the tablet to your PC. It's possible to configure Windows not to display that dialog box. However, if you haven't messed with the AutoPlay settings, an AutoPlay dialog box shows up.

✔ Even if the AutoPlay dialog box doesn't appear, you can still access media and files stored on the tablet from your computer. The later section "Files from Here, Files to There" has details.

 ✔ When the tablet is connected to a computer using the USB connection, the USB notification appears at the top of the screen, as shown in the margin.

 ✔ If you're nerdy, you can open the tablet's icon in the Computer window; press the Win+E keyboard shortcut on your PC to see the Computer window. You'll find the tablet listed as either Portable Media Player (MTP) or Digital Camera (PTP).

Connecting your tablet to a Mac

You need special software to goad your Galaxy Note or Galaxy Tab and Macintosh into communicating; the Mac doesn't natively recognize the tablet. That's probably because the Mac would prefer you had an iPad. As if.

To do the file transfer thing between your Mac and Galaxy tablet, you need to obtain special software, the Android File Transfer app. Download that software from this website: www.android.com/filetransfer.

Install the software. Run it. From that point on, when you connect your Galactic tablet to the Macintosh, you see a special window, similar to what's shown in Figure 17-2. It lists the tablet's folders and files. Use that window for file management, as covered later in this chapter.

MicroSD card storage

Internal storage

Figure 17-2: The Android File Transfer program.

You can also transfer files easily between your tablet and a Macintosh (or a PC) by using Dropbox. See the later section, "Sharing files with Dropbox."

Configuring the USB connection

A Windows computer utterly refuses to recognize your Galaxy tablet as a tablet. In fact, the concept confuses Microsoft. Therefore, when you connect your tablet to a PC, it assumes that the device is either some type of external storage or a digital camera. Sad but true.

The good news is that it doesn't matter how the PC looks at your Galaxy Note or Galaxy Tab. Either way, you can still move files back and forth and sync information. The better option is external storage, which is what the tablet does automatically.

- ✔ The external storage option is MTP, which stands for *Media Transfer Protocol*.
- ✔ The digital camera option is PTP, which stands for *Picture Transfer Protocol*.

To set one option or the other, follow these steps after connecting your tablet to the computer:

1. **Choose the USB notification.**

   The USB notification icon is shown in the margin.

2. **Select either Media Device (MTP) or Camera (PTP).**

   Making the selection instantly reconfigures the tablet. You don't need to disconnect the tablet from the computer.

The USB notification appears when the tablet is connected to a computer. That's the only time you can configure the USB connection.

These steps apply also when you attach your tablet to a Macintosh. Even so, the Mac recognizes the tablet only when it's configured as an MTP device.

Disconnecting the tablet from a computer

The process of disconnecting your tablet from a computer is cinchy: When you're done transferring files, music, or other media between your computer and the tablet, close all the programs and folders you have opened, specifically those you've used to work with the tablet's storage. Then you can disconnect the USB cable. That's it.

It's a Bad Idea to unplug the tablet while you're transferring information or while a folder window is open on the computer. Doing so could damage the tablet's internal storage, rendering some of the information kept there unreadable. So just to be safe, before disconnecting, close those programs and folder windows you've opened.

Unlike other external storage on the Macintosh, there's no need to eject the tablet's storage when you're done accessing it. Quit the Android File Transfer program on the Mac, and then unplug the tablet. The Mac won't get angry.

Files from Here, Files to There

The point of making the USB connection between your Galaxy Note or Galaxy Tab and the computer is to exchange files. You can't just wish the files over. Instead, I recommend following the advice in this section.

 A good understanding of basic file operations is necessary before you attempt file transfers between your computer and the Galaxy tablet. You need to know how to copy, move, rename, and delete files. It also helps to be familiar with what folders are and how they work. The good news is that you don't need to manually calculate a 64-bit cyclical redundancy check on the data, nor do you need to know what a parity bit is.

Transferring files to the tablet

I can think of plenty of reasons why you would want to copy a file from your computer to the tablet. You can copy over your pictures and videos, and you can copy over music or audio files. You can even copy vCards that you export from your e-mail program, which helps you build your tablet's address book.

Follow these steps to copy a file from your computer to the tablet:

1. **Connect the Galaxy Note or Galaxy Tab to the computer by using the USB cable.**

   Specific directions are offered earlier in this chapter.

2. **On a PC, if the AutoPlay dialog box appears, select the Open Folder/ Device to View Files option.**

   When the AutoPlay dialog box doesn't appear, open the Computer window, then open the Galaxy tablet's icon, and then touch the Tablet icon, which represents internal storage.

   The tablet's folder window you see looks like any other folder in Windows. The difference is that the files and folders in that window are on the Galaxy tablet, not on your computer.

   On a Macintosh, the Android File Transfer program should start and appear on the screen (refer to Figure 17-2).

3. **Locate the files you want to copy to the tablet.**

   Open the folder that contains the files, or somehow have the file icons visible on the screen.

4. **Drag the file icon from its folder on your computer to the tablet's folder window.**

If you want to be specific, drag the file to the Download folder; otherwise, you can place the file in the Galaxy tablet's root folder, as shown in Figure 17-3. Try to avoid dragging the file into other, specific folders, which would make the file more difficult to locate in the future.

The same file-dragging technique can be used for transferring files from a Macintosh. You need to drag the icon(s) to the Android File Transfer window, which works just like any folder window in the Finder.

5. **Close the folder windows and disconnect the USB cable when you're done.**

   Refer to specific instructions earlier in this chapter.

Drag files to here to
copy to the root folder

Galaxy tablet

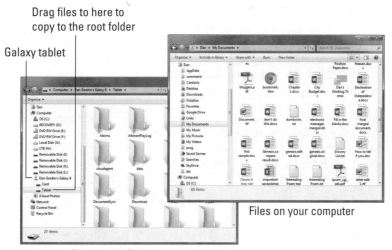

Files on your computer

Files on the Galaxy tablet

Figure 17-3: Copying files to a Galaxy tablet.

Any files you've copied are now stored on the tablet. What you do with them next depends on the reasons you copied the files: to view pictures, use the Gallery, import vCards, use the Contacts app, listen to music, or use the Music app, for example.

The best way to move music and pictures over to your Galaxy tablet from the computer is to synchronize them. See Chapter 13.

The media card transfer

Another way to get files between a computer and your Galactic tablet is to use the microSD card. It can be removed from the tablet and then inserted into a computer. From that point, the files on the card can be read by the computer just as they can be read from any media card.

See Chapter 1 for details on how to remove the microSD card from your tablet. You can't just yank out the thing! You also need a microSD adapter to insert the card into a media reader on the computer. Or you can get a microSD card thumb drive adapter, in which case you merely need a USB port to access the card's information.

Copying files to your computer

After you've survived the ordeal of copying files from your computer to your Galaxy tablet, copying files in the other direction is a cinch: Follow the steps in the preceding section, but in Steps 3 and 4 drag the File icons from the tablet's folder window (or the Android File Transfer window on a Mac) to your computer.

My advice is to drag the files to your computer's desktop, unless you know of another location where you want the files copied.

- Files you've downloaded on the Galaxy tablet are stored in the Download folder.

- Pictures and videos on the Galaxy tablet are stored in the DCIM/Camera folder.

- Music on the Galaxy tablet is stored in the Music folder, organized by artist.

- Quite a few files can be found in the *root folder,* the main folder on the tablet, which you see when the tablet is mounted in your computer's storage system and you open its folder.

Connecting wirelessly with Kies Air

A perfectly wireless way to connect your Galaxy Note or Galaxy Tab with a computer is to use the Kies Air app. Provided that both the tablet and computer can access the same Wi-Fi network, the connection can be made and files can be transferred with relatively little pain.

Both your computer and Galaxy tablet must be connected to the same wireless (Wi-Fi) network for the connection to work.

Follow these steps to use Kies Air to share files with your computer:

1. **Ensure that your tablet is connected to the same Wi-Fi network as your computer.**

2. **Start the Kies Air app.**

    It's found on the Apps screen.

3. **Touch the Start button.**

    Kies Air should immediately recognize your Wi-Fi network. It now sits and waits for an incoming request from your computer.

4. **On your computer, open the web browser app, such as Internet Explorer, Chrome, or Safari.**

5. **On your computer, type in the web browser's address box the URL listed on your tablet's touchscreen.**

    On my screen, I see the URL `http://192.168.1.143:8080`. What you see will probably be different.

    After typing the URL in your computer's web browser, you'll see an Access Request prompt on the tablet. The prompt should state the name of the computer requesting access.

6. **In the proper location on the web page shown on your computer, type the PIN listed on the tablet's touchscreen, and then click the OK button.**

    The tablet and computer are now connected via the Wi-Fi network.

A web page appears on the computer in the web browser's window, similar to what's shown in Figure 17-4. That web page is being hosted by your tablet. It allows access to the device's resources, as illustrated in the figure.

Browse the various categories on the web page to explore files and media on your tablet.

To download an item, or copy it from the tablet to your computer, click to select the item (as shown in Figure 17-4) and then click the Download link. The item is transferred to your computer just like any file you download from the Internet, although the download comes from your Galaxy Note or Galaxy Tab.

To send a file to the tablet, click one of the Upload links, as illustrated in Figure 17-4. Click the Choose File button and use the Upload dialog box to find a file. Click to select that file, and then click the OK button to send it from the computer to the tablet.

Download from the
tablet to the computer

Upload from the
computer to the tablet

Select items

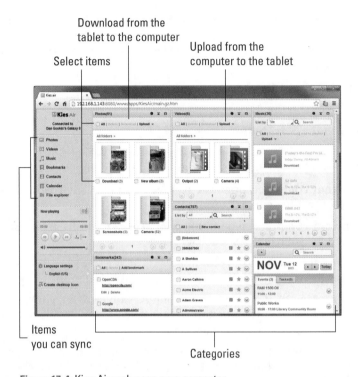

Items
you can sync

Categories

Figure 17-4: Kies Air web page on a computer.

To end the Kies Air connection, touch the Stop button on the tablet's touchscreen. You can then close the web browser window on your computer.

- While the connection is active, you can quickly switch to the Kies Air
  app on the tablet by choosing the Kies Air notification.

- My guess is that Kies is pronounced "kees." I have no idea what it stands
  for or whether it's even an acronym at all.

- Don't click the Back button on your computer's web browser screen
  when using the Kies Air website. Just use the controls on the web page
  itself to navigate.

Sharing files with Dropbox

A handy way to share files between a computer and your Galaxy Note or
Galaxy Tab is to use the Dropbox app. Once installed, any files saved to your
Dropbox folders are immediately synchronized across both your computer
and the tablet. That makes sharing files a snap.

If Dropbox isn't already installed on your tablet, obtain the Dropbox app by
visiting the Google Play Store. It's free. See Chapter 15 for details on using the
Play Store app.

On a computer, obtain a copy of Dropbox by visiting the Dropbox website at `www.dropbox.com` and downloading the program. Dropbox is free and comes with a generous amount of online storage at no extra charge.

Dropbox is used on your computer just like any other storage. You can create folders and files, manage files, and do anything else you'd normally do using Windows Explorer on a PC or the Finder on a Mac. The difference is that all the files and folders you create in your Dropbox folder are duplicated on other computers and devices that share your Dropbox account.

For example, files you save to your Dropbox folder on a PC are instantly available via the Dropbox app on your Galaxy tablet. To move a file back and forth, just save it to a Dropbox folder. The process is nearly instantaneous.

✔ File management on your Galaxy tablet is done by using the My Files app. See the later section, "Managing files."

✔ You can configure the tablet so that pictures and videos you take are instantly uploaded to Dropbox. See Chapter 12.

Galactic Storage

Somewhere, deep in the bosom of your Galaxy tablet, lies a storage device. It's like the hard drive in your computer. The thing can't be removed, but that's not the point. The point is that the storage is used for your apps, music, videos, pictures, and a host of other information. This section describes what you can do to manage that storage.

✔ The Galaxy Note and Galaxy Tab come with either 16GB or 32GB of internal storage. Future tablets may have even more storage.

✔ Removable storage is also available in the form of a microSD card.

✔ A GB is a gigabyte, or one billion bytes (characters) of storage. A typical 2-hour movie occupies about 4GB of storage, but most things you store on the tablet — music and pictures, for example — take up only a sliver of storage. Those items do, however, occupy more storage space the more you use the tablet.

Reviewing storage stats

To find out how much storage space is available on your tablet, follow these steps:

1. **On the Home screen, touch the Apps icon.**

2. **Open the Settings app.**

3. **Choose Storage.**

If necessary, choose the General category from atop the screen. Otherwise, you'll find the Storage item listed on the left side of the screen.

The right side of the screen details information about storage space in the tablet's internal storage, shown as Device Memory in Figure 17-5.

Used space   Free space

What's consuming storage

Figure 17-5: Galaxy tablet storage information.

You can choose a category to see more information or to launch a program. For example, touching Used Space (refer to Figure 17-5) displays a list of items occupying that chunk of memory. You can choose a subcategory, such as Applications, Pictures, or Videos, to view more details.

When a microSD card is installed, information about its storage appears in the SD Card area, shown in Figure 17-5. Alas, further detail is unavailable. You'll have to use a file manager app to review the storage device's contents. See the next section.

✔ Things that consume the most storage space are videos, music, and pictures, in that order.

✔ To see how much storage space is left, refer to the Available Space item.

✔ Don't bemoan that the Total Space value is far less than the tablet's or media card's capacity. For example, in Figure 17-5, my 16GB media card shows only 14.83GB available. The missing space is considered overhead, as are several gigabytes taken by the government for tax purposes.

Managing files

You probably didn't get a Galaxy Note or Galaxy Tab because you enjoy managing files on a computer and wanted another gizmo to hone your skills. Even so, you can practice the same type of file manipulation on the tablet as you would on a computer. Is there a need to do so? Of course not! But if you want to get dirty with files, you can.

The main tool for managing files is the My Files app. It's a traditional type of file management app, which means if you detest managing files on your computer, you'll experience the same pain and frustration on your Galaxy tablet. The My Files app is shown in Figure 17-6.

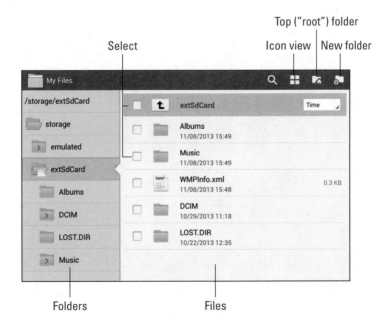

Figure 17-6: Galaxy tablet file management.

✔ Other icons appear atop the My Files app screen, depending on what you're doing in the app. For example, to remove a folder or file, touch its check box and then choose the Delete (trash can) icon.

✔ If your tablet doesn't come with the My Files app, you can obtain one of many similar file management apps at the Play Store.

18

Taking the Galaxy with You

In This Chapter

▶ Bringing the Galaxy tablet on a trip

▶ Taking the tablet on an airplane

▶ Using the Galaxy tablet overseas

▶ Avoiding those data-roaming charges

*L*ast time I checked, the Galaxy Note and the Galaxy Tab didn't have a rolling tread, like a tank. That would be nifty, and I'm sure that more Real Men would buy a Samsung Galaxy tablet with a tank tread, but it's not my point: Your tablet is a mobile device. It's wireless. It runs on battery power. You can take the Galaxy tablet with you everywhere you go and not get those peculiar looks you get when you take the washing machine with you.

How far can you go with your tablet? As far as you want. As long as you can carry the tablet with you, it goes where you go. How it functions may change depending on your environment. You can do a few things to prepare before you go, which are all covered in this chapter.

Before You Go

Unless the house is on fire, you should prepare several things before leaving on a trip with your Galactic tablet. First and most important, of course, is to charge the thing. I plug my tablet in overnight before I leave the next day.

Another good thing to do is to synchronize media with your computer. This operation isn't so much for taking media with you but rather to ensure that you have a backup of the tablet's media on your computer. See Chapter 17 for synchronization information.

Consider getting some e-books for the road. I prefer to sit and stew over the Play Books online library before I leave, as opposed to wandering aimlessly in some airport sundry store, trying hard to focus on the good books rather than on the salty snacks. Chapter 14 covers reading e-books on your Galaxy tablet.

Another nifty thing to do is to save some web pages for later reading. I usually start my day by perusing online articles and angry editorials in the local paper. Because I don't have time to read that stuff before I leave, and I do have time on the plane and I'm extremely unwilling to pay for in-flight Wi-Fi, I save my favorite websites for later reading. Here's how to save a web page by using the Internet app:

1. **Navigate to the page you want to save for later reading.**

2. **Touch the Menu button.**

3. **Choose the Save for Offline Reading command.**

   The page is downloaded, saved to the tablet's internal storage.

Repeat these steps for each web page you want to read when offline.

To view the page, touch the Bookmarks icon, and then touch the Saved Pages tab. You see the web page listed, along with other items you've downloaded.

The online problem with saving a website is that not every version of the Internet app offers this feature. If you don't see the Save for Offline Reading command in Step 3, you can't save the web page.

Galaxy Travel Tips

I'm not a frequent flier, but I am a nerd. The most amount of junk I've carried with me on a flight is two laptop computers and three smartphones. I know that's not a record, but it's enough to warrant my list of travel tips, all of which apply to taking the Galaxy tablet with you on an extended journey:

- ✔ Take the Galaxy tablet's AC adapter and USB cable with you. Put them in your carry-on luggage. Many airports feature USB chargers, so you can charge the tablet in an airport if you need to.

- ✔ At the security checkpoint, place your tablet in a bin by itself or with other electronics.

- ✔ Use the Calendar app to keep track of your flights. The event title serves as the airline and flight number. For the event time, use the takeoff and landing schedules. For the location, list the origin and destination airport codes. And, in the Description field, put the flight reservation number. If you're using separate calendars (categories), specify the Travel calendar for your flight.

✔ See Chapter 14 for more information on the Calendar app.

✔ Some airlines feature Android apps you can use while traveling. Find those apps by searching for the airline's name in the Play Store app. You can use the apps to not only keep track of flights but also to check in: Eventually, printed tickets will disappear, and you'll merely show your "ticket" on the tablet's touchscreen, which is then scanned at the gate.

Into the Wild Blue Yonder

It truly is the most trendy of things to be aloft with the latest mobile gizmo. Like taking a smartphone on a plane, however, you have to follow some rules. Although the Galaxy tablet isn't a smartphone, you still have to heed the flight crew's warnings regarding smartphones.

First and foremost, turn off the Galaxy tablet when instructed to do so. Directions are given before takeoff and landing, so be prepared. This rule may change in the future, so simply obey the flight crew.

Before takeoff, you'll most likely want to put the tablet in Airplane mode. Yep, it's the same Airplane mode you see on a smartphone: The various scary and dangerous wireless radios on the tablet are disabled in that mode. With Airplane mode active, you are free to use the tablet in-flight and face little risk of your tablet causing the plane's navigational equipment to fail and the entire flight to end as a fireball over Wyoming.

To enter Airplane mode on the Galaxy tablet, follow these steps just before takeoff:

1. **Open the Settings app.**

   It's found on the Apps screen, though if you're an old pro, consider using the shortcut found atop the notifications shade.

2. **If your tablet's version of the Settings app features tabs, touch the Connections tab.**

3. **Select the Airplane Mode item. If you don't see that item, select More Settings first.**

4. **Touch the OK button if prompted.**

   The tablet turns off Wi-Fi and Bluetooth if they were on when you first activated Airplane mode.

 When the tablet is in Airplane mode, a special icon appears in the status area at the top of the screen.

And now, for the shortcut: To put the Galaxy tablet into Airplane mode, press and hold down the Power button and choose the Airplane Mode command.

Or pull down the notifications shade and touch the Airplane Mode Quick Setting.

By the way, you can reactivate Wi-Fi in Airplane mode. It's okay to do so, especially when you plan on overpaying for in-flight Wi-Fi.

To exit Airplane mode, repeat the steps in this section but remove the green check mark by touching the square next to Airplane Mode.

- ✔ Officially, the Galaxy tablet must be powered off when the plane is taking off or landing. See Chapter 2 for information on turning off the tablet.

- ✔ You can compose e-mail while the tablet is in Airplane mode. The messages aren't sent until you disable Airplane mode and connect again with a data network.

- ✔ Bluetooth networking is disabled in Airplane mode. Even so:

- ✔ Many airlines now feature wireless networking onboard, which you can use with the Galaxy tablet — if you're willing to pay for the service. Simply activate Wi-Fi on the tablet, per the directions in Chapter 17, and then connect to the in-flight wireless network when it's available.

The Galaxy Goes Abroad

You have no worries taking the Wi-Fi Galaxy tablet abroad. Because it uses Wi-Fi signals, your biggest issue is simply finding Wi-Fi Internet access so that you can use your tablet's communications capabilities. That rule also holds true for the cellular tablet, which can also use Wi-Fi abroad. But for the digital cellular signal, more precautions need to take place. After all, you don't want to incur data-roaming charges, especially when they're priced in *zloty* or *pengö*.

Traveling overseas with the tablet

The Galaxy Note and Galaxy Tab both work great overseas. The two resources you need to heed are a way to recharge the battery and a way to access Wi-Fi. As long as you have both of them, you're pretty much set. (Data roaming is covered in the next section.)

The tablet's AC plug can easily plug into a foreign AC adapter, which allows you to charge the tablet in outer Wamboolistan. I charged my tablet nightly while I spent time in France, and it worked like a charm. All you need is an adapter. You don't need a transformer or power converter, just the dongle that allows you to plug into a wall socket. That's it. You're good.

Wi-Fi is pretty universal, and as long as your location offers this service, you can connect the tablet and pick up your e-mail, browse the web, or do whatever other Internet activities you desire. Even if you have to pay for Wi-Fi access, I believe that you'll find it less expensive than paying a data-roaming charge.

If you want to use Skype, you need to set up international credit on Skype, even when you have Wi-Fi. See Chapter 9 for more information on making Skype calls.

Disabling data roaming

When I've taken my cellular Galaxy tablet abroad, I've kept it in Airplane mode. If you do that, there's no chance of data-roaming charges, and you can still enable Wi-Fi. Even so, and just to be sure, you can disable data roaming on the Galaxy tablet by obeying these steps:

1. **On the Home screen, touch the Apps icon.**

2. **Open the Settings app.**

3. **Select the Connection tab from the top of the screen.**

    It's okay if you don't see the tab; not every Galaxy tablet uses the same Settings app.

4. **Choose the More Settings or Mobile Network command.**

5. **Select Global Data Roaming Access.**

6. **Select Deny Data Roaming Access.**

There's a chance that the Mobile Network screen may not show the Deny Data Roaming Access option. Each cellular provider may place the option in a different spot, or even on a different screen. If you can't find it, try touching the Menu button to see if it appears on a menu.

Of course, you don't need to disable data roaming or keep the tablet stuck in Airplane mode. You can simply wait for your data bill's arrival in the mail. I prefer not to have such a surprise.

Before you travel abroad, contact your digital cellular provider and ask about overseas data roaming. A subscription service or other options may be available, especially when you plan to stay overseas for an extended length of time.

19

Customize Your Galaxy

· ·

In This Chapter

▶ Changing the background image

▶ Putting apps and widgets on the Home screen

▶ Rearranging things on the Home screen

▶ Managing Home screen panels

▶ Removing the screen lock

▶ Adding a pattern lock, PIN, or password

▶ Changing the notification ringtone

▶ Adjusting the brightness

· ·

t's entirely possible to own the amazing Galaxy Note or the spectacular Galaxy Tab for the rest of your life and never even once bother to customize the gizmo. It's not only possible, it's sad. That's because there exists great potential to create your own tablet. You can alter so many things, from the way it looks to the way it sounds. The reason for customizing is not simply to change things because you can but to make the tablet work best for how you use it. After all, it's *your* Galaxy tablet.

Home Screen Decorating

Lots of interesting doodads festoon your tablet's Home screen, like bugs on a windshield after a long trip. You can set the background, add an icon or a widget, and rearrange everything to your heart's content. Or when your heart isn't content, you choose to make your gall bladder content. Either way, directions and suggestions are offered in this section.

Hanging new wallpaper

The Home screen has two types of backgrounds, or *wallpapers:* traditional and live. *Live* wallpaper is animated. A not-so-live *(traditional)* wallpaper can be any image, such as a picture you've taken and stored in the Gallery app.

To set a new wallpaper for the Home screen, obey these steps:

1. **Long-press any empty part of the Home screen.**

   The empty part doesn't have a shortcut icon or widget floating on it.

   Upon success, you see the Home Screen menu, shown in Figure 19-1.

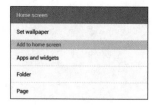

Figure 19-1: The Home Screen menu.

2. **Choose Set Wallpaper.**

   The Set Wallpaper menu appears. You can choose to set wallpaper for the Home screen, the Lock screen, or both screens at once.

3. **Choose on which screen to set the wallpaper.**

   Choose Home Screen or Lock Screen to set separate wallpapers for each screen. Choose Home and Lock Screens to set both to the same image.

4. **Choose the wallpaper image source.**

   Use the Select Wallpaper From menu to select a wallpaper type. You'll find at least three types:

   - *Gallery:* Choose a still image from the Gallery app.

   - *Live Wallpapers:* Choose an animated or interactive wallpaper from a list.

   - *Wallpapers:* Choose a wallpaper from a range of images preinstalled on the tablet.

   Additional types may show up, depending on the apps installed on the tablet.

5. **Select a wallpaper type.**

   For the Gallery option, browse the albums in the Gallery app to select an image. Crop the image to select the portion you want included on the Home screen.

   For certain live wallpapers, the Settings icon may appear. The settings let you customize certain aspects of the interactive wallpaper.

6. **Touch the Done or Set Wallpaper button to confirm your selection.**

   The new wallpaper takes over the Home screen, the lock screen, or both screens.

Live wallpaper features some form of animation, which can often be interactive. Otherwise, the wallpaper image scrolls slightly as you swipe from one Home screen panel to another.

✔ If prompted, be careful how you crop the wallpaper image. When both Home and Lock screens are chosen, zoom out (pinch your fingers on the touchscreen) to ensure that the entire image is cropped properly.

✔ The Zedge app is an über-repository of wallpaper images, collected from Android users all over the world. Check out Zedge at the Google Play Store; see Chapter 15.

✔ See Chapter 12 for more information about the Gallery app, including information on how to crop an image.

Adding apps to the Home screen

The first thing I did on my Galaxy tablet was to place my most favorite apps on the Home screen. Here's how that works:

1. **Touch the Apps icon on the Home screen.**

2. **Long-press the app icon you want to add to the Home screen.**

   After a moment, the Home screen panel overview is displayed at the bottom of the screen, as shown in Figure 19-2. The Remove and Create Folder icons may appear atop the screen, as opposed to the left side. Other icons may join them as well.

3. **Drag the app to a position on the Home screen.**

   The app icon remains stuck under your fingertip.

4. **Position the app where you want it to go and then lift your finger.**

Drag here to move
one panel left

Drag the icon to a
position on the
Home screen

Drag here to move
one panel right

Home screen panel   Add panel
previews

Figure 19-2: Stick an app on the Home screen.

Don't worry if the app isn't in the exact spot you want. The later section "Moving and removing icons and widgets" describes how to rearrange icons on the Home screen.

The app hasn't moved: What you see is a copy, or a shortcut. You can still find the app on the Apps screen, but now the app is — more conveniently — available on the Home screen.

✔ Everything on the Home screen is movable. If you don't want an app or a widget on the main Home screen panel, move it. See the later section "Moving and removing icons and widgets."

✔ Keep your favorite apps, those you use most often, on the Home screen.

✔ Icons on the Home screen are aligned to a grid. You can't stuff more icons on the Home screen than will fit in the grid, so when a Home screen panel is full of icons (or widgets), use another Home screen. You can also add Home screen panels, as described in the "Managing multiple Home screen panels" section.

Building app folders

The Galaxy tablet has room for only seven Home screen panels, maximum. Each panel has room for so many icons, depending on the size of the tablet. For example, a Galaxy Note 10.1 has room for 48 icons on each Home screen panel. An 8-inch Galaxy Tab 3, on the other hand, has room for only 30 icons on each Home screen panel. Obviously, at some point, you're going to run out of room for apps on the Home screen.

Actually, you won't run out of room for app icons as long as you employ the concept of app folders.

An *app folder* is simply a collection of two or more apps, both in the same spot on the Home screen. Figure 19-3 illustrates an app folder on the Home screen, shown both closed and open.

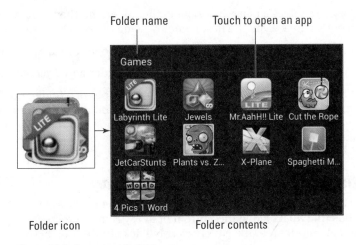

Figure 19-3: Anatomy of a folder.

To create a folder, follow these steps:

1. **On the Home screen, touch the Menu button.**

2. **Choose Create Folder.**

3. **Type a name for the folder.**

   Be short and descriptive.

4. **Touch the OK button to create the newly named folder.**

   The folder is created, but it's empty.

5. **Drag icons into the folder.**

   Move icons from the Home screen into the folder. You can drag icons into the folder also from the Apps screen.

Open a folder by touching it. You can then start an app by touching its icon.

- ✓ With some tablets, you can quickly build a folder by dragging one app icon over another. The two icons appear inside a black oval, as shown in Figure 19-3.

- ✓ Folders can be created also by dragging an app icon to the Create folder icon (shown in Figure 19-2).

- ✓ Folders are managed just like other icons on the Home screen. You can drag them around by long-pressing them, and you can delete them. See the later section "Moving and removing icons and widgets."

- ✓ Change a folder's name by opening the folder and then touching the folder's name. Type the new name by using the onscreen keyboard.

- ✓ Add more apps to a folder by dragging them over the folder's icon.

- ✓ To remove an icon from a folder, open the folder and drag out the icon.

- ✓ When the second-to-last last icon is dragged out of a folder, the folder should be removed. If not, drag the last icon out, and then remove the folder as described in the later section "Moving and removing icons and widgets."

Putting an app on the Favorites tray

Some Galaxy tablets feature a Favorites tray on the Home screen. It's a row of app icons that floats along the bottom of every Home screen panel. Or when the tablet is reoriented, the Favorites tray sticks to the side of the screen. Either way, the same icons still appear on every Home screen panel.

To add an icon to the Favorites tray, first move off an existing icon: Long-press the icon and drag it to the Home screen. Then you can drag into the blank spot any other icon. Or you can do both actions at once: Drag an icon onto the Favorites tray and one of the existing icons swaps places with it.

- ✓ Unlike on the Home screen, you cannot create folders on the Favorites tray.

- ✓ To determine whether your Galaxy tablet features a Favorites tray, swipe the Home screen left or right. If the bottom row of icons remains on both screens, you are looking at the Favorites tray.

Slapping down widgets

Just as you can add apps to the Home screen, you can also add widgets. A *widget* works like a tiny, interactive or informative window, often providing a gateway into another app on the tablet.

Both the Galaxy Note and Galaxy Tab come with a smattering of widgets preaffixed to the Home screen, possibly just to show you how they can be used. You can place even more widgets on the Home screen by following these steps:

1. **Touch the Apps icon on the Home screen.**

2. **Touch the Widgets category atop the screen.**

   The widgets appear on the Apps screen in little preview windows. Pay attention to their size: Some widgets are bulky and can fit only on fairly empty Home screen panels.

3. **Scroll the list to find the widget you want to add.**

4. **Long-press the widget, and drag it to a Home screen panel.**

   The widget is plopped on the Home screen, as shown in Figure 19-4.

Long-press the widget   Position the widget   Resize the widget
on a Home screen panel

Figure 19-4: Adding a widget to the Home screen.

You can resize some widgets after they're on the Home screen or anytime. Touch the widget until you see an orange border, as illustrated in the figure, and then drag your finger on the touchscreen to resize the widget. Touch elsewhere on the touchscreen when you're done resizing.

✓ The variety of available widgets depends on the apps installed. Some apps come with widgets; some don't. Some widgets are independent of any app.

✓ More widgets are available at the Google Play Store. See Chapter 15.

✔ You cannot install a widget when the Home screen has no room for it. Choose another panel or remove icons or widgets to make room.

✔ To remove a widget, see the next section, "Moving and removing icons and widgets."

Moving and removing icons and widgets

Icons and widgets are fastened to the Home screen by something akin to the same glue they use on sticky notes. You can easily pick up an icon or a widget, move it around, and then restick it. Unlike sticky notes, the icons and widgets never just fall off, or so I'm told.

To move an icon or a widget, long-press it. Eventually, the icon seems to lift and break free, as shown in Figure 19-5.

Long-press to lift the icon   Delete the icon or widget

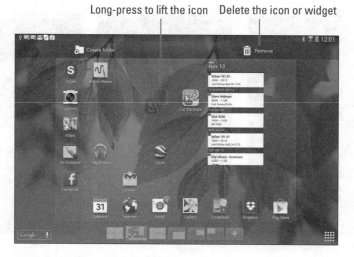

Figure 19-5: Moving an icon about.

You can drag a free icon to another position on the Home screen or to another Home screen panel, or you can drag it to the Remove (trash can) icon that appears on the Home screen, as shown in Figure 19-5.

Widgets can be moved around or deleted in the same manner as icons.

✔ Dragging a Home screen icon or widget to the Remove icon ousts that icon or widget from the Home screen. It doesn't uninstall the app or widget, which is still found on the Apps screen. In fact, you can always add the icon or widget to the Home screen again, as described earlier in this chapter.

✔ When an icon hovers over the Remove icon, ready to be deleted, its color changes to red.

- ✔ See Chapter 15 for information on uninstalling applications.

- ✔ The Create Folder icon, shown in Figure 19-5, is used to create app folders. Simply drag an app to that icon and name the folder. Also see the earlier section "Building app folders."

- ✔ Your clue that an icon or a widget is free and clear to navigate is that the Remove icon appears (refer to Figure 19-5).

Managing multiple Home screen panels

Your Galactic tablet ships with a small smattering of Home screen panels, probably three. But that's not the limit of your Home screen neighborhood. It's possible to expand the number of panels to seven. You can add new panels as you need them, remove empty panels, and even set which is the primary one.

I know: It's difficult to handle such flexibility while not wearing your yoga pants. You can manage.

To add or remove Home screen panels, heed these directions:

1. **At the Home screen, touch the Menu button.**

2. **Choose the Edit Page command.**

   You can also pinch the Home screen to summon the Edit Page command. Either way, you'll see an overview of all Home screen panels, similar to what's shown in Figure 19-6.

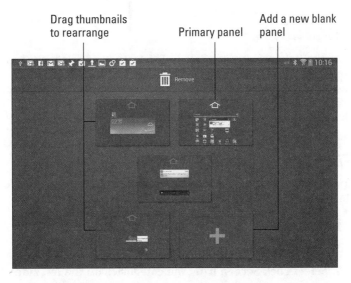

Figure 19-6: Manipulating Home screen panels.

3. **Work with the Home screen panels.**

   You can do four things:

   - *Remove:* To remove a Home screen panel, drag it to the Remove icon. If the panel has icons or widgets, you'll see a warning. If prompted, touch the OK or Yes button to confirm the deletion.

   - *Add:* To add a Home screen panel, touch the thumbnail with a plus icon, as illustrated in Figure 19-6. If you don't see a thumbnail with a plus icon, you can't add any additional panels.

   - *Rearrange:* Drag a panel around to change the order in which it appears.

   - *Set the primary Home page:* The thumbnail with the highlighted Home icon is the primary Home screen panel. To set that primary panel, touch the Home icon.

4. **Touch the Back button or press the Home key when you're done editing.**

You cannot undo a Home screen panel deletion. You have to add a new blank panel and then populate it with icons and widgets.

- ✔ The primary Home screen panel is the one you're returned to when you press the Home key.

- ✔ You can add a new panel to the Home screen also by choosing the Page command from the Home Screen menu, shown in Figure 19-1.

Lock Your Tablet

Both the Galaxy Note and Galaxy Tab feature a basic lock screen: Simply slide your finger across the touchscreen and the tablet is unlocked and ready to use. If you prefer to have a lock that's not so easy to pick, you can choose from one of several types of secure lock screens: Pattern, PIN, and Password, as well as the less secure Face and Voice lock screens.

Finding the locks

Lock screen security is set on the Set Screen Lock or Lock Screen window. Here's how to get there:

1. **On the Home screen, touch the Apps icon.**

2. **Open the Settings app.**

3. **Select Lock Screen from the categories on the left side of the window.**

   If you don't see the Lock Screen item, touch the Device tab atop the screen.

4. **On the right side of the screen, select Screen Lock.**

5. **If a secure screen lock is already set, you must trace the pattern or input the PIN or password to continue.**

The window lists several types of lock settings:

- ✓ **Swipe:** Unlock the tablet by swiping your finger across the screen. Next to not having a lock, this is the least secure lock.

- ✓ **Pattern:** Trace a pattern on the touchscreen to unlock the tablet.

- ✓ **PIN:** Unlock the tablet by typing a personal identification number (PIN).

- ✓ **Password:** Type a password to unlock the tablet.

- ✓ **None:** The screen doesn't lock. Choosing this option disables all locks.

Two additional items might also be found on some Galaxy tablets:

- ✓ **Face Unlock:** Use the tablet's front camera and your adorable face as the unlocking mechanism.

- ✓ **Face and Voice:** Add a vocal utterance to the face unlock feature, which doesn't make the lock more secure but does make it more interesting.

To set or remove a lock, refer to the following sections.

Removing the screen lock

You use the Screen Lock window not only to place a lock on the tablet but also to remove existing locks.

After visiting the Screen Lock window, as described in the preceding section, you can choose the None option to remove all screen locks. To restore the original screen lock, choose Swipe.

Setting a PIN

Perhaps the most common and (according to the Screen Lock window) the second most secure method of locking the tablet is to use a PIN, or personal identification number. This type of screen lock is also employed as a backup for the less-secure screen unlocking methods.

A *PIN lock* is a code between 4 and 16 numbers long. It contains only numbers, 0 through 9. To set a PIN lock, follow the directions in the earlier section "Finding the locks" to reach the Set Screen Lock window. Choose PIN from the list of locks.

Use the onscreen keyboard to type your PIN once, and touch the Continue button. Type the PIN again to confirm that you know it. Touch OK. The next time you turn on or wake up the tablet, you'll need to type that PIN to get access.

To disable the PIN, reset the security level as described in the preceding section.

Assigning a password

The most secure — and therefore the most arduous — way to lock the tablet is to apply a full-on password. Unlike a PIN (refer to the preceding section), a *password* can contain numbers, symbols, and both uppercase and lowercase letters.

Set a password by choosing Password from the Screen Lock window; refer to the earlier section "Finding the locks" for information on getting to that screen. The password you select must be at least four characters long. Longer passwords are more secure.

You're prompted to type the password whenever you unlock the tablet or whenever you try to change the screen lock. Touch the OK button to accept the password you've typed.

Creating an unlock pattern

One of the most common ways to lock a Galaxy tablet is to apply an *unlock pattern:* The pattern must be traced exactly as it was created to unlock the device and get access to your apps and other tablet features.

1. **Summon the Screen Lock window.**

   Refer to the earlier section "Finding the locks."

2. **Choose Pattern.**

   If you've not yet set a pattern lock, you may see a tutorial describing the process; touch the Next button to skip over the dreary directions.

3. **Trace an unlock pattern.**

   Use Figure 19-7 as your inspiration. You can trace over the dots in any order, but you can trace over a dot only once. The pattern must cover at least four dots.

4. **Touch the Continue button.**

5. **Redraw the pattern.**

   You need to prove to the doubtful tablet that you know the pattern.

6. **Touch the Confirm button.**

7. **Type a PIN to back up the pattern lock in case you forget.**

   Specific details on setting a PIN lock are found earlier in this chapter.

I began the
pattern here

Keep tracing

The pattern so far

Figure 19-7: Setting an unlock pattern.

And the pattern lock is set.

To ensure that the pattern shows up, check that the Make Pattern Visible option is selected on the Lock Screen window. For even more security, you can deselect the option, but you have to be sure to remember how — and where — the pattern goes.

✔ The unlock pattern can be as simple or as complex as you like. I'm a big fan of simple.

✔ Wash your hands! Smudge marks on the display can betray your pattern.

Unlocking the tablet with your face

The Face Unlock setting allows you to get access to your Galaxy tablet simply by looking at it. You don't even need to make a funny face; your normal visage does the job. The only downside is that not every tablet features this locking mechanism.

Delaying the screen lock

The lock screen shows up right away whenever you unlock your tablet. It shows up also after a sleep timeout or a period of inactivity. When that happens, the touchscreen automatically turns off and the tablet locks. You can control the timeout delay for the screen lock as well as whether the tablet locks automatically when you press the Power Lock key.

To see the screen lock timeout delay, get to the Lock Screen window: Open the Settings app and choose the Lock Screen category (if necessary, touch the Device tab first). Choose the Lock Automatically option to set how long the touchscreen waits to lock after the tablet

has a sleep timeout. This option appears only when a secure screen lock is set, so if you don't see it, first set a secure lock. The value can be adjusted from 0 to 30 minutes.

Both the Galaxy Note and Galaxy Tab are configured to immediately lock the screen whenever the Power Lock key is pressed. To change this option, remove the check mark by the Lock Instantly with Power Key item, also found in the Lock Screen window. (This option appears only when a secure screen lock is set.) With this option off, the tablet uses the sleep timeout value to specify when the lock screen kicks in.

To set the face unlock, follow these steps:

1. **Get to the Screen Lock window.**

   Refer to the earlier section "Finding the locks" for specific directions.

2. **Touch the Next button at the warning because you're not silly enough to try to use Face Unlock while you're driving your car.**

3. **Choose Face Unlock.**

   In the directions on the screen that you probably didn't read, it says that Face Unlock is less secure than other forms of locking the phone. But it's fun, so what the heck?

4. **Touch the Set It Up button.**

5. **Hold up the tablet so that it's facing you at eye level — as though you were using it as a mirror.**

6. **Touch the Continue button.**

7. **Line up your face with the oval dots on the screen, and then hold the tablet steady as the dots change from white to green.**

8. **Upon success, touch the Continue button.**

9. **Choose Pattern or PIN to set a backup lock for those frequent times that Face Unlock fails.**

   Refer to later sections in this chapter for how to set up these types of locks.

10. **After confirming the pattern or PIN lock, touch the OK button.**

    Face Unlock is now ready for action.

Most of the time, Face Unlock works fine. When it doesn't, you need to use the backup pattern or PIN lock. You also need to use the pattern or PIN whenever you need to change the lock, as discussed in the earlier section "Finding the locks."

Setting face and voice unlock

The Face and Voice screen lock adds a vocal dimension to the Face Unlock feature, covered in the preceding section. It's basically the same lock but with the addition of a voice command. If it fails, the fallback is the pattern or PIN lock, which is nice because it does occasionally fail.

To add vocal commands to the Face Unlock feature, choose the Face and Voice option from the Select Screen Lock screen. Work through the same steps as for Face Unlock, enumerated in the preceding section. Eventually you'll be asked to utter an unlocking phrase four times. Do so. Then set the optional pattern or PIN lock.

Adding owner info text

When you can no longer contain your desire to scribble text on the tablet's lock screen, follow these steps:

1. **Visit the Settings app.**

2. **Choose Lock Screen.**

   If need be, first touch the Device category atop the screen.

3. **On the right side of the screen, choose Lock Screen Widgets.**

4. **Choose Owner Information.**

5. **Type text in the box.**

   You can type more than one line of text, though the information is displayed on the lock screen as a single line.

6. **Ensure that the Show Owner Info on Lock Screen option is selected.**

7. **Touch the OK button.**

Whatever text you type in the box appears on the lock screen. Therefore, I recommend typing something useful, as the command suggests: your name, address, phone number, and e-mail address, for example. This way, should you lose your tablet and an honest person finds it, that person can get it back to you.

Various Galactic Adjustments

You have plenty of things to adjust, tune, and tweak on your Samsung Galaxy tablet. The Settings app is the gateway to all these options, and I'm sure you could waste hours there if you had hours to waste. My guess is that your time is precious; therefore, this section highlights some of the more worthy options and settings.

The information in this section is specific to the Settings app. Not every Galaxy tablet uses the same Settings app. The newer tablets feature a Settings app with categories along the top of the screen. Older versions of the app lack the category tabs.

Singing a different tune

The Sound screen is where you control which sound the tablet plays as a ringtone, but it's also where you can set volume and vibration options.

To display the Sound screen, choose Sound from the list of categories on the left side of the Settings app screen. If you don't see the Sound category, first choose the Device tab.

Here are the worthy options on the Sound screen:

Volume: Though you can set the Galaxy tablet volume using the Volume key on the side of the gizmo, the Volume command on the Sound screen lets you set the volume for a number of sound events. Table 19-1 describes what the various volume items control.

Table 19-1	Various Noisy Things
Volume Setting	*Sounds It Controls*
Music, video, and so on	The web, YouTube, movie and TV rentals and purchases, games, and so on
Notification	New notifications, such as new e-mail messages, calendar appointments, alarms, or whatever else produces an alert
System	Sounds generated by the Android operating system, such as when locking the screen or connecting the dock or USB cable, warnings, as well as other alerts

For example, if you want video games to be quiet and alarms to be loud, adjust each slider accordingly.

Default Notification Sound/Notifications: Choose which sound you want to hear for a notification alert. You can optionally choose an app to use after touching the Notifications entry. For example, you might see a Complete

Action Using menu showing both Media Storage and Zedge Ringtones listed. Choose an app, and then touch either Just Once or Always. Select a sound from the list, or choose Silent for no sound.

Also check individual apps for their own notification sounds. For example, Facebook and Twitter set their sounds by using the Settings command in those individual apps.

See the sidebar "Always or just once" for more information on the Complete Action Using menu.

Vibration Intensity: Tablets that sport the vibration feature use this category to control vibration settings. Two sliders appear on the Vibration Intensity menu: Notification and Haptic Feedback.

The Notification item is a general vibration setting. It's used specifically when you've muted the tablet.

The Haptic Feedback item applies to other tablet activities, such as long-pressing an icon or using the onscreen keyboard. That slight vibration you feel during those actions is set by adjusting the Haptic Feedback slider.

Touch the OK button after messing with the various vibration settings.

Always or just once?

During your Galaxy tablet day, you may occasionally see the Complete Action Using menu. It lists a slew of apps (or sometimes just two) plus two buttons, Always and Just Once. Your job is to choose an app to complete an action, such as cropping an image or playing music. Choose the app first, and then touch Always to always use that app. Or touch Just Once to choose the app and complete the action but be prompted to make the same choice the next time.

If you choose the Always option and down the road change your mind, you can reset your choice. The key is to remember which app you chose, such as the Gallery for viewing images or Zedge for choosing ringtones. In the Settings app, visit Application Manager. Choose the app from the list on the right side of the screen. In the app's information window, touch the Clear Defaults button.

Changing visual settings

Probably the key thing you want to adjust visually on the Galaxy tablet is screen brightness. This task is deftly handled by swiping down the notifications shade: Adjust the Brightness slider right (brighter) or left (dimmer).

You can also touch the Auto button next to the slider to have the tablet automatically adjust its brightness based on the ambient light.

Brightness can be set also by using the Settings app: Select the Display category on the left side of the screen. (If you don't see that category, touch the Device tab.) Choose Brightness.

Another item worthy of note is the Screen Timeout setting. Select this item to see the Screen Timeout menu, from which you can set the inactivity duration, after which the Galaxy tablet touchscreen turns itself off. I prefer a value of 1 Minute.

✔ The Timeout setting is the setting that the tablet uses to automatically lock itself.

✔ See Chapter 3 for more information on Quick Settings.

Maintenance and Troubleshooting

In This Chapter

▶ Cleaning the tablet

▶ Checking the battery

▶ Saving battery power

▶ Solving annoying problems

▶ Searching for support

▶ Troubleshooting issues

▶ Getting answers

I hear that the maintenance on the Eiffel Tower is arduous. Once a year, the French utterly disassemble the landmark; individually scrub every girder, nut, and bolt; and then put it all back together. The entire operation is performed early in the morning, so when Paris wakes up, no one notices. Well, people notice that the Tower is cleaner, but no one notices that it was completely disassembled, cleaned, and rebuilt. Truly, the French are amazing.

Fortunately, maintenance for your Galaxy tablet isn't as consuming as maintenance on one of the world's great monuments. For example, cleaning the tablet takes mere seconds, and no disassembly is required. It's cinchy! Beyond covering maintenance, this chapter offers suggestions for using the battery, plus it gives you some helpful tips and Q&A.

Regular Galactic Maintenance

Relax. Maintenance for your Galaxy Note or Galaxy Tab is simple and quick. Basically, I can summarize it in three words: Keep it clean. Beyond that, another maintenance task worthy of attention is backing up the information stored on your tablet.

Keeping it clean

You probably already keep your tablet clean. Perhaps you're one of those people who use their sleeves to wipe the touchscreen. Of course, better than your sleeve is something called a *microfiber cloth.* This item can be found at any computer- or office-supply store.

✔ Never clean the touchscreen by using a liquid — especially ammonia or alcohol. Those substances damage the touchscreen, rendering it unable to read your input. Further, such harsh chemicals can smudge the display, making it more difficult to see.

✔ If the screen keeps getting dirty, consider adding a screen protector. This specially designed cover prevents the screen from getting scratched or dirty while also letting you use your finger on the touchscreen. Be sure that the screen protector is designed for use with your model Samsung Galaxy tablet.

Backing up your stuff

A *backup* is a safety copy of information. For your tablet, the backup copy includes contact information, music, photos, video, and apps, plus any settings you've made to customize your tablet. Copying that information to another source is one way to keep the information safe in case anything happens to your Galaxy tablet.

Yes, a backup is a good thing. Lamentably, there's no universal method of backing up the stuff on a Galaxy tablet.

Your Google account information is backed up automatically. That information includes the tablet's address book, Gmail inbox, and calendar appointments. Because that information automatically syncs with the Internet, a backup is always present.

To confirm that your Google account information is being backed up, heed these steps:

1. **At the Home screen, touch the Apps icon.**

2. **Open the Settings app.**

3. **View your Google account information.**

    If the Settings app features tabs along the top, touch the General tab, and then choose Accounts from the left side of the screen. Choose your Google account.

    If you don't see tabs along the top of the Settings app, choose your Google account from the list of accounts on the left side of the screen.

4. **On the right side of the screen, select your Gmail address.**

5. **Ensure that check marks appear by every item in the list.**

   On my tablet, the list includes Calendar, Contacts, Gmail, Google Photos, Google Play Books, and Google Play Music.

   You're not done yet!

6. **On the left side of the screen, select the Backup and Reset item.**

7. **Ensure that both items shown on the right side of the screen have green check marks.**

   There. Now you can rest easy.

Beyond your Google account, which is automatically backed up, the rest of the information can be manually backed up. You can synchronize information on the tablet with your computer by using an app such as Samsung Kies or Dropbox (both covered in Chapter 17), or you can manually copy files from the tablet's internal storage to the computer as a form of backup.

Yes, I agree: Manual backup isn't an example of technology making your life easier.

- ✔ See Chapter 17 for information about exchanging files between your computer and your Galaxy tablet.

- ✔ A backup of the data stored on the tablet would include all data, including photos, videos, and music. Specifically, the folders you should copy are DCIM, Download, and Music. Additional folders to copy include folders named after apps you've downloaded, such as Kindle, Kobo, and Layar.

Updating the system

Every so often, a new version of the Android operating system becomes available. It's an *Android* update because Android is the name of the operating system, not because your Galaxy tablet thinks that it's some type of robot.

When an automatic update occurs, you see an alert or a message, indicating that a system upgrade is available. My advice: Install the update and get it over with. Don't dally.

- ✔ If possible, connect the tablet to a power source. You don't want the battery to die during a software update.

- ✔ You can check for updates manually: In the Settings app, choose the General tab (if it's there), and then select About Device. Touch the Software Update item. When the system is up-to-date, the screen tells you so. Otherwise, you find directions for updating the Android operating system.

- ✔ Non-Android system updates might also be issued. For example, Samsung may send an update to the Galaxy tablet's guts. This type of update is often called a *firmware* update. As with Android updates, my advice is to accept all firmware updates.

Battery Care and Feeding

Perhaps the most important item you can monitor and maintain on your Galactic tablet is its battery. The battery supplies the necessary electrical juice by which the device operates. Without battery power, your tablet is basically an expensive trivet. Keep an eye on the battery.

Monitoring the battery

You can find information about the Galaxy tablet's battery status in the upper-right corner of the screen, next to the current time in the status area. The icons used to display battery status are shown in Figure 20-1.

 Battery is fully charged; the tablet is happy.

 Battery is starting to drain.

 Battery is very low; stop using and charge at once!

 Battery is being charged.

Figure 20-1: Battery status icons.

You might also see an icon for a dead battery, but for some reason I can't get my tablet to turn on and display that icon.

 Heed those low-battery warnings! The Galaxy tablet alerts you when the battery level gets low, at about 15 percent capacity.

Another warning shows up when the battery level gets seriously low, below 5 percent — but why wait for that? Take action at the 15 percent warning.

- ✔ When the battery level is too low, the Galaxy tablet shuts itself off.

- ✔ The best way to deal with low battery power is to connect the tablet to a power source: Either plug it into a wall socket or connect it to a computer by using a USB cable. The tablet begins charging itself immediately; plus, you can use the device while it's charging.

- ✔ You don't have to fully charge the tablet to use it. When you have only 20 minutes to charge and you get only a 70 percent battery level, that's great. Well, it's not great, but it's far better than a lower battery level.

- ✔ I have no idea what the red X means on the battery icon (refer to Figure 20-1). I'm pretty sure it doesn't mean that anything is wrong.

- ✔ Battery percentage values are best-guess estimates. The typical Galaxy tablet has a hearty battery that can last for hours. But when the battery meter gets low, the battery drains faster. So, if you get 8 hours of use from the tablet and the battery meter shows 20 percent left, those numbers don't imply that 20 percent equals 2 more hours of use. In practice, the amount of time you have left is much less than that. As a rule, when the battery percentage value gets low, the battery appears to drain faster.

Determining what is sucking up power

The Galaxy tablet is smart enough to know which of its features use the most battery power. You can check it out for yourself:

1. **At the Home screen, touch the Apps icon.**

2. **Open the Settings app.**

3. **Choose the General tab, if available.**

   Not every version of the Settings app displays a General tab.

4. **Choose Battery from the list of categories on the left side of the screen.**

   You see a screen similar to the one shown in Figure 20-2.

The number and variety of items listed on the Battery screen depend on what you've been doing between charges and how many apps you're using.

Carefully note which apps consume the most battery power. You can curb your use of these programs to conserve juice — though, honestly, your savings are negligible. See the next section for battery-saving advice.

Current battery charge and state   Usage and time chart

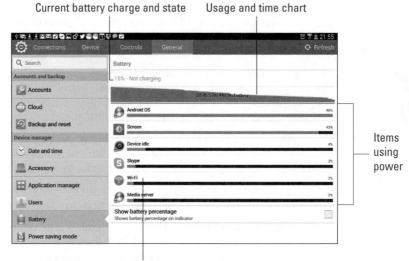

Items
using
power

Touch to view usage and change settings

Figure 20-2: Things that drain the battery.

✔ You can touch any item listed on the Battery screen to see further details for that item. On the Use Details screen, you can review what is drawing power. Buttons are available on some screens that let you disable features that may be drawing too much power.

✔ Not everything you've done shows up on the Battery screen (refer to Figure 20-2). For example, even after I read a Kindle book for about half an hour, Kindle didn't show up. Also, I've seen the Gallery app show up from time to time, even though I didn't use it.

Extending battery life

A surefire way to make a battery last a good long time is to never turn on the device in the first place. But rather than let you use your Galaxy tablet as an expensive paperweight, I offer a smattering of suggestions you can follow to help prolong its battery life:

Turn off vibration options: The tablet's vibration is caused by a teensy motor. Although you don't see much battery savings by disabling the vibration options, a minuscule savings is better than no savings. See Chapter 19 for information on disabling vibration options.

Lower the volume: Consider lowering the volume for the various noises the tablet makes, especially notifications. Information on setting volume options is found in Chapter 19.

Dim the screen: If you look at Figure 20-2, you see that the display (labeled Screen) sucks down quite a lot of battery power. Although a dim screen can be more difficult to see, especially outdoors, it definitely saves on battery life.

Adjust the screen timeout: Make the screen sleep at a shorter interval to save valuable battery life. Or manually lock the tablet, especially if you're just listening to music. See Chapter 19 for information on display settings.

Turn off Bluetooth: When you're not using Bluetooth, turn it off. See Chapter 16 for information on Bluetooth, though you can turn it off easily from the Quick Actions at the top of the notifications shade.

You'll find a Power Saving Mode item in the Settings app. (You might need to touch the General tab first). Select the item on the left side of the screen. Then touch the button atop the screen to activate Power Saving Mode, and select items shown on the screen to help manage how the tablet uses battery juice.

Help and Troubleshooting

Wouldn't it be great if you could have an avuncular, Mr. Wizard–type available at a moment's notice? He could just walk in and, with a happy smile on his face and a reassuring hand on your shoulder, diagnose the problem and tell you how to fix it. Never mind that such a thing would be creepy — getting helpful advice is worth it.

Fixing random and annoying problems

Here are some typical problems you may encounter on your Galaxy Note or Galaxy Tab and my suggestions for a solution:

General trouble

For just about any problem or minor quirk, consider restarting the Galaxy tablet: Long-press the Power Lock key and choose the Restart command from the Device Options menu. This procedure will most likely fix a majority of the annoying problems you encounter.

Signal weirdness

As you move about, the cellular signal can change. In fact, you may observe the status icon change from 4G LTE to 3G to even the dreaded 1X or — worse — nothing, depending on the strength and availability of the cellular data service.

My advice for random signal weirdness is to wait. Oftentimes, the signal comes back after a few minutes. If it doesn't, the cellular data network might be down, or you may just be in an area with lousy service. Consider changing your location.

For Wi-Fi connections, you have to ensure that the Wi-Fi is set up properly and working. This process usually involves pestering the person who configured the Wi-Fi router or, in a coffee shop, bothering the cheerful person with the bad haircut who serves you coffee.

Perhaps the issue isn't with the tablet at all, but rather with the Wi-Fi network. Some networks have a "lease time" after which your tablet might be disconnected. If so, follow the directions in Chapter 16 for turning off the tablet's Wi-Fi and then turn it on again. That often solves the issue.

Music is playing and you want it to stop

It's awesome that the Galaxy tablet continues to play music while you do other things. Getting the music to stop quickly, however, requires some skill. Primarily, you need skill at pulling down the notifications shade and touching the Pause button that appears in the currently playing song's notification.

An app has run amok

Sometimes, apps that misbehave let you know. You see a warning on the screen announcing the app's stubborn disposition. When that happens, touch the Force Quit button to shut down the app. Then say, "Whew!"

When you don't see a warning or when an app appears to be unduly obstinate, you can shut 'er down the manual way, by following these steps:

1. **From the Apps screen, open the Settings app.**

2. **On the left side of the screen, select the Application Manager item.**

   Choose the General tab from the top of the Settings app screen if you don't readily see the Application Manager item.

3. **Select the app that's causing you distress.**

   For example, the program doesn't start or says that it's busy or has some other issue.

   If you swipe the right side of the screen over to the Running item, you see only currently running apps. That helps narrow the list.

4. **Touch the Stop button.**

   The program stops.

You've reached your wit's end

When all else fails, you can do the drastic thing and reset your Galaxy tablet, essentially returning it to the state it was in when you first popped it out of the box. Obviously, you need not perform this step lightly. In fact, consider finding support (see the next section) before you start the following process:

1. **Start the Settings app.**

2. **On the left side of the screen, select Backup and Reset.**

   The Backup and Reset item is found under the General tab. If you see the General tab atop the screen, touch it.

3. **Choose Factory Data Reset.**

4. **Touch the Reset Device button.**

5. **Touch the Delete All button to confirm.**

   All the information you've set or stored on the tablet is purged, including all your accounts, any apps you've downloaded, music, everything.

Again, do not follow these steps unless you're certain that they will fix the problem or you're under orders to do so from someone in tech support.

You can also choose to wipe everything should you ever return or sell the tablet. Of course, you probably love your tablet so much that the mere thought of getting rid of it makes you blanch.

Getting support

You can use two sources for support for your Galaxy tablet. For cellular tablets, the first source of support is your cellular provider. The second source, or the only source if you have a Wi-Fi tablet, is Samsung. Or, perhaps, if you were suckered into a long-term service agreement at some Big Box store, you can try getting support from it.

Before you contact someone about support, you need to know the device's ID:

1. **From the Home screen, touch the Apps icon.**

2. **Open the Settings app.**

3. **Choose About Device.**

   The About Device command is located under the General tab.

   The tablet's model number is listed, as well as the Android version.

On my Galaxy Note 10.1, the model number is listed as SM-P600 and the Android Version is 4.3. Look up the names and numbers for your tablet, and then jot down that information right here:

Model Number: _____

Android Version: _____

For app issues, contact the developer in the Play Store app, which is covered in Chapter 15. For issues with the Play Store, contact Google at `support.google.com/googleplay`.

If you have a cellular tablet and are an active mobile data subscriber, you can get help from the cellular provider. Table 20-1 lists contact information on US cellular providers.

Table 20-1		US Cellular Providers
Provider	*Toll free*	*Website*
AT&T	800-331-0500	www.att.com/esupport
Sprint Nextel	800-211-4727	mysprint.sprint.com
T-Mobile	800-866-2453	www.t-mobile.com/Contact.aspx
Verizon	800-922-0204	http://support.vzw.com/clc

For hardware and other issues, you have to contact Samsung. The support number is (800) 726-7864. The Samsung support website is www.samsung.com/us/support.

No one likes wading through bottomless automatic customer support systems. Odds are good that you merely want to speak to a human. I've found that the fastest way to do that is to keep pressing the zero key after you phone into the system. This process eventually turns you over to a live person who, I hope, can either deal with your problem or connect you with someone who can.

Valuable Galaxy Tablet Q&A

I love Q&A! Not only is it an effective way to express certain problems and solutions, but some of the questions might also cover things I've been wanting to ask.

"I can't turn the tablet on (or off)!"

Yes, sometimes a Galaxy tablet locks up. I even asked Samsung about this issue specifically, and the folks there told me it's impossible for a Galaxy tablet to seize! Despite this denial, I've discovered that if you press and hold down the Power Lock key for about 8 seconds, the tablet turns off or on, depending on which state it's in.

I've had a program lock the Galaxy tablet tight when the 8-second Power Lock key trick didn't work. In that case, I waited 12 minutes or so, just letting the tablet sit there and do nothing. Then I pressed and held down the Power Lock key for about 8 seconds, and the tablet turned itself back on.

"The touchscreen doesn't work!"

A touchscreen, such as the one used on a Galaxy tablet, requires a human finger for proper interaction. The tablet interprets the static potential between the human finger and the device to determine where the touchscreen is being touched.

You cannot use the touchscreen when you're wearing gloves, unless they're specially designed, static-carrying gloves that claim to work on touchscreens.

The touchscreen might also fail when the battery power is low or when the tablet has been physically damaged.

I've been informed that there is an Android app for cats. That implies that the touchscreen can also interpret a feline paw for proper interaction. Either that or the cat can hold a human finger in its mouth and manipulate the app that way. Because I don't have the app, I can't tell for certain.

"The battery doesn't charge!"

When your battery isn't charging, start at the source: Is the wall socket providing power? Is the cord plugged in? The cable may be damaged, so try another cable.

When charging from a USB port on a computer, ensure that the computer is turned on. Most computers don't provide USB power when they're turned off.

"The tablet gets so hot that it turns itself off!"

Yikes! An overheating gadget can be a nasty problem. Judge how hot the tablet is by seeing whether you can hold it in your hand: When it's too hot to hold, it's too hot. If you're using your Galaxy tablet to cook an egg, it's too hot.

Turn off the tablet and let the battery cool.

If the overheating problem continues, have the tablet looked at for potential repair. The battery might need to be replaced. As far as I can tell, there's no way for you to remove and replace the battery in a Galaxy tablet.

Do not continue to use any gizmo that's too hot! The heat damages the electronics. It can also start a fire.

"It doesn't do landscape mode!"

Not every app takes advantage of the Galaxy tablet's capability to orient itself in landscape mode, or even upside-down mode. For example, many games set their orientations one way and refuse to change, no matter how you hold the tablet. So, if an app doesn't go into landscape mode, that doesn't mean anything is broken.

Confirm that the orientation lock isn't on: Check the Quick Actions on the notifications shade to ensure that the Screen Rotation item is on; otherwise, the screen doesn't reorient itself.

Part V
The Part of Tens

 Enjoy another part of ten chapter online at www.dummies.com/extras/samsunggalaxytabs.

In this part...

- ✔ Discover ten tips, tricks, and shortcuts.
- ✔ Work with ten things to remember.
- ✔ Explore ten free apps.

Ten Tips, Tricks, and Shortcuts

In This Chapter

▶ Adding lock screen widgets

▶ Employing the Smart Screen

▶ Activating the dream feature

▶ Creating shortcuts on the Home screen

▶ Removing the vocal dirty word filter

▶ Telling the tablet what to do

▶ Changing TV channels with the tablet

▶ Setting locations for your schedule

▶ Finding the task manager

▶ Monitoring online data access

A tip is a small suggestion, a word of advice often spoken from experience or knowledge. A *trick,* which is something not many know, usually causes amazement or surprise. A *shortcut* is a quick way to get home, even though it crosses the old grave-yard and you never quite know whether Old Man Witherspoon is the groundskeeper or a zombie.

I'd like to think that just about everything in this book is a tip, trick, or shortcut for using a Galaxy Note or Galaxy Tab tablet. Even so, I've distilled a list of items in this chapter that are definitely worthy of note.

Add Widgets to the Lock Screen

Just as you can adorn the Home screen with widgets, you can also slap down a few right on the lock screen. In fact, the time display on the tablet's lock screen is a widget. It's only one of several.

To add a lock screen widget, heed these directions:

1. **Open the Settings app.**

   It's found on the Apps screen.

2. **Choose the Device category from the top of the screen.**

   Don't sweat if you don't see that category; not every Settings app features the category tabs.

3. **On the left side of the Settings app screen, select Lock Screen.**

4. **Select the Multiple Widgets item.**

   That's it.

Normally you'd be disappointed at this point because you don't see the lock screen brimming with widgets. Silly. You have to add them. To do that, you need to first lock the tablet.

Lock the tablet.

Unlock the tablet, but on the lock screen, swipe the Clock widget (it's really a widget) to one side or the other. You'll see a large plus icon. Touch that plus icon, and then choose a lock screen widget from the displayed list, such as Calendar, Gmail, Digital Clock, or what-have-you.

- Multiple widgets can be placed on the lock screen, though you can see only one at a time. Swipe the screen to see others.

- To remove a lock screen widget, long-press it. Drag the widget up to the Remove icon and it's gone. You can even remove the Clock widget, in which case only the large plus icon appears on the lock screen.

Smart Screen Tricks

Some Galaxy tablets feature a slew of Smart Screen tricks. These tricks greatly increase your fear of the device by making it frighteningly smarter than you would otherwise think.

Ensure that the Smart Screen repertoire of tricks is active by visiting the Settings app. Select the Controls category, and then touch the Smart Screen item on the left side of the screen. You'll behold four basic Smart Screen actions:

- **Smart Stay:** This item directs the tablet not to dim the screen or automatically lock as long as you're looking at the screen.

- **Smart Rotation:** This item keeps the screen oriented in relation to your face. It's perfect for watching movies or reading in bed.

> ✓ **Smart Pause:** This item is used when viewing movies on the tablet. If you look away from the screen, the movie is automatically paused.

> ✓ **Smart Scroll:** This item watches how you tilt your head, scrolling information on the screen accordingly.

Select the box by various items to turn them on. Some items may sport an on-off icon: Touch the icon to activate that item. You can then touch the same entry to make specific settings. (As this book goes to press, only the Smart Scroll item features an on-off icon.)

I've had mixed results with the various Smart Screen tricks. I suppose my third eye probably messes up the tablet's human face sensor.

Watch the Tablet Dream

Does a Galaxy tablet fall asleep or does it just lock? A locked tablet seems rather restrictive, so I prefer to think of the tablet as taking a snooze. But does it dream? Of course it does! You can even see the dreams, providing you activate the Daydream feature — and you keep the tablet connected to a power source or in a docking station. Heed these steps:

1. **Start the Settings app.**

2. **Touch the Device tab.**

   Not every tablet's Settings app has a Device tab.

3. **Choose Display.**

4. **Ensure that the Daydream on-off icon is in the on position.**

   The Daydream feature is activated.

5. **Touch the Daydream item to view the various types of daydreams available.**

   I'm fond of Colors.

   Some daydream items feature a Settings icon, which can be used to customize how the daydream appears.

6. **When you're done, touch the Back button or touch the Home key to return to the Home screen.**

The daydreaming begins when the screen would normally timeout and lock. So, if you set the tablet to lock after 5 minutes of inactivity, it daydreams instead.

> ✓ To disrupt the tablet's dreaming, swipe the screen.

> ✓ The tablet doesn't lock when it daydreams. To lock the tablet, press the Power Lock key.

Add Shortcuts to the Home Screen

Don't bother looking: You won't find a something called a "shortcut" to add to the Home screen. Older versions of the Android operating system had such a feature. Today, you apply shortcut widgets instead.

For example, say you desire a Bluetooth shortcut icon on the Home screen. You can use that icon to turn the Bluetooth radio on or off. Here's how to add that shortcut, which is really a widget:

1. **Touch the Apps icon to visit the Apps screen.**

2. **Choose the Widgets category.**

3. **Choose the Settings Shortcut widget.**

   It's *way* over there on the left, although not every tablet may have this widget.

4. **Apply the widget to the Home screen.**

   Specific directions are provided in Chapter 19.

5. **Choose an action for the widget by selecting an item from the scrolling menu.**

   In this case, you could choose the Bluetooth item to create a Bluetooth settings shortcut on the Home screen.

The shortcut icon provides a direct link to a specific entry in the Settings app. So although the shortcut doesn't turn something on or off, it quickly gets you to the screen that does so.

Another popular Home screen shortcut is a contact shortcut: Repeat Steps 1 and 2 but choose the Contact widget in Step 3. Continue working Step 4, but in Step 5 you choose a specific person from the tablet's address book. To use the shortcut, touch the widget; you'll see information about that contact.

Add Spice to Dictation

I feel that too few people use dictation, despite how handy it can be. Whether or not you use it, you might notice that it occasionally censors some of the words you utter. Perhaps you're the kind of person who won't put up with that kind of s***.

Relax, b******. You can lift the vocal censorship ban by following these steps:

1. **At the Home screen, touch the Apps icon.**
2. **Open the Settings app.**
3. **Choose the Controls tab, if you see it on the Settings app screen.**

   Not every Settings app uses the tabs across the top of the screen.
4. **On the left side of the screen, select Language and Input.**

5. **Touch the Settings icon next to Google Voice Typing.**
6. **Deselect the Block Offensive Words option.**

And just what are offensive words? I would think that *censorship* would be an offensive word. But no, apparently the words s***, c***, and even innocent little old a****** are deemed offensive by Google Voice. What the h***?

Command the Tablet with Your Voice

I just tried this trick for my son, and he was really impressed. On my Galaxy tablet, I touched the Microphone icon on the Home screen's Google Search widget. I uttered, "Phone Obama." In less than five seconds, the tablet started the Skype app and phoned the White House.

Chapter 14 covers the Google Now feature, which is really the heart of this trick: The Google Search widget on the Home screen hooks you into the Google Search or Google Now app. Once started, you can bark out various commands.

What makes the "Phone Obama" command work, however, are two things. First, I have President Obama in my tablet's address book. No, I don't know him personally; I just always keep the current US president in my address book.

Second, I have the Skype app installed. Skype is covered in Chapter 9. Both apps — Google Now and Skype — work tougher on the tablet to carry out voice commands.

You can try similar tricks as well. Say, "Watch a video" or "Send e-mail to *someone*" or "Go to *address/map location*." The tablet is uncanny.

Use the Galactic TV Remote

I didn't point it out back in Chapter 1, but located on your tablet's edge is an infrared remote. It's a dark, glassy area about the size of a grain of rice. You can use that infrared hardware and the WatchON app as a super genius TV remote.

This is an order: Go into your TV room with your Galaxy Note or Galaxy Tab. Sit down in front of the TV. Start the WatchON app and follow the directions on the screen. Configure the app to match your local cable or satellite provider. Set up your TV set based on its brand name.

Eventually, you'll be able to use the tablet running the WatchON app as your TV remote, but that's only a minor trick. The big deal is the program guide that appears on the screen, such as the one shown in Figure 21-1.

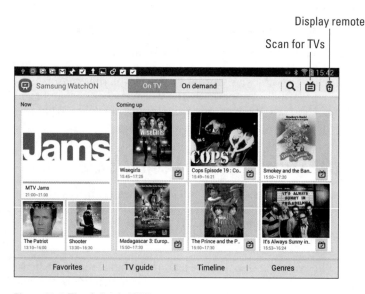

Figure 21-1: The Galactic TV Remote app.

As long as the tablet is pointing at the TV, you can touch a show on the screen to instantly switch to that channel on your TV. Or use the remote feature (refer to Figure 21-1) to control the TV's volume or manually cruise the channels.

Enter Location Information for Your Events

When you create an event for the Calendar app, remember to enter the event location. You can type either an address (if you know it) or the name of the location. The key is to type the text as you would type it in the Maps app when searching for a location. That way, you can touch the event location and the tablet displays it on the touchscreen. Finding an appointment couldn't be easier.

✔ See Chapter 10 for more information about the Maps app.

✔ See Chapter 15 for details about the Calendar app, which may also be called the S Planner on some tablets.

Use the Task Manager

One app that seems to be missing from both the Galaxy Note and Galaxy Tab is a task manager app. One may be added in the future, but until then you have a handy substitute. To view running apps on your tablet, follow these steps:

1. **Open the Settings app.**

2. **On the left side of the screen, select the Application Manager item.**

   If you don't see this item, choose the General tab from atop the screen.

3. **Swipe the list of apps on the right side of the screen until you see the Running heading.**

   You see a list, similar to what's shown in Figure 21-2, left. Some of the items are apps currently active on your tablet, such as Samsung WatchON, but others are services, such as the MTP Application. Some apps may even have double entries, showing that the apps are doing more than one thing at a time.

4. **Select an app to examine more details.**

   The details break down the app's usage of the tablet's resources into an organized list of exhaustive information that few people understand (see Figure 21-2, right).

And now, the shortcut: When you long-press the Home key, you see a list of recent apps. At the bottom of the screen, you'll find three buttons. The button on the far left accesses the official Task Manager window. Like the Application Manager, it shows running apps, but it also shows an End button next to each app.

Choosing an app from the Applications Manager window reveals a Stop button. Like the End button in the Task Manager, you can use the Stop button to halt an app.

Even though you can use the End or Stop buttons to halt apps run amok, I don't recommend that you go about and randomly stop apps and services. The end result could render the tablet unstable, requiring you to power off or reset the tablet to regain control.

Running apps

Memory usage   Details

Figure 21-2: Apps running on the Galaxy tablet.

Check Your Data Usage

Whether you have a Wi-Fi–only Galaxy tablet or one that can also access the mobile data network, you can use the Data Usage screen to check Internet activity and even control how much data is sent and received.

To visit the Data Usage screen, open the Settings app and choose Data Usage, which is found in the Connections tab if your tablet's Settings app features tabs. You'll see a graph charting data usage over time. Cellular tablets also feature red and orange limit bars, which you can adjust to set warnings when your mobile data usage gets too close to your monthly limit.

To review network access for a specific app, select it from the list. You'll see an overlay of the app's data usage, as well as a delicious pie chart. If you notice that the app is using more data than it should, touch the View App Settings button. You may be able to adjust some of the settings to curtail unintended Internet access.

Ten Things to Remember

In This Chapter

▶ Switching apps quickly

▶ Using Multi Window

▶ Choosing Quick Actions

▶ Speaking to the tablet

▶ Locking orientation

▶ Improving your typing with suggestions

▶ Minding the battery hogs

▶ Making phone calls

▶ Checking your schedule

▶ Taking a picture of a contact

*H*ave you ever tried to tie string around your finger to remember something? I've not attempted that technique just yet. The main reason is that I keep forgetting to buy string and have no way to remind myself.

For your Galaxy Note or Galaxy Tab, some things are definitely worth remembering. Out of the long, long list, I've come up with ten good ones.

Summon a Recently Opened App

I have to kick myself in the head every time I return to the Apps screen to, once again, page through the panels o' icons to dig up an app I just opened. Why bother? Because I can summon the list of recently opened apps by long-pressing the Home key. Up pops the Recent Apps list, from which I can easily switch to a previous app.

Using the Recent Apps list is the best way to switch between two running apps. So when you need to switch, for example, between Email and the web browser, just long-press the Home key and select the bottom item on the list. It's effectively the same thing as the Alt+Tab key combination in Windows.

View Multiple Apps at Once

Your Galactic tablet features a Multi Window mode. It doesn't allow you to run multiple apps at once; the tablet already does that. What Multi Window mode does is let you view two apps running at once, side-by-side. When you find yourself switching between two apps over and over, just hop into Multi Window mode instead.

Another Multi Window mode tip is to disable it when you don't use it. If you see that tab loitering off on the left side of the screen and you've never used it, disable Multi Window mode by selecting the Multi Window item from the Quick Actions, which are on the notifications shade.

See Chapter 3 for more information on Multi Window mode.

Take Quick Actions

Shortcuts exist for many of the common things you do on the Galaxy tablet. Especially for those items that can be turned on or off, you'll probably find a Quick Action.

To view the Quick Actions, pull down the notification shade. The Quick Action icons march across the screen, left to right. On some tablets, you can scroll the actions left and right. On other tablets, the Quick Action icons cannot be scrolled. That's okay. You can touch the Grid button in the upper-right corner of the screen to view all the Quick Actions on one screen.

Use Dictation

Dictation is such a handy feature, yet I constantly forget to use it. Rather than type short text messages, use dictation. You can access dictation from any onscreen keyboard by touching the Microphone icon. Speak the text; the text appears. Simple.

See Chapter 4 for information on dictation.

Lock the Orientation

It's nice to be able to rotate the tablet, alternating between portrait and landscape orientations. Some apps look good one way; others the other way. The orientation lock feature prevents the apps from switching when you don't want them to: The screen stays fixed in whichever orientation it was in when you set the orientation lock.

To set the orientation lock, pull down the notifications shade. In the Quick Settings area, locate the Screen Rotation item. Touch it to lock orientation. Touch it again to unlock.

See Chapter 3 for more information about the Quick Settings.

Use the Keyboard Suggestions

Don't forget to take advantage of the suggestions that appear above the onscreen keyboard when you're typing text. In fact, you may not even need to type much text at all: Just keep choosing a word from the list presented. It's fast.

To ensure that suggestions are enabled, follow these steps:

1. **Open the Settings app.**
2. **On the left side of the screen, select Language and Input.**

   You may need to choose the Control tab atop the screen so that you can find the Language and Input item.

3. **Touch the Settings icon to the right of the Samsung Keyboard entry.**

   The icon is found on the right side of the screen, similar to the one shown in the margin.

4. **Ensure that the on-off icon that appears by the Predictive Text option is green, or on.**

Also refer to Chapter 4 for additional information on using the keyboard suggestions.

Avoid Things That Consume Lots of Battery Juice

Three items on your Galaxy tablet suck down battery power faster than a massive alien fleet is defeated by a plucky antihero who just wants the girl:

- ✔ A bright display
- ✔ Wi-Fi networking
- ✔ Bluetooth

It takes a lot of power for the tablet to give you a nice, bright touchscreen, so don't make the screen any brighter than you have to. If possible, set the brightness to Auto. That setting saves a lot of power. See Chapter 19 for more information on properly setting the touchscreen brightness.

Both Wi-Fi networking and Bluetooth require extra power for their wireless radios. The amount isn't much, but it's enough that I would consider shutting them down when battery power gets low.

- ✔ See Chapter 20 for more information on managing the Galaxy tablet's battery.

- ✔ Another item that can draw a lot of power is turn-by-turn navigation. This feature is found in the Maps app but not readily used on a tablet as much as it is on a smartphone. If you do use the Navigation feature on your Galactic tablet, ensure that the tablet is connected to the car's 12-volt power supply. An adapter can be found at any electronics or phone store.

Make Phone Calls

Yeah, I know: It's not a phone. I wish it were (and I'm sure Samsung might as well), but your Galaxy tablet lacks a native capability to use the cellular system for making phone calls. Even so, with apps such as Hangouts and Skype, you can make phone calls and even video chat with others. Refer to Chapter 9 for details.

Keep Up with Your Schedule

The Calendar app can certainly be handy to remind you of upcoming dates and generally keep you on schedule. A great way to augment the calendar is to employ the Calendar widget on the Home screen.

The Calendar widget lists the current date and then a long list of upcoming appointments. It's a great way to check your schedule, especially when you use your tablet all the time. I recommend sticking the Calendar widget right on the main Home screen.

See Chapter 19 for information on adding widgets to the Home screen; Chapter 14 covers the Calendar app, which is called the S Planner app on some tablets.

Snap a Pic of That Contact

Here's something I always forget: Whenever you're near one of your contacts, take the person's picture. Sure, some people are bashful, but most folks are flattered. The idea is to build up your Contacts list so that all contacts have photos.

When taking a picture, be sure to show it to the person before you assign it to the contact. Let her decide whether it's good enough. Or, if you just want to be rude, assign a crummy looking picture. Heck, you don't even have to do that: Just take a random picture of anything and assign it to a contact. A plant. A rock. Your cat. Just keep in mind that the tablet can take a contact's picture the next time you meet up with that person.

See Chapter 11 for more information on using the tablet's camera. Assigning contact pictures is covered in Chapter 5.

Ten Great Apps

*H*undreds of thousands of apps are available at the Google Play Store — so many that it would take you more than a relaxing evening to discover them all. Rather than list every single app, I've culled from the lot some apps that I find exceptional. They show not only the diversity of the Google Play Store but also how well the Galaxy Note and Galaxy Tab can run Android apps.

Every app listed in this chapter is free; see Chapter 15 for directions on finding them using the Google Play Store.

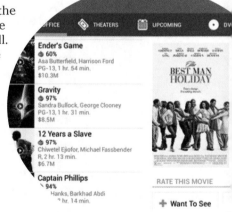

Chrome

Samsung's Galaxy tablets are based on the Android operating system, which is the spawn of Google. The Google-preferred way to browse the web is to use the Chrome web browser. Your tablet came with the Internet browser. It's like Chrome, but Chrome has some features you may want to take advantage of.

Yes, it's okay to have more than one web browser app on your tablet.

Because Chrome is a Google invention, it plays well with other Google apps and services. If you have and use Chrome as your computer web browser, Chrome on your tablet will be familiar to you. Not only that, Chrome on your tablet coordinates your bookmarks, forms, and maybe even passwords on various websites. It can be a handy feature — but, again, only when you use Chrome as your computer's web browser.

Google Finance

The Google Finance app is an excellent market-tracking tool for those of us who are obsessed with the stock market or want to keep an eye on our portfolios. The app offers you an overview of the market and updates to your stocks as well as links to financial news.

To get the most from this app, configure Google Finance on the web, using your computer. You can create a list of stocks to watch, which is then instantly synchronized with your Galaxy tablet. Visit Google Finance on the web at `www.google.com/finance`.

As with other Google services, Google Finance is provided to you for free, as part of your Google account.

Google Gesture Search

The Gesture Search app provides a new way to find information on your tablet. Rather than use a keyboard or dictate, you simply draw on the touchscreen the first letter of whatever you're searching for.

Start the Gesture Search app to begin a search. Use your finger to draw a big letter on the screen. After you draw a letter, search results appear on the screen. Touch a search result or continue drawing more letters to refine the search.

Gesture Search can find contacts, music, apps, and bookmarks in the Chrome app.

Movies by Flixster

The Movies by Flixster app is your Galaxy tablet's gateway to Hollywood. It lists currently running films and films that are opening, and it has links to your local theaters with showtimes and other information. The app is also tied into the popular Rotten Tomatoes website for reviews and feedback. If you enjoy going to the movies, you'll find the Movies app a valuable addition to your tablet's app library.

Netflix

It's not the big screen. It's not even the little screen (which I'm guessing is TV), but it's still something to watch. The Netflix app gives you access to a streaming library full of television and movies. You can hook up the headphones, turn on the tablet, and sit back and enjoy your favorite show or a flick from the golden era of Hollywood.

The Netflix app is free, but to get the most from it you need a subscription to Netflix's streaming video service. The subscription doesn't cost much, plus the Galaxy tablet can count as one of the three devices you can use to access your Netflix account. So you can still watch on the TV or the computer while you enjoy taking movies with you anywhere.

Notepad

The Galaxy Note comes with the S Memo app, which I suppose you could work on a Galaxy tablet by using your finger instead of the S Pen. Never mind! When you need to jot down a quick note and don't mind using the onscreen keyboard (or dictation), get the Notepad app, also known as GO Notepad.

For example, before a recent visit to the hardware store, I made (dictated) a list of items I needed by using Notepad. I also keep some important items as notes — things that I often forget or don't care to remember, such as frequent flyer numbers, my dress shirt and suit size (like I ever need that info), and other important notes I might need handy but don't want cluttering my brain.

Sky Map

Ever look up into the night sky and say, "What the heck is that?" Unless it's a bird, an airplane, a satellite, or a UFO, the Sky Map can help you find what it is. You may discover that a particularly bright star in the sky is, in fact, the planet Jupiter.

The Sky Map app is elegant. It basically turns the tablet into a window you can look through to identify things in the night sky. Just start the app and hold the Galaxy tablet up to the sky. Pan the tablet to identify planets, stars, and constellations.

Avoiding Android viruses

How can you tell which apps are legitimate and which might be viruses or evil apps that do odd things to your tablet? Well, you can't. In fact, most people can't because most evil apps don't advertise themselves as such.

The key to knowing whether an app is evil is to look at what it does, as described in Chapter 15. If a simple grocery-list app uses the tablet's cellular signal and the app doesn't need to access the Internet, it's suspect.

In the history of the Android operating system, only a handful of malicious apps have been distributed, and most of them were found in Asia. Google routinely removes these apps from the Google Play Store, and a feature of the Android operating system even lets Google remove apps from your tablet, so you're pretty safe.

Generally speaking, avoid "hacker" apps, porn, and those apps that use social engineering to make you do things on your Galaxy tablet that you wouldn't otherwise do, such as text an overseas number to see racy pictures of politicians or celebrities.

Also, I highly recommend that you abstain from obtaining apps from anything but the official Google Play Store, the Amazon Market, and Samsung's own app store. Other markets are basically distribution points for illegal or infected software. Avoid them.

Sky Map promotes using the tablet without touching it. For this reason, the screen goes blank after a spell, which is merely the tablet's power-saving mode. If you plan extensive stargazing with the Sky Map, consider resetting the screen timeout. Refer to Chapter 19.

TuneIn Radio

I know I mentioned this app in Chapter 13, but I want to recommend it again. One of my favorite ways that my Galaxy tablet entertains me is as a little radio I keep by my workstation. I use the TuneIn Radio app to find a favorite Internet radio station, and then I sit back and work.

While TuneIn Radio is playing, you can do other things with your tablet, such as check Facebook or answer an e-mail. You can return to the TuneIn Radio app by choosing the triangle notification icon. Or just keep it going and enjoy the music.

Voice Recorder

Your tablet can record your voice or other sounds, and the Voice Recorder is a good app for performing this task. It has an elegant and simple interface: Touch the big Record button to start recording. Make a note for yourself or record a friend doing his Daffy Duck impression.

Previous recordings are stored in a list on the Voice Recorder's main screen. Each recording is shown with its title, the date and time of the recording, and the recording duration.

Several voice recording apps can be found at the Google Play Store. I recommend the one by Mamoru Tokashiki.

Zedge

The Zedge program is a helpful resource for finding wallpapers and ringtones — millions of them. It's a sharing app, so you can access wallpapers and ringtones created by other Android users as well as share your own. If you're looking for a specific sound or something special for Home screen wallpaper, Zedge is the best place to start your search.

Index

• *H* •

About the Author

Dan Gookin has been writing about technology for over 25 years. He combines his love of writing with his gizmo fascination to create books that are informative, entertaining, and not boring. Having written over 140 titles with 12 million copies in print translated into over 30 languages, Dan can attest that his method of crafting computer tomes seems to work.

Perhaps his most famous title is the original *DOS For Dummies,* published in 1991. It became the world's fastest-selling computer book, at one time moving more copies per week than the *New York Times* number-one bestseller (though, as a reference, it could not be listed on the *Times'* Best Sellers list). That book spawned the entire line of *For Dummies* books, which remains a publishing phenomenon to this day.

Dan's most popular titles include *PCs For Dummies, Word For Dummies, Laptops For Dummies,* and *Android Phones For Dummies.* He also maintains the vast and helpful website www.wambooli.com.

Dan holds a degree in Communications/Visual Arts from the University of California, San Diego. He lives in the Pacific Northwest, where he enjoys spending time with his sons playing video games indoors while they enjoy the gentle woods of Idaho.

Publisher's Acknowledgments

Acquisitions Editor: Katie Mohr

Senior Project Editor: Susan Pink

Copy Editor: Susan Pink

Editorial Assistant: Annie Sullivan

Sr. Editorial Assistant: Cherie Case

Project Coordinator: Patrick Redmond

Cover Image: Front Cover Image: ©iStockphoto.com/pixalot; Galaxy Tab 3 courtesy of Samsung; Back Cover Images: courtesy of author